D1125913

The ECONOMICS *of* MOBILIZATION *and* INFLATION

The ECONOMICS *of* MOBILIZATION *and* INFLATION

Seymour E. Harris

GREENWOOD PRESS, PUBLISHERS
NEW YORK 1968

First Greenwood reprinting, 1968
LIBRARY OF CONGRESS catalogue card number: 68-28586

PRINTED IN THE UNITED STATES OF AMERICA

For Ruth

CONTENTS

Part Five. THE RATE OF INTEREST AND THE NATIONAL DEBT

Part Six. CONTROLS

Part Seven. THE INCIDENCE OF INFLATION

Part Eight. WELFARE ASPECTS

PREFACE

THIS BOOK, my twenty-fourth, I hope is the last in a long series of (ten) books dealing exclusively or in a substantial part with problems of mobilization and war.

In 1926, I finished a doctorate thesis (published in 1930) on the assignats, the paper money issued to finance the Revolution and Napoleon's fourteen armies. This was the classic experience with paper money, the assignat falling in value over a period of about five years by 200 times. Among the interesting features of this experience was a control of prices which worked well so long as the penalty of infraction was the guillotine; a flight from the currency measured by a rise of prices of about 200 times as against an expansion of money of but 20 times; an attempt to redress inequities by requiring repayments of debts adjusted to value of currency at time of incurring and repaying debt.

In 1931 appeared *Monetary Problems of the British Empire,* and in 1933, *Twenty Years of Federal Reserve Policy* (2 volumes). These books also dealt with the problems of a war economy. The major problems were much different from those discussed in recent years. In World War I, the large contributions of bank credit to the financing of war were in the forefront. The problem was, in part, one of discovering techniques for increasing the reserve base so that with large additional supplies of money manufactured to pay the bills of government, the public would still retain its confidence in the monetary unit. There was, of course, an awareness of the importance of taxes and savings. But controls were in the background, and prices were a matter of a relationship of *money* and *output.* The attack on rising prices was to moderate the expansion of monetary supplies, rather than to concentrate on total spending. When expansion was greater than in other countries (e.g., Great Britain), much attention was devoted to maintaining exchange rates—e.g., by borrowing dollars.

In World War II, the emphasis was different, though my first two books (*Economics of American Defense,* 1941, and *Economics of America at War,* 1942) still largely reflected the economics of World War I, improved to some extent by the Keynesian analysis.

In addition to the two volumes, I was responsible for *A Manual of Price Control* (as Editor and Chairman of the Training Committee of the Office of Price Administration), 1943; *Price and Related Controls in the United States,* 1945; *Inflation and the American Economy,* 1945; *Problems in Price Control: Stabilization Subsidies, 1942–46* (Historical Reports of War Administration, OPA), 1947; *The National Debt and the New Economics,* 1947. In addition, as editor I devoted much space to wartime problems in four other volumes (*Post-War Economic Problems,* 1943, *Economic Reconstruction,* 1945, *The New Economics,* 1947, and *Foreign Economic Policy for the United States,* 1948).

The major emphasis in these books was on the contribution of controls, the relation of direct and indirect controls, the technical problems of controls, the treatment of inflation, the problems raised by a rising national debt, the manner of supplementing price and related controls through subsidies, and the analysis and treatment of the economic "hang-over" following a war. The last two books dealt primarily with problems other than those arising from mobilization.

To understand the economics of war and mobilization, active participation helps. I have had occasion to study these problems as an operational officer, as a member of the Policy Committee of the Board of Economic Warfare, as Director of the Export-Import Price Control Office, as adviser on stabilization to several Latin-American countries, as economic adviser to the Vice-Chairman on Civilian Requirements of the War Production Board, and as adviser on stabilization to the National Security Resources Board. I am now a Consultant to the President's Council of Economic Advisers, a member of the Board appointed by the President to advise the Secretary of Agriculture on the operation of the Commodity Credit Corporation, and a member of the Agricultural Mobilization Policy Board. Of course, I write as a private citizen, and no one shares any responsibility for my views.

Despite a good deal of experience, I am still impressed by how difficult the problems remain. What happened in the French Revolution, in World War I, or in World War II is interesting and often relevant; but one who depends too much on past episodes of mobilization and war will be badly misled. That is why I have written a new book.

The peculiar state of war and nonwar, the resulting difficulties of allocating resources, the need of mobilizing after ten years of inflation and from a high level of employment, the peculiar problems raised by the divided world, the shortages of materials, the large national debt outstanding with relatively small reductions since 1945, the almost insoluble manpower problems, the increased influence of well-organized groups not averse to inflation, the limited success of World War II controls from the perspective of 1950–51, the special obstacles to adequate tax programs (e.g., the high level of taxes in 1950) and to required savings programs (e.g., the questions raised concerning fixed-interest securities by those who have become aware of ten years of steady inflation)—these and many other problems raise a host of questions which must be discussed in a new approach and arrangement. As historians we know we learn much from the past, but we know also that each effort brings new problems.

I am indebted to many government officials for help. I

should mention particularly Ewan Clague, Director of the Bureau of Labor Statistics, for making much material available, and Elmer Staats, Assistant Director of the Budget. The latter kindly read Chapter 11 on "Economies of Public Outlays" with great profit to the writer. Secretary of Agriculture Brannan generously criticized Chapter 5 on "Farm Resources and Farm Policy," and members of the U.S. Treasury Tax Staff, Chapter 15. I am also indebted to the Council of Economic Advisers for their excellent report of January, 1951, and to their able chairman, Leon Keyserling, with whom I have discussed many of the issues of mobilization. The responsibilities are all mine, however.

I owe much to my secretary, Miss Lillian Buller, to Mrs. Anna Thorpe for typing, and to Mrs. Daniel Cheever for reading the manuscript.

SEYMOUR E. HARRIS

Cambridge, Mass.
July 7, 1951

Part One

THE MAIN ISSUES

ABBREVIATIONS

BLS	Bureau of Labor Statistics
BEW	Board of Economic Warfare
CCC	Commodity Credit Corporation
CED	Committee on Economic Development
DPA	Defense Production Act
ECA	Economic Cooperation Administration
EPCA	Emergency Price Control Act
ERP	European Recovery Program
ESA	Economic Stabilization Administration
FEA	Foreign Economic Administration
GI	Government Issue
GNP	Gross National Product
HOLC	Home Owners' Loan Corporation
MLR	*Monthly Labor Review*
NAM	National Association of Manufacturers
OEEC	Office of European Economic Cooperation
OES	Office of Economic Stabilization
OPA	Office of Price Administration
OWMR	Office of War Mobilization and Reconversion
PC	President's Commission on Higher Education
RFC	Reconstruction Finance Corporation
SCB	*Survey of Current Business*
TNEC	Temporary National Economic Committee
TVA	Tennessee Valley Authority
WFA	War Food Administration
WPB	War Production Board
WMC	War Manpower Commission

1. MAJOR ECONOMIC PROBLEMS OF MOBILIZATION

THE PROBLEM

IN A STATE of war or semiwar, the military requires additional raw materials, food, plant, equipment, and manpower. These resources can come from the following sources: additional output, reduced consumption, reduced investment for nonwar or nondefense purposes, increases of imports and/or curtailed exports.

Acquisition of supplies and manpower by the military is the number one problem, the main objective of a military or semimilitary economy. In general, this objective takes precedence over all others. As a preliminary, of course, it is necessary to determine the resources to be made available for stockpiling, for the military, for consumption, for investment, and for nonmilitary government use. This is the programing problem, and here decisions have to be made from highest authority and should reflect the wishes of the people.

The second problem is that of distribution of the burden. Who works harder? Who gives up what? This is largely a problem of distributive justice. To impose the burden with the minimum sacrifice is the goal. Yet it is a mistake to assume that the two problems are unrelated. Excessive burdens on labor may kill incentives and induce absenteeism. Confiscatory tax rates on business will dull the interest of executives and owners.

A SHORT-RUN OR LONG-RUN EFFORT?

Ordinarily a country embarking on war mobilizes resources on the assumption that the war will be over in a few years. That it is next to impossible to know whether the contest is to last five or twenty-five years, and whether a major contest will break forth in 1957, 1960, or not at all, makes planning largely a matter of judicious guessing.

This uncertainty colors the programs proposed. The mobilization is on a gradual basis—e.g., $5 billion additional at the end of 1950 (annual rate), $35 billion additional by the end of 1951, $65 billion by the end of 1952, $120 billion additional in an all-out effort (annual rates). The technique is to emphasize the accumulation of stockpiles and increase the capacity and reserves of manpower, both military and industrial, rather than to seek an all-out flow of goods and military men now. In his first report to the nation, February 23, 1951, the Director of the Office of Defense Mobilization anticipated outlays of 100 to 150 billion dollars for defense in 2 to 3 years. Yet, though this involved sacrifices by civilians in 1951 and 1952, Mr. Charles Wilson anticipated that civilians, by 1953, would have as much as in 1949 or 1950. In other words, Mr. Wilson adhered to the theory that, short of an all-out war, a rise of output would ultimately provide the required resources.

Peculiarities of timing and growth are reflected in the sources of the war machine and the manner of imposing the burdens. Despite the high level of output and employment that prevailed in June, 1950, prior to the Korean War, the authorities are inclined to rely heavily on an increase of output. They envisage a normal rise of output of 2 to 3 per cent per year and on top of that an additional increase of 2 to 3 per cent associated with extraordinary mobilization measures:

inflow of additional manpower, increase of hours, special financing of increased capacity, etc. A 5 per cent rise of output per year would yield about $15 billion additional output, or a substantial part of the new resources required by the military. This emphasis on gradualness explains the anticipated rise of 25 per cent of output in five years by the President's Council,[1] * the 10 per cent rise of output from the third quarter of 1950 to the third quarter of 1951 by Dr. Woodlief Thomas, Adviser of the Board of Governors of the Federal Reserve System,[2] and of the rise of gross national product (GNP) of 8, 4, and 8 per cent for the years 1951, 1952, and 1953 presented by the Harvard Business School group of economists. The last envisage a rise of GNP from $279 billion in 1950 to $337 billion in 1953. In their thoughtful and stimulating analysis, the Harvard Business School group can thus reconcile federal military outlays of $84 billion in 1953 with a decline of consumption and of private investment of but a few billion dollars each from 1950 to 1953.[3]

THE RISE OF OUTPUT?

The extent of the rise of output is crucial. Unless output expands greatly, the public will have to reduce consumption and/or private investment (future consumption) substantially. Thus a $50-billion effort with a rise of output of but $20 billion requires cuts of $30 billion in consumption and/or investment. The required reduction of consumption would be especially large when measured against man-hours of work—as the latter rise.

Can we, then, expect large increases in output? Those who are optimistic underline the average gains since 1900, the 50 to 70 per cent gain of World War II, the continued modernization of our plant, the untapped labor sources, the movements of labor into more highly productive industries as mobilization proceeds.

* Notes are arranged by chapters in the Appendices, pp. 295–302.

They base their conclusions in part upon the continued high level of investment with accompanying gains of man-hour output.

An example of the "optimistic school" is the following excerpts from an advertisement by McGraw-Hill.[4]

Can even the United States add a $40 billion miracle of production on top of what it is already doing?

Our answer is "Yes"—and within two years. It can be done by adding about $6 billion each year to our program of capital investment which now runs about $22 billion a year.

Part of this added production will come from expanding our industries. The steel companies, for example, already have plans to increase their capacity almost ten per cent in the next two years.

But by far the largest part of that $40 billion of added production must come from higher productivity—raising industry's efficiency.

To meet our goals we need to raise our productivity five per cent a year.

Can it be done?

The answer is an emphatic "Yes."

McGraw-Hill's studies of industry's equipment show that there are countless opportunities for improving efficiency. Our manufacturing industries alone need at least $35 billion of new equipment to raise their facilities to first class technical standards.

Here are some of the broad possibilities reported by the trained editors of McGraw-Hill's business magazines:

In many manufacturing plants as much as 40 per cent of the workers' time goes into moving materials and parts—shifting things about within the plant between processes and to and from shipping platforms.

FACTORY *estimates that improved materials handling equipment and methods will cut handling costs twenty-five per cent and save annually over 650,000 man-years of unnecessary labor.*

Modern machine tools, designed since World War II, are 40 per cent more productive, on the average, than is old equipment. But

American Machinist surveys show that 95 per cent of industry's machine tools are designs at least ten years old. Replacing them could raise productivity of the metalworking industries at least ten per cent—enough to absorb a major share of the metalworking industries' part of the defense program as now planned.

In coal mining, latest equipment and methods can raise productivity sharply. The editors of *Coal Age* estimate that production of bituminous coal could be raised from seven tons per man-shift to ten within three to five years.

Many new textile production techniques are 50 per cent to 75 per cent more efficient than those in use now. If plants could be fully modernized, and full use made of latest management methods, *Textile World* estimates that output-per-manhour would rise 20 per cent. A *Food Industries* study indicates *that modern equipment plus the best management techniques could raise productivity in food processing at least 20 per cent.*

Aware of the unexpected miracles of 1942–45, I nevertheless am less optimistic than the current "guns-and-butter" school.

It is easy to exaggerate the significance of the rise of output in World War II. In wartime the GNP seems to rise more than it actually does. The war industries need to attract labor and materials, and, therefore, they bid high prices for the factors of production. Less efficient than the peacetime industries and bidding extravagantly for labor and materials, the war industries account for a large dollar value of output which seems larger in real terms than it actually is. Considerations of this kind explain Dr. Simon S. Kuznets' deflation of official appraisals of the wartime rise of output by one-third or more.[5]

In short, the official indexes tended to exaggerate the rise of output: the dollar value is not deflated adequately by the price index which, in turn, did not reflect appropriately the "inflation" ingredient in the dollar value of war output.

For example, assume that GNP rises from 100 to 200 million dollars. The genuine rise of prices, once allowance is made for the relative inefficiency in new war industries and higher relative prices paid by these industries for factors of production, is 150. But since the index used reveals a 25 per cent rise, the deflated rise is found to be 60 per cent instead of the actual rise of 33⅓ per cent.

The counterpart of this problem in the fifties is that the "optimists" frequently include excessive gains of GNP associated with an increased proportion of military and related output in potential output: part is fictitious.

Even by 1950, it was evident that as war output rose, the GNP would rise disproportionately. High pay for war workers, increased pressure on the markets for raw materials needed, loose pricing and weak bargaining by government procurement officers—all of these would raise prices and war outlays and give an exaggerated impression of the rise of GNP. These factors explain in part the much higher costs of war supplies; though, of course, part of the problem is, as President Truman suggested in his *State of the Union* speech of January 8, 1951, that weapons are much more complicated.

> We used to think that the B-17 was a huge plane, and the block-buster it carried was a huge load. But the B-36 can carry five of these block-busters in its belly, and it can carry them five times as far. Of course, the B-36 is much more complicated to build than the B-17 and far more expensive. One B-17 costs about $275,000, while now one B-36 costs about 3½ million dollars.

According to an interesting survey by *Fortune,* the initial equipment of a full-strength infantry division would have cost about $80 million in June, 1950, as compared to only $19.3 million in World War II. Within the fiscal year 1950–51 the Budget Bureau estimated a further increase of 10 per cent. The explanation of the rise since 1945 is higher prices and the assignment of more and heavier weapons to a division.

Ultimate costs would, of course, depend partly on the number of divisions required.

Here are a few examples.[6]

	Unit Price		Number per Division	
Equipment	*1945*	*1950*	*1945*	*1950*
50 cal. machine gun . . .	$ 249	$ 720	237	354
105 mm. howitzer	8,262	13,672	54	54
Light tank (M-24) T41	39,652	126,029	0	9

What does all of this mean? Simply that the cost of warfare is on the rise. In World War II a million men in the military service added $7.5 billion per year to the government's budget. We shall be fortunate if the required outlay in 195? is but $15 billion per one million men. The result is that a $50-billion military program will not achieve as much as a $25-billion program did in 1944. In order to reach targets, the government will have to raise the costs of the military budget—probably much more than was contemplated in 1950–51. The significance of this fact lies in the point that any genuine rise of output will be quickly absorbed by the military demands, and also that to a substantial extent the direct and indirect outlays for the military will conceal an inflationary bias in output value figures not revealed by the usual index number.

Our first reservation (among several) to the optimistic estimates of the rise of output and the continued high level of investment and consumption is that the dollar figures give an exaggerated impression of the increase of GNP, and also suggest large rises in dollar outlays to yield a given military objective. In short, we shall have to depend more on economies of private spending and less on increases of output than so far anticipated.

The second reservation stems from the much smaller degree of unemployment in the economy of 1950. Whereas the country could increase its man-hours by about 55 per cent in World War II, the probable rise in the early fifties would be only 20 per cent. Those who anticipate large gains of output are generally well aware of this limitation.

They fail, however, to allow adequately for the relation of this fact to the man-hour productivity—our third reservation. The economy started in 1950 from a high level of employment, and, therefore, the additional workers to be added in the early fifties were, on the whole, less efficient workers than those at work in 1950. Insofar as the economy could raise man-hour output in World War II, the explanation largely was that, with the vast expansion of output and with the large amount of unemployment and of reserve labor, the average employed worker *added* could still be an efficient worker and, more important, the rise of output per hour and per plant from a low level of output would account for a reduction in unit costs. Both in terms of the quality of the added worker and the changes in the ratio of output to capacity, American industry could not look forward in 1950 to the productivity record of World War II. A rise of output from operation at 60 per cent of capacity is one thing, from 90 to 95 per cent of capacity, another.

Our fourth point relates to resources. Serious shortages confront this nation: e.g., in nonferrous metals, in lumber, in all kinds of critical and strategic materials, and in power. To some extent, projected rises of capacity (e.g., in iron and steel) and diversions from civilian to military use (e.g., aluminum) will solve the problems of shortages. But the supply of many items is not adequate even to meet large military demands; and in other instances deprivation of the civilian economy may reduce total GNP. Plundering of the forties accounts for danger in the fifties.

Finally, it is well to stress the fact that most estimates in 1950–51 relate to an armed personnel of 3 to 4 million. In World War II, the country had 11 to 12 million under arms. In the early fifties, the corresponding number would be about 14 million. With a mobilization of this magnitude, the man-hours available for production would be substantially less than in 1950, and, therefore, total output might well fall—even in the absence of bombing, a possibility which should not be left out of account in any forecasts of total output.

THE PROBLEM OF FINANCE AND DISTRIBUTION

Attack on Income

Income is the starting point of any analysis. This approach marks the difference of analysis between World War II and World War I and reflects the influence of the Keynesian Revolution.

Perhaps the greatest advance since World War II is the *general* recognition that a rise of output alone does not solve the inflation or the distribution problems. It is not likely that citizens will march to Washington in hordes, as they did in 1945, pleading that, if the economy were freed of controls, the inflation problem would be solved. In government publications, in technical journals, in semipopular media (*Fortune*), there is a recognition of the fact that the higher the output and income and the less the consumption goods and services made available (the more required for war or investment), the greater the inflationary pressures. The problem of inflation is acute when incomes are high as in the forties, not when they are low as in the thirties. Thus, with incomes rising by $50 billion by 1952 and with an unchanged supply of consumption goods available, obviously there would be an excess of demand over supply for consumption goods.

Our first attack is, then, on income. It is imperative that money incomes should not rise any more than is absolutely imperative to elicit required output. Even with wage rates frozen as of June, 1950, the rise of labor income would be a threat to stability. It is well to recall that the rise of basic wage rates in World War II accounted for about one-sixth of the increase of labor income. The need of stabilizing income, insofar as is practical, is an argument against wage adjustments in response to increases in the cost of living, or any improvement in productivity.

I am aware, of course, of the difficulties of freezing wage rates. On the basis of World War II experience, I would conclude that a wage freeze would be unwise and in any case not enforceable. To some extent, as I argue elsewhere, some flexibility of wage rates is necessary to assure required reallocation of workers. Indeed, in a full-employment economy, the wage incentive can only play a subsidiary part. But it will be necessary to correct inequities (e.g., in 1942 a wage "freeze" was introduced when about two-thirds of the workers had received substantial wage increases). The pressure to allow wage increases in response to rises in the cost of living and productivity is bound to be great. The best attack here is to stabilize the cost of living as much as possible, to introduce an over-all limit to the rise of wage rates (as under the Little Steel Formula in World War II), and to base wage increases on rises in the cost of living (e.g., to apply adjustments only to an "iron ration" of say $25 per week).[7]

The burden of stabilizing income should not rest with labor alone. Provisions in the Defense Production Act (DPA) spiral incomes of farmers; and the parity formula for farmers allows them to pass increased taxes on to buyers. Restraint on the part of businessmen may also keep prices and profits down. At least in the semicompetitive fields of large-scale business enterprise, there is a disposition not to charge what the traffic will bear. Unfortunately, such restraints will do little good unless sellers all along the line are equally circumspect. Charging less than the traffic will bear by General Motors largely results in higher profits for automobile dealers, who succumb to the law of supply and demand and, according to *Fortune,* average $50,000 profits per year.

The conclusion is that incomes must be kept down; that in a democratic society with large and influential pressure groups, it is not easy to keep them down; and that if income recipients are not restrained in their demands, then the burden on other anti-inflationary weapons becomes too great. Our success in moderating the rise of incomes will determine the tax effort required and in large part the degree to which our economic society will become a controlled one.

The rise of income in part is reflected in higher costs, and in part in increased demands. From both angles, the pressure on the price level rises.

Fiscal Problems

Our greatest expectations lie in a bold and courageous tax policy. Taxes are necessary for two reasons. The first is that they provide the Treasury with the resources which are needed to pay for the defense program; the second, that they deprive potential spenders of cash which they might have used in competition with the government, the increased taxes thus serving as an anti-inflationary force.

Higher taxes are the tools of those who would stabilize the economy and yet preserve the free pricing system. Remove the excess purchasing power through rises of taxation, and then it will not be necessary to sterilize purchasing power through controls—e.g., rationing—which demonetize part of the monetary supply. For example, Marriner S. Eccles would balance the budget by raising $75 billion in taxes out of a GNP of $300 billion. Apparently about $10 billion would reflect an automatic response to higher incomes and higher taxes imposed in 1950, and $20 billion a further rise of tax rates and the imposition of new taxes. Eccles' program announced in October, 1950, was similar to the Administration's program of January, 1951.[8]

All who are interested in preserving a stable economy should support a pay-as-you-go plan of defense or war finance. They should not give the politicians any moral support for doing what is easiest: not voting heavy taxes. It is well to recognize that the average citizen, unaware of the creeping inflation, would resent a large rise of taxes; that many businessmen, farmers, and debtors generally (e.g., the home builders and consumers generally who owe $60 billion) profit from inflation at least temporarily. Even those in favor of vigorous taxes want the taxes to be paid by others. This tax program should fall on all classes: business should pay higher income and corporation and profits taxes; labor and farmers, higher income, excise, and payroll taxes.

Should this country succeed in putting through a pay-as-you-go program even with a $75-billion budget (more than $50 billion for defense), this would be a unique experience in economic history. Here are six obstacles to adequate taxes.

1. The opposition to paying higher taxes—particularly in view of the growing acceptance of the myth of a ceiling on taxes equal to 25 per cent of income.

2. Restraint on income growth, partly related to the rise of taxes, in itself would cut tax receipts. In World War I, taxes accounted for about 25 per cent of war outlays; in World War II, about 40 per cent. In both experiences, the inflation and large rise of income contributed greatly even to these modest gains. The rise of taxes from 5 to 45 billion dollars in World War II would not have prevailed in the absence of a very large money rise of income. In the fifties, a pay-as-you-go plan, with its goal of price stability, means that an increase of income of about 25 per cent over five years would be the maximum expectation.

3. The gestation period of a new tax program is long. It is, therefore, imperative that in launching a pay-as-you-go plan taxes should rise much more rapidly than expenditures. The experience of the early years of the mobilization for

World War II, when the rise of personal taxes was but 4 and 10 per cent of the gains of personal income, in 1941 and 1942 respectively, is a warning.

	$ Billion	
	1941	*1942*
Rise of personal income	17.0	26.9
Rise of personal taxes	0.7	2.7

Source: *Survey of Current Business,* July, 1947, p. 19.

4. As the mobilization proceeds, what the military gets will increasingly be at the expense of the civilian economy. Therefore, taxes will come increasingly *out* of current spending, not out of *additional* income. In this sense, taxation will mean much greater genuine sacrifices than in World War II. It is easier to share gains than to make positive sacrifices. In World War I, the government's additional drains of resources exceeded the rise of income, and this partly explains the poor tax record of that war. In 1918, war output was 26 per cent of GNP, but the rise of GNP from 1914 to 1918 was but 20 per cent. In contrast, World War II yielded more guns and more butter.[9]

5. So far we have assumed that the task of the tax collector would be merely to cover the government's bills. But if the responsibility of the tax collector is to prevent inflation, then the government may well have to obtain more than it pays out.

As noted, the income payments are likely to be inflationary. To restrain inflation the Treasury has to intercept part of the additional income; but to avert inflation, the tax haul should be adequate to offset the income inflation.

6. Related to fiscal policy is the problem of savings. In World War II, large savings contributed toward the containment of inflation. The experience since 1945 does not suggest that savings are going to play the part they did in World War II: First, because savings in 1950 were surprisingly low

in relation to income, a reflection in part of an increased awareness of the effects of continued inflation and, therefore, a disposition to spend before the dollar loses further in purchasing power; and second, because savings will not flow into the market for Treasury issues in the proportion of World War II, a fact explained partly by the losses suffered by the holders of the $257-billion national debt in 1950—$75 billion, or 30 per cent, in goods value as compared to the goods value of the debt at time of acquisition.[10]

Concentration of responsibility for fiscal policy on the Treasury means also that any inflationary effects resulting from an excess of investment over savings is offset by an excess of public receipts over expenditures. In view of the large investments of business in relation to savings in recent years, the government will have to prune private investments through controls or additional taxes, thus relating investments to savings and removing the inflationary effects of business spending in excess of funds available to business. Incidentally, taxpayers offset taxes in part by reduced savings, and, therefore, taxes have to increase by more than $1 in order to reduce spending by $1.

From all of this, it is evident that the task for the tax collector is formidable. He may receive a little help from any reductions of expenditures by all governments and any increase of taxes by state and local governments. There is every reason for stringent public economy in periods of mobilization. The gains are not likely to be large, however, if allowance is made for (1) fixed commitments, (2) the effects of over-all rise of prices on public expenditures (offsetting economies), and (3) the economies which are not really budgetary savings (e.g., reduction of loans on housing). Savings on a cash basis, whatever their effect on the budgetary situation, are important, however, in their anti-inflationary effect.

So far I have contended that the government should embark on a pay-as-you-go policy as a condition for solving the inflation problem. Should savings rise greatly, however, in response (say) to unavailability of consumer durables and a growing conviction that prices are to be stabilized, and should the government restrict private investments to 20 to 30 billion dollars, then savings and investments may be kept in balance and inflation be contained, and a substantial part of all public expenditures may be financed by borrowing. But in this case, the public debt would continue to rise.

THE CONTRIBUTION OF CONTROLS

In the writer's opinion, an outstanding lesson of the forties is that controls as a weapon in the stabilization arsenal have been deflated. Perhaps the most important reason for this is that wartime controls proved, in part, that they postpone inflation rather than suppress it. Given the attitude of the public toward controls, they are almost certain to be scrapped once the emergency is over. Inflation, spared the country in 1942–43, spread in 1946–50.

Reluctance on the part of the public to be anti-inflationary in their income and tax policies is reflected also in a reluctance to accept controls. In espousing all these policies, authorities seek to impose and allocate sacrifices; and each group and individual tries to shed his rightful share.

As difficult as it was to enlist adequate controls in World War II, it will be much more difficult to mobilize them in the fifties. I do not mean paper controls but controls that are acceptable and enforceable. With the country short of full mobilization and the crisis of uncertain duration, the fist-pounding type of controls will not prove very effective. With the public reluctant to abide by regulations, the only way out would be a Stabilization Gestapo, for which the American people are certainly not prepared.

Another lesson we learned from World War II is that in the absence of a strong income, fiscal and saving policies, the pressure on commodity markets becomes so great that enforcement of controls encounters all kinds of obstacles. It is, therefore, imperative to provide a restrained income and a courageous tax policy. They are necessary not only to avert a widely controlled economy, but to assure the success of any controls to the extent that income and tax policy cannot do the job unaided. Here is the case for stressing the contribution of the pricing system against that of the mimeographing machine—as one writer characterized controls.

We should not assume that recourse to proper income and fiscal policies means the substitution of voluntary for compulsory policies—as *Fortune* does in an able and eloquent defense of the pricing system as the guide of mobilization economics. Taxes are a compulsory weapon as are the restraints on consumers' credit supported by *Fortune*.[11]

The espousal of the fiscal approach and the insistence that fiscal policy should play a larger part vis-à-vis controls than in World War II does not mean that the country can wage a major mobilization effort without controls. The real issue is how far controls should go.

World War II experience again guides us. Surely, it will be necessary ultimately to control prices, wages, man-hours, and supply and demand of scarce materials. The real issue is when, how, and how far.

It may not be necessary to control virtually all prices as in World War II, although the exemption of *x* items from millions may raise more problems than it settles. Perhaps the best approach might be price controls of essential items only—though their definition is a herculean task. To prevent excessive migration of labor, capital, and materials to nonessential areas where prices and profits would be high, control over movement of scarce factors and heavy taxes on nonessentials would be required.

Professor J. K. Galbraith[12] has suggested an ingenious approach: price and wage control in the crucial industries which set the pace in the determination of prices and wages. In this manner, Dr. Galbraith proposes to tolerate suppressed inflation and exclude overt inflation, the latter endangering the economy with its wage-price spiral.

Clearly, the solution is not the one provided by the Defense Production Act (DPA): no price-fixing unless accompanied by wage-fixing. The effect of this provision is to give the Stabilization Director two alternatives and two only: no price or wage determination by government, as the DPA requires, or a comprehensive freeze. Obviously, it is not practical to relate the wages of a steel worker (say) to the price of steel rather than to the price of what he buys. One effect of the deficiencies in the DPA was a premature general freeze of prices and wages early in 1951.

Above all, we should know by now that controls are interrelated. Control of the demand for aluminum helps maintain price ceilings. With wage control, price control is made easier. But we should also recognize the fact that insofar as we remove the price incentive, the movement of materials and manpower in desired directions is discouraged—though we should not assume that the price incentive is the exclusive motivating force. Limited fluctuations in prices and wages are desirable and helpful. The failure to obtain rigid price and wage freezes contributed toward an improved distribution of factors of production in World War II. Rigid wage control, for example, with primitive manpower control might well have been disastrous.

THE APPROACH TO THE INFLATION PROBLEM

In going so far, I do not, however, subscribe to Professor Sumner Slichter's 10 per cent a year inflation program. I am sure that a 2 to 4 per cent rise could be consistent with required movements. I object to all programs of *built-in inflation:* the automatic response of wages to rising cost of living; the rise in the price of government bonds in response to higher prices; of farm prices to increased costs of what farmers buy. There is no more certain way of bringing about a destructive inflation. Lags, though symbolic of injustices, are an essential mechanism for fighting inflation.

Finally, I am not convinced that the limited controls required are destructive of production gains. Surely World War II experience or British experience since 1946 (vis-à-vis Belgian and Italian which scorned controls) do not support Professor Slichter's position.

I am convinced, however, that the departure of policy in the fifties should be a greater dependence on income and fiscal policy and a lesser reliance on controls. Controls will not salvage the economy should income and fiscal policy fail. Rather, controls are likely to fail in the absence of vigorous policies in these other areas. We should consider controls as a supplement to income and fiscal policy, not the other way around. And the choice is not really between controls and no controls, but rather between kinds of controls; it is largely a matter of the extent to which we apply controls that interfere minimally with choices of investors and consumers (income and fiscal policies), and controls that impinge directly—e.g., allocations, price control.

Not a word has been said so far about monetary policy, and I do not intend here to discuss the relevance of monetary policy in the forties. Perhaps fiscal policy has advanced too far and monetary policy was discarded too soon. Perhaps rates of interest should have been higher and more uncertain in the last five years, with the result that savings might have been higher, sales of securities to obtain additional credit less important (as securities declined in value), investment and even consumption on a less ambitious scale (with the discouragement resulting from the rise of rates), and the total supply of money less, as these restraints were imposed.[13]

But whatever the merits of the controversy in the last five years, monetary policy is likely to play a limited role in the next 5 to 10 years. Neither income policy nor output will be substantially determined by any feasible changes in the rate of interest. (In 1950, as I suggest in Chapter 7, monetary authority might have been helpful.) Rather fiscal policy and the demand of the war economy will largely determine the supplies of money. (I do not include as monetary policy the general measures to control the supply of money—e.g., the control of consumer credit, which really belongs under control measures.) Even savings are much more likely to be a function of the availability of consumers' goods, the level of taxes, and the assurances given investors of protection against rising prices than of monetary policy and any practical rise of interest rates. Insofar as other policies fail to contribute as they should toward the goals of the mobilization economy, then monetary policy may be helpful. A balanced budget or a budgetary surplus and some control, directly or indirectly, of private investment are the best possible assurances that the monetary system will not create excessive supplies of money.

Part Two

RESOURCES FOR MOBILIZATION

2. ADDITIONAL OUTPUT AND/OR SACRIFICES

COMPARISON OF WORLD WAR II AND THE FIFTIES

OBVIOUSLY resources for war or mobilization must come from additional output and/or current consumption and/or from investment or from abroad. We include in current consumption government outlays for nonwar goods and services. We shall not discuss foreign sources here (see Chapter 6), for this country is likely to export more than it imports.

A comparison of the allocation of the nation's GNP in 1939 and 1950 (just prior to the Korean War) will suggest the sources in World War II and in the emergency of the fifties:

GROSS NATIONAL PRODUCT ON EXPENDITURES (GNP) *
($ BILLION)

	GNP	*Personal Consumption Expenditures*	*Gross Private Domestic Investment*	*Net Foreign Investment*	*Government Purchases of Goods and Services*
1939	91.3	67.5	9.9	0.9	13.1
1944	213.7	111.6	7.7	—2.1	96.5
1950 (2nd quarter)	268.0	184.5	44.0	—2.0	41.5

* *Economic Report of the President,* July, 1950.

This table suggests that the resources for waging World War II came out of additional output, and it also suggests that the major contribution of a great effort is likely to come in the future through diversions from consumption, investment, and government purchases of goods and services for nonwar purposes. The last is not likely to make an important contribution since outlays for defense, foreign aid, veterans' benefits, and interest on debt are largely fixed and account for about 85 per cent of the budget. (Cf. Chapter 11.)

The major developments from 1941 to June, 1945, were as follows:

	$ Billion
Resources made available: *	
Excess of GNP over 1940	332
Reduction of private investment over 1940	29
	361
Resources used up: *	
War	269
Additional consumption	110
	379

* Calculated from my *Inflation and the American Economy* and the *Annual Reports of the Secretary of the Treasury on the State of the Finances.*

In short, about nine-tenths of the additional resources came from additional output and one-tenth from cutting investment. More than 30 per cent of the additional resources made available were, however, "dissipated" in a rise of consumption.

CONSUMPTION IN WORLD WAR II

Dissipation is of course a strong word to be used here. The gain of consumption was not so large as is suggested by these figures, since prices rose to some extent. Furthermore, the number of workers had increased greatly and hours were longer. By 1944 the civilian employed labor force was 8 million or 18 per cent greater than in 1939 and hours of work about 20 per cent more. Allow for the rise of prices, of number of employed and hours of work, and the consumption per hour of work proves to be less in 1944 than in 1939—actually about 10 per cent less.

The rise of consumption is a mirage when put in terms of rewards per hour of work. But this conclusion also is misleading. The fact is that the consumption of 11 million in the armed services, not included in private expenditures for consumption, may well have accounted for 10 per cent of consumption. At any rate, the private economy saved roughly 10 per cent of their prewar consumption by allowing the military to feed, clothe, and house part of the population. When allowance is made for this factor and also for the excess of *actual consumption* over consumption expenditures, then we conclude that consumption per hour of work was somewhat above prewar levels. Consumption tends to exceed consumption expenditures in periods of war, for in such periods the production of consumption goods and especially durables is curtailed, and consumption (using up) exceeds new outlay on consumption goods.

In summary, the incentive lay not primarily in additional consumption per hour of work although, in response to more time put in, the economy possibly yields a somewhat greater flow of consumption goods. The large rise of personal income (128 per cent in dollars and 81 per cent in stable dollars from 1939 to 1944) was absorbed primarily not in additional consumption but in rising taxes and savings.

THE SOURCES OF RESOURCES FOR THREE STAGES OF MOBILIZATION: A PESSIMISTIC VIEW

For the future, the resources for war will have to come primarily from consumption and private investment. As the mobilization effort advances, the contribution of additional output will taper off. (Should the country, however, stabilize military outlays at 50 to 60 billion dollars, then a large effort without large sacrifices in 1952 and 1953 is certainly possible —as Charles Wilson has contended.)

On the following three assumptions we can make some informed guesses:

1. Manpower available will gradually rise by an equivalent of 10 million. This will come from (a) Three and one-half million entrants into the labor market. At the peak of the war manpower was about as high as in June, 1950. Since 1944 about 3 to 4 million new potential recruits became available (the excess of those becoming of working age over deaths and retirements). A number equal to these 3 to 4 million have retired from the labor market: the influx into educational institutions, return to the home from factories, etc. We may assume that in the event of a great emergency these will return to the labor market or military service. (b) In addition, we can count on a reduction of unemployment of 1½ million from the June, 1950, level. (c) Finally, we allow for an increase of hours by 4 to 5 in order to bring the working week up to the war level again. This provides the equivalent of 5 million additional workers. (In Chapter 3, we assume larger gains of manpower.)

2. We assume the gradual recruiting of manpower and rise of hours.

3. We assume that for each $15 billion of war outlay, one million additional manpower will be required in the military services. The amount rises as prices go up. At the peak of World War II, the cost was 7 to 8 billion dollars per million men and women. We estimate our costs per man about double World War II; first, because of the rise of prices and, second, because of the increased use of expensive arms.

The table below suggests the manner of obtaining resources and the effects upon consumption as mobilization proceeds.

Allocation of Resources for Mobilization and Manpower Allocation (All dollars in pre-Korean values)

Changes from pre-Korean War Period	*Stage I* (*1950 Program*)	*Stage II* *Substantial Mobilization* (*1952 Program*)	*Stage III* *Mobilization close to World War II Peak* * (*1954 Program*)
Additional war outlay, $ billion	20	55	125
Rise of GNP, $ billion	10	25	25
Decline of consumption, per cent	8	14	48
Rise of total hours worked, per cent	5	10	10
Decline of consumption per hour of work, per cent	12	22	53
Rise of civilian manpower, million (inclusive of allowance for changes of hours worked)	3	6	6
Rise of military manpower, million	1½	4	8

* Ninety per cent of 80 billion raised by 75 per cent to cover rise of prices.

Once we reach Stage III, we account for 14 million additional members on the labor market, 6 million for the civilian and 8 million for the military. We assumed, however, that only 10 million additional would become available—half from new entrants and half as a result of the rise in hours. (For a more optimistic assumption on potential manpower, see Chapter 3.)

Hence the solution promised for Stage III is possible only on one of the two following conditions (or combinations of these):

1. A much greater mobilization of manpower than in World War II—through withdrawals from the schools, home, or from retirement, and through a further rise of hours (cf. Chapter 3).

2. A rise of man-hour output of about 7 per cent to offset the deficiency of 4 million on the labor markets.

Should these not obtain, then the contemplated war effort

will not be attained or the sacrifices in consumption and investment will have to be greater than so far suggested.

SACRIFICES REQUIRED

The important point to note is that in the successive stages of the war effort, consumption *per hour of work* will have to decline by 12, 22 and 53 per cent, respectively, from the 1950 level. This is an entirely different situation than in World War II when consumption per hour of work did not change greatly. These sacrifices would require a high devotion to the cause for which we are fighting and, also, a heroic fiscal policy. Taxation would have to be on an unprecedented level to reduce consumption per hour of work by 12, 22 and 53 per cent in these stages without a large dose of inflation; and especially since we shall not be able to rely on savings proportionately as much as in the last war. In the absence of a heroic tax policy, the government will be able to obtain the required resources only by competing with private purchasers through an inflationary process: new government money competing with old private money. Even a thorough central program will not solve the problem, for price-fixing, for example, will not work so long as large excesses of money obtain. Here are the changes assumed.

	$ Billion	
	Consumption	*Private Investment*
1950, second quarter	184	44
Reduction from 1950, Stage I	15	5 (rise)
Reduction from 1950, Stage II	25	5
Reduction from 1950, Stage III	88	12

A MORE OPTIMISTIC VIEW

So far we have taken a pessimistic viewpoint. But it is possible to be more optimistic. Should we assume, for example, a rise of output of 25 per cent over five years (as the

Council of Economic Advisers) or 27 per cent ($70 billion) by 1953 over the first half of 1950 (by Harvard Business School Economists in the *Harvard Business Review,* January, 1951), and a larger paring of investment, then the sacrifices required of consumption would be much less; and those required would be disproportionately in consumers' durables and housing where the stocks available are large and hence where reduction in buying would involve smaller sacrifices of consumption. Thus, the Business School group envisaged consumption in 1951 at 7 per cent in excess of that of the first half of 1950 and 3 per cent above that of 1950 entire; and in 1952 and 1953, only 5 to 6 per cent below the record level of 1951. In short, their view is that a major effort of $84 billion, or $70 billion above 1949 military, etc., outlays (cf. my $55 billion in Stage II) can be provided for by an expansion of output of $70 billion.

On the assumption that, in my second stage, output rises by $40 billion and investment is reduced by $15 billion (instead of $5 billion), then total consumption would be unchanged from the second quarter of 1950 and consumption per hour of work would decline by 9 per cent.

In Stage III, we might assume a rise of output of 25 per cent (as the Council does) and the gain in output would be about $70 billion. With investment down by $25 billion, it would be necessary to cut consumption by only $30 billion, or 16 per cent ($70 + 25 + 30 = 125$) in order to achieve a $125-billion effort. The reduction of consumption per hour of work would then be 23 per cent.

It is clear that the sacrifices required depend upon the magnitude of the effort, upon the gains of output and upon investment policy, the last in turn being determined by assumptions concerning the duration and intensity of the crisis. Great inflationary pressures result from the concomitance of high levels of consumption, of investment, and of military preparations. Insofar as investment is pruned, more becomes available either for consumption or the military. But the uncertainty concerning the duration of the crisis makes the government less willing to curtail investment sharply as in World War II (gross private investment was 4 per cent of GNP as compared with almost 20 per cent in the last quarter of 1950). In my opinion, however, in cutting nonessential investment in 1950–51 the government moved too slowly.

Perhaps the best estimate I could make is a reduction of consumption from the middle of 1950 of 5 to 10 per cent (15 per cent per hour of work) in Stage II and 25 per cent in Stage III (a reduction of consumption of about 32 per cent per hour of work).[1]

3. MANPOWER

SOURCES OF ADDITIONAL MANPOWER

EXPERTS almost universally consider a shortage of manpower one of the most serious obstacles to a large mobilization. A first source of manpower is the unemployed. The 1950 effort started with unemployment of 3.4 million. On the assumption that unemployment can be reduced to 1 to 2 per cent of the labor force in 1949, the active labor market may draw about 2½ million from the ranks of the unemployed. In World War II, the previously unemployed accounted for about 9 million additional employed or in the military, or about 16 per cent of the 55 million in the labor market at the outset of the mobilization. In the mobilization program of the fifties, the unemployed can provide but 2½ million, or less than 4 per cent of the 66 million on the labor market in June, 1950. It is clear that, in comparison with 1940–44, the economy will be able to draw on the unemployed only to a small degree in the fifties.

In World War II, the second major source of additional manpower, in response to improved demand and higher wages, was the rise of *numbers on the labor market.* The young and the old and the housewife were the most important new recruits. From 1939 to 1944, the expansion was 10.3 million, of which increase about 2 million were normal.

It is now clear how important this source of additional manpower will be in the fifties. In June, 1950, the labor force amounted to 66.1 million, or roughly equal to the 65.9 million in 1944. The appropriate figure in 1950, corrected for seasonal, would be 1 million less, or 65 million. It follows from this that the labor market retained a large part of the "abnormal accessions" of 1940–44. In the six years 1944 to 1950, the normal net accessions (the excess of new members over retirements and death) were about 3 million. Apparently 4 of the 8 million of abnormal accessions were still on the labor market in June, 1950 (see summary below). A complete mobilization on the 1944 standards would then elicit 4 million additional workers, plus ½ million additional per year.

SUMMARY

	Million
Numbers on labor market, 1944 and June, 1950	66
Correct for seasonal excess in June, 1950, over 1950 average in normal year	1
	65
Correct for normal rise of manpower, 1944–50	3
	62
Normal numbers, 1944	58
Difference = abnormal accessions, June, 1950	4

Since the labor market in June, 1950, had retained about 4 million of the 8 million abnormal accessions of 1940–44 (likewise, on 1940 standards an excess of 4 million was still on the labor market), therefore, a mobilization on the scale of 1944 would yield 4 million additional workers. In addition, there would be a growth of the labor force of 1 million; and, if we assume that the abnormal accessions would be in proportion to the numbers on the labor market in 1944 and 1950, the seasonally corrected labor force in June, 1952, would be 71 million.

A third source of additional manpower would be a rise in working hours. In 1950, weekly hours of work were still above prewar, but about 5 hours below wartime peaks. (The decline in railroads was substantially greater.) An increase from an average of 41 to 46 hours or even somewhat less under "peacetime" conditions, say 10 per cent, that is to 45 hours, might raise the available manpower by the equivalent of 5 million.[1] (The increase is not applicable or is meaningless for many groups: the military, young workers, and old workers.)

From these three sources, the rise of man-hours within two years might be put optimistically at 13½ million, or above 20 per cent, as follows:

	Million
Unemployed	2½
Additional workers	6*
Additional hours	5
	13½

* 4 million = abnormal rise on basis of 1944 absolute abnormal rise
1 million = additional abnormal rise associated with larger labor force in 1950
1 million = normal accessions

REDISTRIBUTION ON THE BASIS OF ESSENTIALITY

World War II was far from an all-out war; and, therefore, all possible sources of additional manpower were far from exhausted. It might be helpful to examine the manpower potential on the assumption that an all-out war may have to be fought.

Let us consider first the possibility of a redistribution of manpower under which manpower might be withdrawn from the less essential employments. In World War II the distribution and service trades, which might have been an important source of additional manpower, yielded very little. In contrast, the industries *manufacturing* luxury goods contributed a great deal. Thus an estimate for the four years ending July, 1944, showed that the military and war industries absorbed 19.4 million. Aside from 7.4 million from unemployed, and 9.7 million from additional workers, the only significant contributions were 900,000 from agriculture and 1.3 million from construction. In the first two years of this period, the major source of additional labor was from the unemployed (6.5 million) and a rise in the labor force (3.2 million). In the second two years, the unemployed accounted for but 1.8 million and new members, 5.7 million. In the latter period, the armed forces absorbed more than twice as many as in the earlier period, and civilian employment remained almost unchanged. Genuine shortages developed in many areas.[2]

In Chapter 2, the possibilities of reducing consumption as much as 50 per cent and investment by a very large percentage is discussed. With reduction of private spending of these proportions, it would be possible to release labor from nonessential civilian employments. Even if we assume that the required cut in private spending (both consumption and investment) were to be only about one-third and the economies of labor only about one-quarter, *then it would be possible to release about 15 million workers occupied in less essential work from the 57.6 million engaged in industry in 1949.* The result would be, of course, a great redistribution of labor occupationally or geographically. The largest gains would be for government (inclusive of military) and manufacturing, the former including a shift from nonwar to war activities and the latter in part the shift from nonessential civilian to war and essential civilian output. Wholesale and retail trade, finance, services, and contract construction would suffer the largest losses—say one-third or about 8 million. In contrast, from 1939 to 1944 the persons engaged in these occupations were relatively unchanged at 18 million.[3] This was scarcely evidence of all-out war.

In considering the manpower problem, we should also allow for the fact that the distribution of manpower by industries and occupations is substantially different than ten years ago. Thus, in 1939, those engaged in manufacturing accounted for 22 per cent of the total engaged in production; in 1949, 25 per cent. The 1949 percentage was less than the 1944 figure of 27 per cent; but nevertheless the higher percentage in manufacturing than prewar (as well as the absolute rise of 4.26 million) would facilitate the preparation for war.

Occupationally, the advantage again is with the fifties. Agriculture and services account for a much smaller proportion of the labor supply than in 1940; and professional and semiprofessional workers, clerical and kindred workers, and factory workers a larger part. Skilled workers now form a larger part and unskilled a smaller part. The relative absorption in the proprietor and managerial and in white-collar occupations generally may point to higher productivity; but it may also point to smaller availability in the actual production process.

OCCUPATIONAL CHANGES: MARCH, 1940, TO APRIL, 1949

	Millions	
Reductions:		
Farm management and workers	4.7	17.4 to 12.7
Service workers	1.5	12.2 to 10.7
Professional and semiprofessional workers	0.3	7.0 to 6.7
Laborers	2.8	9.1 to 6.3
Increases:		
Proprietors, managers, officials	2.9	7.6 to 10.5
Clerical and kindred workers	2.7	10.0 to 12.7
Craftsmen, foremen, operatives, etc.	3.8	30.4 to 34.2

Source: U.S. Census, *Annual Report on the Labor Force,* 1949, p. 9.

ADDITIONAL MANPOWER FURTHER CONSIDERED

Aside from the increase in numbers as suggested by World War II experience, the reduction of unemployment, the increase of hours, and the diversion from nonessential industries related to substantial cuts in consumption, are there any other possibilities of increasing manpower?

Now let us consider the sources of additional manpower. At the peak of World War II, the abnormal influx into the labor market was as follows:

Abnormal Influx into the Labor Market, by April, 1944 (Millions)

Females	
Girls and young women normally students	1.1
Young women, 20–24	0.4
Women over 35	1.5
	3.0
Males	
Boys and men normally students	2.2
Handicapped and other marginal workers	0.7
Older workers who postponed retirements	0.8
	3.7

Source: W. Haber and E. Welch, "Labor Force during the Reconversion," *Review of Economics and Statistics*, November, 1944, p. 198.

In what respects can we exceed this record in the fifties? In October, 1949, the numbers in school and college were substantially less than in April, 1940:

Aged 14–17	Decline of	830,000
Aged 18–19	Decline of	420,000
Aged 20–24	Rise of	240,000
Total	Decline of	1,010,000

Source: U.S. Census, *School Enrollment of the Civilian Population, October, 1949*, April 26, 1950.

In October, 1949, there were 1.0 million less in schools and colleges, than in April, 1940. In World War II, about one-third of the 9.9 million deserted school and college for industry or military service. Despite the school reservoir of 1 million less, there are actually about 1 million more on the labor market who are enrolled in school or college. Whereas 790,000 in schools and college were members of the labor market in April, 1940, in October, 1949[4] 1,877,000 students were members of the labor market.

We draw the four following conclusions from these figures:

1. A substantial part of the "abnormal accessions" of World War II still on the labor market in 1949–50 were students —approximately 1 million. Incidentally, since about 45 per cent of the 1.46 million aged 14 to 19 worked less than 15 hours, 42 per cent 15 to 34 hours, and 13 per cent 35 hours or over, the gain of numbers on the labor market is overdone to some extent. Roughly, the additional million probably account only for one-half million additional full-time jobs.

2. A loss of one-third from the schools and colleges would yield but 2.9 million, not the 3.3 million in World War II. The net gain would be less, insofar as we allow for the additional million of school and college students now employed —on the average one-half time.

3. An all-out war might require a loss of three-fourths of the 1950 college enrollment to the military and industry (seven-eighths of the men and five-eighths of the women), and a serious depletion of the high schools. It is possible to envisage the withdrawals of one-half of the high school students and three-quarters from institutions of higher learning; then the schools and colleges could contribute about 5 million, or 1.7 million in excess of World War II. Since they are already contributing about ½ million (1 million at half time), the net gain would be 4½ million.

4. One reservation is required here, though we have already largely taken it into account. In the fifties, the low

birth rate in the depression will be reflected in a reduced number of school and college age. The small number at high school already reflects this factor. The Executive Director of the Office of Manpower pointed out recently that there has been a loss of approximately 2 to 3 million in the number of people between 10 to 19 years of age. "And there are no more men and women in the age range 20–24 than there were 10 years ago. . . . The practical effect is that for the next 8 years or so we will not have as many men reaching the age of 19 as we had during the 1940–45 period. And yet this is the age group that is so much in demand by both the armed services and industry." [5]

We can assume that the contribution from the handicapped will roughly equal that of World War II. It is not likely that the women not at school and college will desert the home in larger numbers than in World War II. Against the possibility of a greater mobilization effort, we must put the much larger number of children to be cared for.

INCREASED PARTICIPATION OF OLDER WORKERS

In the older age group, the contributions may be substantially larger. The first reason for this is that there are many more old people in the population, both relatively and absolutely, and the proportion tends to rise. Thus, in 1950, the estimated numbers aged 45 to 65 were 4.53 million in excess of the numbers in 1940; and, in 1960, the rise would be 8.52 million over 1941. For the 65-and-over group, the increases are estimated at 2.23 and 5.02 million, respectively. For both groups, the percentage of the population was estimated as follows: [6]

	Per Cent
1940	26.7
1950	28.8
1960	31.9

These increases, absolutely and relatively, give a large base to draw upon. The participation of the aged in the labor market also tends to rise. In response to longer lives and improved labor-market demand, the older workers tend to remain in the labor market in larger numbers. The increased participation of older workers in 1947 vis-à-vis 1940 means many more years of working life to be expected at age 40 or age 60. In fact, the stationary male population in 1947 could be expected to yield 9 per cent more man-years of work than the corresponding population in 1940.[7] The explanation of this fact is the increased participation of older workers as well as earlier entry into the labor market.

AVERAGE NUMBER OF REMAINING YEARS IN LABOR FORCE, MALES

Year	*At Age 40*	*At Age 60*
1940	23.8	9.2
1947	24.8	9.7
1975—On basis of 1940 labor participation	24.5	7.9
1975—On basis of 1947 labor participation	27.2	10.5

Source: Bureau of Labor Statistics, *Tables of Working Life,* p. 42.

Older workers participated in much larger relative numbers in the labor market in 1949 than in 1940. The 1949 rate of participation applied to the 1949 numbers accounts for 1.2 million additional workers in age group 45 to 64 in 1949 over the numbers that would have obtained at 1940 rates of participation, and 450,000 additional for age group 65 and over. This total of 1.65 million is about twice the number estimated as the contribution of the previously retired to the labor market in World War II. Of course, part of the gain of 1.65 million is to be associated with the increased participation of the younger older workers, in turn related to improved economic conditions.

INCREASED PARTICIPATION OF ALL WORKERS

Incidentally, there was an increased participation in the labor market by all groups except those aged 20 to 24 and 25 to 34—the decline being associated with the increased college population and young mothers.

LABOR FORCE PARTICIPATION RATES BY AGE, FOR THE UNITED STATES (PERCENTAGE OF TOTALS IN EACH AGE GROUP)

	1940	*1949*
Total, 14 years and over	55.9	58.0
14 to 19 years	33.0	43.1
20 to 24 years	73.3	66.3
25 to 34 years	66.1	63.8
35 to 44 years	63.4	67.4
45 to 54 years	60.6	65.4
55 to 64 years	53.4	56.3
65 years and over	26.1	27.3

Source: U.S. Census, *Annual Report on the Labor Force*, 1949, p. 3. The total population by age groups upon which calculations above are made were derived from U.S. Census, *Forecasts of the Population of the United States, 1945–1975*, p. 74.

It is significant that for the whole adult population (14 and over), the increased numbers on the labor market associated with increased relative participation from 1940 to 1949 was but 2.3 million; for those aged 45 and over, 1.65 million, or two-thirds of the total. Moreover, the rise of about 1 million associated with increased relative participation for those aged 14 to 19 was in fact a rise of but half that amount, if allowance is made for part-time work. It is clear that the old can increase its contribution.

For every 1 per cent rise of participation for those aged 14 and over, the labor force rises by more than 1 million. In

1940, the participation was 56 per cent; in 1944, 62 per cent; in 1949, 58 per cent. A return to the peak of 62 per cent would yield a total of 70 million in 1951.

MISCELLANEOUS GAINS AND ESPECIALLY LONGER HOURS FOR SHORT-TIME WORKERS

An additional ½ million at work might be obtained at the expense of the 1.619 million (October 8–14, 1950) who were *employed but not at work.* The major causes were: vacation (443,000), illness (671,000), temporary layoff and new job or business (137,000), industrial dispute (84,000), all other (276,000).[8]

We have already suggested the possibility of increasing weekly hours by five. In 1948, the average number of weekly hours in nonagricultural employment was 41.6; in 1949, 40.9; and in October, 1950, 41.5 hours. By early 1951 there was already some progress toward the 4-hour increase to 45 hours.

Here I have in mind increases beyond an over-all rise of 4 hours. Additional gains might be had as a result of the increase of hours for part-time workers—a substantial part of whom would like to work longer hours. Since 1.8 million of those in school and college are on the labor market, most of them part time, any estimate of gains from a conversion of part time to full time should not include those already considered in the efflux from the colleges and schools. The gross gain for the 13.4 million working less than 40 hours would be 5 million additional workers. From this should be deducted 1 million for the full-time equivalent for part-time workers at school and college, who either would stay at school or college or would enter the labor market and hence are considered above; and those working part time who cannot (or possibly will not) work full time even under a full-blown emergency —possibly another 1½ million. Then 2½ million would be the net gain.[9]

In all we might then add 3 million to the 31½ million above, with potential gains then rising to 34½ million.

CONCLUSION

In the mobilization of the fifties, efforts roughly paralleling those of 1940–44 would yield the equivalent of 13½ million additional members of the labor market, or about 20 per cent of the total available prior to the Korean War. The contribution of the unemployed would be about 15 per cent; of additional members, 45 per cent; and of additional hours, about 40 per cent. The corresponding rise in 1940–44 was 30 million (inclusive of the rise due to additional hours), with the unemployed contribution playing a much larger relative part than is probable in the fifties. Whereas the gains in 1940–44 were about 55 per cent of the total on the labor market in 1939, the gain in the fifties would be but 20 per cent. Should the military absorb 13½ million ultimately, then any gain of war industries would have to be at the expense of civilian industries.[10]

This expansion of the equivalent of 13 million suggested by World War II experience is not by any means the limit of possible gains for the war economy. In an all-out effort, private consumption and investment might decline by 50 per cent (in stable dollars). Even a reduction of 33⅓ per cent and savings of labor of 25 per cent would release 15 million from the nonessential and make a corresponding number available for the military and essential occupations. In World War II, however, the relatively nonessential occupations (e.g., services, finance, distribution) used 18 million in 1939 and still were absorbing 18 million in 1944. Here, then, is a source of manpower that might yield 10 to 20 million additional.

Despite the fact that enrollment in the schools and colleges was about 1 million less in 1949 than in 1940, they contributed 1 million more to the labor market (working about half time, however). In World War II, the schools and colleges reduced their enrollment by one-third, thus providing 3.3 million for the labor market and the military. A reduction of one-half for those aged 14 to 17 and three-fourths for those aged 18 to 24 would make available 5 million, or 1.7 million in excess of the number in World War II. (Approximately ½ million in full-time equivalent of these 5 million are already on the labor market.)

We may also expect larger contributions from the older workers. In response to longer lives and especially improved demand, the older worker participates much more in economic activity than in 1940. Of about 2.3 million additional workers in 1949 associated with the increased rate of participation as compared with 1940, those aged 45 to 64 accounted for 1.2 million and those aged 65 and over 450,000, or together about two-thirds of the total of 2.3 million associated with the increased relative participation. The older workers may be expected to contribute substantially more than 800,000 *additional* workers as in World War II—in fact, a substantial part of the 1,650,000 (above) has already been contributed by the old.

All in all, advances paralleling those in 1940–44, with 62 per cent of those aged 14 and over on the labor market (as in 1944) would yield at least 70 million in the early fifties. (The percentage was 56 per cent in 1940 and 58 per cent in 1949.)

A summary of the statistics follows:

INCREASES ON THE BASIS OF 1944 ACHIEVEMENT

	Millions
Unemployment	2.5
Additional workers	6.0
Equivalent of additional hours	5.0
	13.5

FURTHER GAINS

Diversions from nonessential occupations, not less than	15
Additional rise at expense of education	1.7
Older workers	1.0
Total	31.2

With the same degree of participation as at the peak of the war, the labor force would rise from 66 million in June, 1950 (64.7 million in December, 1950), to about 69 million. Participation of women would then be somewhat less than in 1944–45; in part, because of the baby boom of the forties. Another obstacle to a rise of participation would be the reduced mobility associated with full employment and pension programs. As an offset, the country has a much larger labor force (both at any one time and the total numbers employed at any time within a period of a few years) and a management much more experienced in effectively using the labor force than in 1940.

It is not likely that in the early fifties the country will be able to raise the numbers on the labor market much beyond 70 million unless stronger measures are taken than those used in World War II, e.g., the certificates of availability, employment ceilings, priorities of employment, sanctions through revocation of contracts and denials of raw materials —all of these undoubtedly helped. Allocation of contracts according to availability of labor also contributed toward an effective use of manpower. But real compulsion was not used, largely because the crisis was not sufficiently great to require such extreme measures. For this reason, labor's view prevailed that direction of labor meant contract and conditions of work by government, and hence was not acceptable.[11]

So far we have suggested how much more labor might be made available on the basis of World War II experience. We have also suggested rich additional sources for an all-out effort, and, in particular, diversion from nonessential industries and full-time work for most part-time workers. Not only would mobilization of (say) the equivalent of 30 million additional workers require strong measures never before used in this country, but there is another reservation to be considered.

Additional labor is of little use unless the complementary factors are available. Additional labor requires additional executives, capital, and materials. The last, in particular, may reduce the number of workers usable in essential output and in the military. Insofar as productivity rises, it is scarcely necessary to add, the additional workers required would be less. Moreover, this figure of 31 to 35 million assumes a much greater degree of mobility of workers both occupationally and regionally than in World War II. In the absence of a high degree of wage flexibility, the government would have to use a vigorous form of labor direction to achieve the necessary redistribution.

Lest there be any misunderstanding, I emphasize the point that the mobilization on the World War II parallel is a goal only if a general war should break out. Then, as the war progresses and bombing follows, the country would ultimately have to look further for manpower than suggested by the World War II experience. For the years 1951 and 1952 the country may obtain the required manpower—given the rate of military spending and the availability of complementary agents—merely by reducing the unemployed by 2 million, increasing hours by the equivalent of 3 million, and adding 2 to 3 million to the labor force (largely youth going into military service), thus providing an increase of the equivalent of about 10 per cent in the labor force.

4. RESOURCE PROBLEMS

INTRODUCTION

ECONOMISTS estimate the available manpower and expected levels of productivity and, on the basis of these, project future output and income. They abstract from the problem of availability of materials, power, plant, etc.

We shall, however, not attain the expected level of output if copper, iron and steel, power, or numerous other items are not available in adequate amounts. The vast consumption of vital materials in the forties aggravates this problem. In recent years, warfare abroad, inroads of communism, lack of capital, labor difficulties, increased competition of other purchasers—all of these have reduced the help to be expected from foreign sources.

The government will have to face up to the problem of how much investment the country will have to make in order to provide more materials and power in the years to come. Much will depend, of course, upon the nature of the mobilization. Should an all-out effort be required over a short period, then large investments which would yield results over a long period would not be practical. It will be necessary to concentrate on short-run results. If, on the other hand, this is likely to be a long-drawn-out struggle, then large investments, both at home and abroad, would probably be expedient.

In the recent report of the President's Water Resources Policy Commission, it was estimated that "an adequate conservation and development program for renewable resources over the next generation might cost the nation in the neighborhood of $100 billion." In the fiscal years 1950, 1951, and 1952, the Federal Budget called for outlays of 1,554 million, 2,117 million, and 2,519 million dollars on resources development, or 3.9, 4.5, and 3.5 per cent, respectively, of total outlays. A substantial part of these outlays, however, were for atomic energy (550 million, 818 million, and 1,277 million dollars in successive years) and also for forestry, recreation, etc. Water-resource development accounted roughly for about two-thirds of the total. The Commission suggested a six-year program, as well as ten- and twenty-year programs. "The rate of investment would be determined by the urgency of need in the various regions, and by the availability of funds for development purposes." [1]

Testifying, in 1949, before the Senate Committee on Interior and Insular Affairs, Secretary of the Interior Krug summarized well some of the issues:

. . . During the last year, the nation consumed over 2,000,000,000 barrels of oil, over 600,000,000 tons of coal, and a record production of 96,000,000 tons of iron and steel, and about 300,000,000,000 kilowatt hours of electric power.

These enormous demands have brought us face to face with shortages of many critical materials which are serious and will affect our output, our employment levels, and our standard of living if they are not handled with the utmost intelligence. . . .

. . . For every two tons of coal mined, one has been left in the ground and lost. More energy is being wasted through the flaring of natural gas in the fields than is being produced by the entire series of TVA dams.

The weight of the average automobile has increased substantially in the face of declining iron ore and petroleum reserves. In harvesting timber, one third has been left as waste in the forests. . . .

The public range land has been overgrazed at the cost of less meat and wool to-morrow. All of the losses we have incurred from unwise and spend-thrift waste contribute in part to many of our present-day shortages, and to the problems of increasing the national income to-morrow. Our mineral position alone threatens to restrict our ability to expand production and employment in the next decade.[2]

DEFICIENCIES

In minerals, any large defense or war economy is going to be confronted with serious problems. The rise of output to meet the needs of a vastly expanding economy has been tremendous. In 1880, the annual value of minerals produced in the United States had reached $367 million; in 1946, $9 billion, or a rise in dollars of about 25 times. By 1944, the production of minerals and raw materials exceeded that of 1919 by 125 per cent and that of 1929 by about 40 per cent. Important changes have occurred in the composition of the index, however. New metals to serve as substitutes or meet new needs (e.g., magnesium and aluminum) have greatly grown in importance. The older and bulkier metals and nonmetallic minerals have experienced declines or slackening in their rate of growth.[3]

A study of important minerals yields the four following conclusions:

1. The reserves of 15 of the minerals were adequate to meet more than 50 years' requirements at the rate of consumption of 1935–44. Included in this category were iron, coal, phosphate rock, potash, nitrogen, salt, and magnesium. We need have little concern for these minerals.

2. Twenty-three items, including copper, lead, zinc, petroleum, bauxite, tin, most of the ferroalloy minerals, and several nonmetallic minerals, are not available in supplies adequate to cover 25 years of consumption at 1935–44 rates.

3. A table prepared by the Department of the Interior shows that virtual self-sufficiency is assured for a long time for 13 minerals (e.g., coal, nitrates, phosphate rock), complete

or virtual dependence (actual and impending) on foreign sources for 10 (including tin), and partial dependence on foreign sources for 16 items (e.g., copper, iron ore, lead, mercury, and bauxite).

4. According to these estimates, at the end of the war, the reserves (in year requirements) were as follows: iron ore, 76; cobalt, 53; bauxite, 23; copper, 19; petroleum, 15; lead, 10; mercury, 2; tin, nickel, mica, quartz crystal—reserves negligible.[4]

It is clear that shortages are serious. Unless adequate supplies of tin, copper, manganese, nickel, industrial diamonds, etc., are found, both the national economy and the mobilization will suffer. In many instances, domestic reserves are inadequate to cover needs for many years, especially when these needs are multiplied by a large mobilization. For some minerals, total world production seems inadequate even if this country could obtain its "rightful" share—e.g., copper, tin. The problem for some minerals is that, although reserves are more than adequate, exploitation has not proceeded sufficiently to build up reserves to cover an emergency—e.g., iron ore and cobalt. It is scarcely necessary to add that new discoveries, the miracle of physics and chemistry (e.g., nuclear power and increased use of plastics), improved methods of exploitation (e.g., a reduction within 25 years of two-thirds in the fuel cost of producing 1 kilowatt hour)—all of these will help solve our problem. *But, nevertheless, there is a genuine danger, much greater than in World War II, that unavailability of crucial materials will impinge on the required growth of our economy.*

STOCKPILING OF STRATEGIC MATERIALS

In order to contend with the problem of shortages, the federal government has inaugurated a stockpiling program for strategic materials. The basic law, Public Law No. 117 of

June 7, 1939, provided that materials held for the military by Treasury procurement could not be released without order of the President. Under Public Law No. 664 of June 25, 1940, the government prepared for stockpiling for World War II: the Reconstruction Finance Corporation (RFC) was to procure, develop, store or release material under The War Production Board (WPB) and other agency orders; and under Law No. 664 the RFC procured more than $300 million worth of strategic and critical materials. Under Public Law No. 457 of October 3, 1944, about $580 million worth of surplus materials were transferred to stock piles, the largest dollar items being in rubber and zinc. By December 15, 1948, about $175 million of materials had been delivered to the government under Public Law No. 520 of July 23, 1946. Finally, under Public Law No. 472, April 3, 1948 and Public Law No. 793, June 28, 1948 [both related to the Economic Cooperation Administration (ECA)], the government was to seek strategic materials for stockpiling in relation to aid given under ECA. The latter provides that 5 per cent of counterpart funds (local currency funds received by ECA countries in exchange for ECA goods provided by the United States) should be used to purchase strategic materials.[5] In a revision of the Act (Public Law No. 47 in 1949), the ECA was requested to take whatever measures were necessary and available under the Act in order to procure materials abroad which were deficient in the United States. The Administrator of the European Recovery Program (ERP) might even enter contracts over a period of 20 years in order to provide materials required by the Bureau of Federal Supply.

On the whole, the stockpiling results have been disappointing. The 5-year Munitions Board objective was estimated at $3.7 billion as of December 15, 1948. Deliveries to this date were as follows: Public Law No. 117—$60 million; transfers of surplus property by War Assets Administration—$580 million; Public Law No. 520—$175 million. These amounted to

22 per cent of requirements; and another 15 per cent ($542 million) were obligated against undelivered contracts.

On the whole, the President's budget statements of 1949, 1950, and 1951 reveal disappointments concerning the stockpiling program, although the opening of hostilities in 1950 is reflected in much larger appropriations. Thus, the outlays in successive fiscal years were: 1949, $299 million; 1950, $438 million; 1951, $900 million (estimated January, 1951); 1952, $1,300 million (estimated January, 1951). Even in early 1951 the modest goal of $3.7 billion announced early in 1949 had not been reached. The large increase proposed for fiscal year 1952 over 1951 largely reflected an increase of prices rather than supplies.[6]

In the first year of ERP, 5 per cent of the dollar equivalent of total local currency deposits of the ERP countries was $197 million. The ECA estimated that only $50 million would be used to obtain strategic materials. Actually, in the first 1¾ years, only $48 million, all in counterpart funds, were spent—as against an estimate of $75 million of procurement in the first year.[7]

As noted (and despite acceleration after June, 1950), the stockpiling program has not achieved what was expected of it. At home, the opposition of owners of competing sources of supplies and the unwillingness of the Munitions Board to interest itself in long-term development, the fear of producers generally of stock piles overhanging the market, and the lack of authority and funds for long-term development, in part corrected recently and perhaps further to be implemented by outlays under Point 4—all of these have jeopardized the program. In foreign activities, the lack of co-operation of the Munitions Board, the unwillingness of foreign countries to make materials available, the competition of other bidders, the reluctance of the ECA to demand materials, the lack of co-ordination among agencies—these have blocked progress.

ENERGY RESOURCES

Before dropping this subject of deficiencies, I must comment on the problem of energy resources. There are widespread fears that power may be a bottleneck, especially in a bombing war. The importance of power is suggested not only by the need of additional power as output rises, but also by the large contribution of power toward any rise of productivity. Thus, according to one writer, the product of an hour's work in 1850 was valued at 23 cents, with the animal contributing 79 per cent, the machine only 6 per cent, and man 15 per cent. In a recent year, the animal, the machine, and man produced $1.36 in an hour's time; but the animal's share was but 1 per cent, the machine's share 96 per cent.[8]

The United States has a great advantage in the amount of power used; and it is important to maintain that advantage. Thus, in 1937, among 12 countries listed, the United States was second in energy consumption per firm engaged in agriculture, first among 26 countries in energy consumption per person employed in mining and manufacturing (U.S.—39,449 kw-hr; U.S.S.R.—11,312 kw-hr). Of 47 countries listed, the gain from 1937 to 1946 in the volume of energy consumed was 35 per cent for the United States. Canada (47 per cent), Mexico (59 per cent), Union of South Africa (36 per cent), Turkey (47 per cent), and New Zealand (58 per cent) revealed larger relative increases than the United States. In the production of hydroelectric power, the gains for the world (30 countries) for these years was 46 per cent; for the United States, 79 per cent. Nine countries showed larger increases than the United States.[9]

Despite these large gains, there is much concern for future supplies of energy. "The Federal Power Commission estimates that by 1970 the Nation will require a total installed central station power capacity of 160 million kilowatts to supply total energy requirements of 725 billion kilowatt-hours a year of electric energy over the next 20 years. . . . If present practices based on the most economical use of water power are followed, this will mean the development of about 25 million kilowatts additional hydroelectric power and 68 million kilowatts additional steam plant capacity." [10]

This estimate of an increased need of more than one-half of current capacity within 20 years means also that as mobilization proceeds, the time when this capacity will be needed will be much earlier than 1970. In January, 1951, President Truman estimated additional capacity needed in the near future at 20 million kilowatts. Our failure to exploit our water resources further in the last generation may prove to be a serious handicap for us in the next generation. One government expert, referring specifically to the year 1947, put the problem as follows: The underdeveloped hydro power of the nation is a great annual waste that can be stopped: [11]

	Million Kilowatts
Generating capacity of all utility systems . .	52.3
Total undeveloped and economic hydro-potential	77.1
	Billion Kilowatt Hours
Energy generated	255.7
Total undeveloped and economic hydro . .	394.0

CONCLUSION

In summary, the country's reserves of many critical and strategic materials are dangerously low. As communism makes further inroads in Asia, the situation becomes more precarious.

In 1948, as expert of the House Foreign Affairs Committee, and even earlier, Professor W. Y. Elliott fought vigorously for an ambitious stockpiling program. At that time, he pointed out the dangers, the lack of reserves, the inroads of the ERP program, the difficulty of substituting high-cost substitutes, and the need of an aggressive stockpiling program.[12]

We shall have to depend on substitutes, on keeping the oceans free, on maintaining free intercourse with much of Asia, Latin America, Australia, Africa, and Europe, on long-range and short-range development programs integrated with our aid and Point 4 programs, on special incentive payments to high-cost producers at home, on subduing the protectionists who would abandon defense to keep their prices up, on improved integration among public agencies, on government monopoly buying abroad, and, *especially, on the most detailed control of production methods and use of the scarce materials.* Controls of supply and demand will have to be much more rigid than in World War II—so far the controls have been inadequate.

There are dangers in a vigorous program also, as is evident in the unfortunate effects on supplies of our allies of accelerated buying in 1950–51 by the United States.

5. FARM RESOURCES AND FARM POLICY

INTRODUCTION

OUR FARMS provide most of the food required by the American people and much of the fiber. It is imperative that in the course of the emergency the farms produce more than in the years 1948–50. Yet serious shortages of wool and cotton threatened even in 1950; and as demands rise in response to mobilization, higher incomes, and reduced availabilities of consumer durable goods, supply of meat and dairy products will be inadequate at 1950 prices.

For many years the problem of agriculture has been excesses, depressed prices, and low incomes for farmers. American farm policy has sought to assure farmers a fair price through control of output, and to achieve a pattern of farm production related to an improved structure of demand. Unfortunately, the policy of treating surpluses is not the appropriate policy in periods of mobilization and war, when shortages harass the nation. Lest this paragraph be misunderstood, I stress the point that policies of curtailment favored in some quarters in the early years of the New Deal gave way to policies of readjustment of output.

Hence, however defensible farm policy of curtailing supplies might have been in peacetime, it is not the correct policy in wartime. In World War II, the government quickly reversed its policies, substituting incentives to encourage farmers to raise production for rewards for cutting output. Once again in 1950–51, the government had to modify its farm program, seeking maintenance of output and even expansion rather than a policy of curtailment which followed a 25 per cent cut of farm income in 1948–49.

As in 1942–45, so in the fifties, the peacetime program was fortunate in that the government had set a floor to farm prices. A guarantee of minimum prices assures the farmer that an expansion of output will not bring in its train a disastrous price drop. Hence he is now disposed to co-operate.

The price support program and the large inventories of farm products accumulated as part of a program for supporting prices were two features of the anti-surplus program which facilitated the carrying through of a mobilization or war program. The large carry-overs in June, 1950, which exceeded those of 1940, were an important asset at the outset of a large mobilization program. On September 30, 1950, the Commodity Credit Corporation (CCC) had $3,014 million invested: one-third in wheat and one-third in corn, and large sums in the following items (in order of importance)—flax and linseed oil; cotton, upland; tobacco; eggs, fresh and dried; butter.[1]

PRODUCTIVITY, INVESTMENT AND OUTPUT

Perhaps the most significant fact about American agriculture in the last 50 years and especially in the last 10 to 20 years has been the vast gains of productivity, which have made possible a rise of output of about two-thirds since 1914 and two-fifths since 1935–39, without any substantial change in acreage. The striking fact has been that output per man in recent years has been rising more rapidly than in industry and mining. Whereas the gains in the latter exceeded those in farming from 1910 to 1930, the reverse has been true since 1930. (In part the explanation may be a somewhat greater reduction of weekly hours in industry.): [2]

GROSS PRODUCTION PER FARM WORKER AND PRODUCTION PER WORKER IN MANUFACTURING AND MINING (1935–39 = 100)

	Farm	*Manufacturing and Mining*
1910	79	62
1930	96	95
1948	142	121

Source: *Agricultural Outlook Charts—1950,* p. 20.

What explains these phenomenal gains in farm output, total and per worker? The major explanations are more machinery, more fertilizer, more and better insecticides (especially organic), and improved strains.

In 1910, the farms of this country had 1,000 tractors, in 1945, 1,545,000, and by 1949, 3,500,000. In the number of tractors, automobiles, grain combines, corn pickers, and milling machines on farms, the increase in the last ten years has greatly exceeded that of the thirty years 1910–40. All farm machinery measured in 1935–39 dollars was of equal value in 1910 and 1939, but had increased by 56 per cent from 1939 to 1949.

Consumption of fertilizers (1935–39 = 100) in terms of plant nutrients was 61 in 1910, 109 in 1939, and 258 in 1948. Here even more than in machinery the gains of the last decade have been phenomenal. The increased use of synthetic organic insecticides—e.g., DDT, benzene hexachloride—reflects a vast expansion of use of insecticides in the last 10 years. A decade ago the farmers used about 145 million pounds of inorganic and botanical insecticides. Now they have substituted 100 million pounds of the synthetic organic insecticides, which are many times as effective pound for pound as the inorganics and which save much manpower.[3]

It is no wonder, then, that with increased use of machinery, fertilizers and insecticides, productivity has increased so much that, with a working force 8 per cent smaller in 1949 than in 1940, output was 27 per cent greater than in 1940 and 38 per cent greater than in 1935–39.[3]

The significance of the rise of productivity for the future is that, in order to maintain and even exceed present high levels of output, agriculture will require machinery, fertilizers, and insecticides in quantities at least equal to amounts obtained in the last few years. In view of the potential drains of manpower to the military and especially to war industries, the required output will not be forthcoming unless productivity continues to rise. For 1951, the Department of Agriculture sought as much machinery and equipment as in 1949. In that year the value of machinery and equipment on the farms rose from 9 to 11 billion dollars, or by $2 billion. In other words, in order to maintain farm output, the economy was required to produce $2 billion of machinery and equipment aside from the amounts required for repairs. These needs impress one with the difficulties of cutting private investment drastically.

Yet, despite the expected drains of manpower in the midst of a great mobilization or war, the farmers will be able to increase output without maintaining present rates of expansion of capital plant—and the more so since, with unusual inventories, the losses resulting from the using up of capital (postponing replacement) may not be great.

Incidentally, a comparison of gains in machinery on the farms in the years 1942–45 and 1946–49 suggests that accumulation of capital goods at a rate much less than the optimum was consistent with an expansion of output of 29 per cent from 1939 to 1944.

INCREASE OF MACHINES ON FARMS (THOUSANDS)

	1942–45	*1946–49*
Tractors	747	1078
Motor trucks	395	510
Automobiles	−178	1098
Grain combines	150	215
Corn pickers	48	197
Milking machines	155	320
Percentage rise, farm machinery (1935–39 dollars)	8	31

Source: *Agricultural Outlook Charts—1950,* pp. 44, 49.

What might be expected is large investment for the farmers in the transitional year 1950–51 (June to June) or possibly in 1951 during which period the economy is being shifted to a semi-military basis. At first the defense resources will come out of additional output; and then they should be maintained at the expense of nonessential civilian output (e.g., housing, automobiles). During this period, it would be well to continue investment on farms at a high level so that, when military outlays become so large as to exclude all but the most essential immediate needs, the farmers' capital stock would be large enough to allow substantial depletion.

POLICY ISSUES

An examination of production figures reveals that despite some restrictionist policies in the thirties, farm production rose. Even in 1939, output was 106 (1935–39 = 100), or 14 per cent in excess of the output of 1934. Fortunately, there had been an improvement in economic conditions, with the result that cash receipts from farm marketings rose, though not so much as income of industrial workers. This substantial rise of total farm production may be associated with (*a*) the large rise of productivity (an increase of gross production of

29 per cent per worker in the years 1934 to 1939); (*b*) related to (*a*), the tendency to farm each acre more intensively in response to reduced allotments; (*c*) shifts of released acreage to production of commodities not under control; (*d*) a response of output to the increased demands in recent years for high-income foods—meats, dairy products, fruits and vegetables; (*e*) the reluctance of farmers to accept regimentation as the price to be paid for supply control and higher prices and incomes.

The failure of farm policy in the thirties to keep the output down more proved to be a blessing when war came. Even the failures in wheat and cotton were a blessing once the high level of output and carry-overs could be adapted to war purposes. In a similar manner, the failure to reduce output in 1948 and 1949 in the face of price pressure and the continued high carry-overs will contribute to the satisfaction of demand and the containment of inflation in the fifties.

For many years there has been much criticism of the government for spending large sums of money in order to curtail farm output and support prices. On the whole, the effects in contracting output do not seem to have been very successful.

What of the outlays involved? In all, government payments to farmers from 1934 to 1947 amounted to $8.5 billion, or 5 per cent of the $156.5 billion of net farm income over this period. From this total, we should deduct $2.1 billion paid to farmers in the years 1943 to 1946 in order to achieve *higher,* not lower production.

But what of the losses sustained by the CCC in its lending and purchasing operations? From 1933 through September 30, 1950, realized losses were $664 million, and valuation reserves for losses, which it was estimated would be sustained on the disposal of commodities then owned or to be acquired from loans, amounted to $653 million.[4]

The total cost of support programs to the government can then be estimated at $7.7 billion. A very liberal estimate, inclusive of aids for the years 1948–50, would be substantially less than $10 billion. The amount involved is much less than 5 per cent of farm income for the years 1933–50; less than 2 per cent of total government outlays in these 18 years; and less than ½ of 1 per cent of the $2,300 billion of national income in these years.

These figures give a rough indication of the direct payments made to farmers and other costs resulting from the support program. Most of the 25 to 32 million on the farms benefited from these outlays in the last 18 years. This form of protectionism given to the farmers should be put against the costs to the nation of the protection given manufacturers over a much longer period.

The cost to the average American is not only the additional taxes paid, but also the higher prices resulting from price support programs. Not only have farm prices risen but they have risen more than the prices of commodities purchased by farmers. Few will contest the fact that the government played a relatively small part (as implied above) in getting prices up, and that the major factors were the increased demand associated with the improved business conditions and especially war and preparation for war.

	Parity Ratio *	*Farm Income ($ Billion)*
1930–33	68	2.7
1934–41	85	4.7
1942–50	108	13.4
1946	113	14.8
1949	100	13.4
1950	100	13.0

Source: *The Economic Report of the President,* January, 1951, pp. 174, 195.

* Index of prices received and prices paid by farmers. Prices Received, August 1909–July 1914 = 100. Prices Paid, 1909–1914 = 100.

To some extent, the government contributed toward higher farm prices and incomes. The degree of approval of these policies will depend upon one's attitude toward government's interference with income distribution and the pricing process.

Our experience with farm policy prior to two great emergencies teaches some lessons:

1. In the semiwar world we live in, too effective control of output in peace periods may be a mistake. Large inventories of nonperishable commodities is a wise precaution and, therefore, as part of a price-support program, maximum inventories should be maintained.

2. A price-support program is a very effective weapon for achieving maximum co-operation of farmers in a program to raise output. For that reason, we do not subscribe to the views expressed in some influential quarters that, since demand was satisfactory in 1950–51, there was no need for a support program.

3. The manner of allocating support among commodities is far from satisfactory. The commodities chosen are determined too much by the influence of particular Congressmen, rather than by the needs of the nation. It is difficult otherwise to understand the inclusion of peanuts as a basic commodity; the failure to deal with perishable commodities on equal terms with *genuine* basic commodities (e.g., through price guarantees and free-market sales as suggested by Secretary Brannan); the haphazard distribution of programs and support dollars with little attention paid to favoring (*a*) the products in which the country has a comparative advantage or a small disadvantage (related to cost and demand conditions) in peace times or (*b*) the commodities which should receive preferential attention because of their importance in war; and finally the indiscriminate provision of subsidies irrespective of profits and size of farms (e.g., 100,000 farms, 2

per cent of the total, account for 25 per cent of all farm products).[5]

On the issue of comparative advantage, we note particularly that a support program which raises prices of a commodity in which the American farmer is especially effective may destroy markets both abroad and at home and aggravate the problem of controls. Nevertheless, the case for price-raising policies is stronger in these areas than for the commodities produced at high cost in the United States.

4. Our past experience with output control points to the need of marketing as well as acreage control as conditions of successful control of output. In view of the uncertain world situation, with a war or quasi-war economy prevailing in "peace" times, the case for further regimentation of farmers is not so great as it otherwise would be. In general, the desired correction is through increased demands rather than a curtailment of output. Then, in emergencies, our output would be high and any reduction of output could be met by pruning demand.

ISSUES DIRECTLY RELATED TO MOBILIZATION

Despite large losses in manpower, limitations on machinery, fertilizers and insecticides made available, and the restrictive effects of price control, agriculture increased its output substantially in World War II.

The problem in the fifties is largely one of maintenance of output rather than increases. In cotton and wool, serious shortages prevailed, however, at the very outset of the mobilization. The carry-over of cotton at the end of the 1950–51 marketing year was estimated late in 1950 at 3.3 million bales, or about one-quarter of that in 1940–41. With the economy twice as large, this shortage disturbed Washington and explained both a rise of prices of 10.2 cents per pound (35 per cent) in the year ending October, 1950, as well as the proposal to expand output from 10 to 16 million bales. In 1950, wool shorn was but 218 million pounds, as compared with 372 million pounds in 1940.

What are the appropriate policies in the course of mobilization and war? The price incentive is bound to play a smaller part than in the forties.

First, because the emergency starts with farm prices much higher absolutely and relatively than in the forties. In June, 1950, prices received by farmers were 2½ times as high as in 1940, and the parity ratio was 97, as compared with 81 + in 1940.

Second, output in 1950 was on a high plateau, close to two-fifths above prewar level. The rise of prices and output explains an increase of farm income of about 1½ times in the first half of 1950 over 1940. It is not likely that output will rise greatly in the fifties; and, in response to large losses of manpower and difficulties of obtaining machinery, fertilizer and insecticides, and less favorable weather conditions than in the forties, it may be difficult even to maintain the levels of output of the years 1948–50. It follows that price rises will contribute less to eliciting additional output than in the forties. (In 1951, farm experts anticipated further gains, although not equal to the rate of the forties.)

Perhaps a word should be said here concerning price-control policy, a subject discussed more fully in Chapter 20. From 1940 to 1945, the prices received by farmers rose by 96 per cent, or 2⅔ times as much as all wholesale prices. This large rise is a testimony of the great political strength of the farmers, but it might also be justified to some extent on the grounds that the large rise contributed toward a substantial increase of output and reflected in part the rise of costs incurred by farmers. Whatever the justification, however, the policy tended to aggravate the stabilization problem, for, as the Price Administrator attempted to stabilize prices, he was frustrated by the pressure of higher prices of food and raw materials. An incentive system, vigorously opposed by farm groups, which attempted to isolate the effects of increases of costs to that part of additional supply costing more, to some extent moderated the rise of farm prices.

As suggested above, a rise of output in the fifties is going to be less important than in the forties. For this reason, we cannot support price rises as a condition for increased output. When additional output is required, the case for differential pricing is as great as it was in World War II. The farmers should, however, be protected against price declines, which might follow in the wake of increased output: the price-support program and the Defense Production Act (DPA) provide the required degree of protection, although unfortunately price incentives for high cost units are excluded.

Perhaps the farmers are overly protected under DPA which precludes price ceilings reflecting prices to farmers below parity or below those prevailing just prior to the Korean War. A high authority in the Agriculture Department estimated for me, however, that in the unlikely event that all prices should rise to parity levels, retail food prices late in 1950 would have risen by 5 per cent and the consumers' price index by but 2 + per cent.

On one score, the farmers are overprotected. Under a major mobilization, what is required is sacrifices by all groups. Just as labor should not expect an increase of wage rates *pari passu* with the increase in the cost of living, so farmers should not expect a rise of prices in response to increases in living costs and taxes paid. Yet the parity program ties prices received by farmers to prices of what farmers buy. As the latter rises, the parity formula operates as an automatic inflationary mechanism. Insofar as stabilization of wages and other costs prevail, this problem will not emerge.

The final point that requires further discussion is the all-important manpower question. From 1940 to 1945, farm employment declined by 7 per cent, and numbers on the farm by 5.1 million or 17 per cent. In the fifties, the farms may be more successful in holding their labor than in the forties, for the following reasons: First, relative wage rates are higher on the farms than in 1940. In 1950, the ratio of farm wages had risen to 0.38 per cent of factory wages, as compared with 0.26 per cent in 1939. Coverage under the Old-age and Survivors' Insurance should also make farm work more attractive. Second, control of wages on the farms should be much more difficult than in the factory.[6] Third, attempts are being made to make more effective use of seasonal workers. Fourth, the proportion of farm workers in the age group demanded by the military, ages 18 to 24, is much less than in 1940: 1940 = 1,323,000; 1945 = 636,000; 1949 = 891,000. Fifth, with serious mobilization, manpower control is likely to be a more potent factor than in World War II.[7]

Against these favorable factors, we should note (*a*) the greater shortages pending, and, therefore, stronger pressures for workers to leave the farms, and (*b*) the increased importance of skilled workers, as farms are more mechanized now —and these are especially the workers in great demand.

CONCLUSION

In general, we are impressed by the large gains of productivity and output on the farms in the forties. The need for continued high output points to the need of adequate machinery and other production factors for the farm and particularly the maintenance of, and a high priority for, machinery—in particular so long as our economy is not fully mobilized for war.

A continuance of price support is a necessary condition for co-operation of farmers. We do not go so far, however, as to demand price rises on the scale of those in World War II. The problem now is more to maintain output than to increase it. And it is important that farmers, like all other groups, should make sacrifices. Therefore, it is not expedient to support built-in inflation as the parity formula allows. By this I mean that to some extent farm prices rise automatically with increases in costs inclusive of some taxes. In inflationary periods, these automatic features may kindle inflationary fires.

6. EXTERNAL ASPECTS

MAXIMIZATION OF SUPPLIES

IN A HIGHLY mobilized or war economy, the first principle of international economics is to import as much as possible and export as little as possible: the less exports and the more imports, the more available for the defense or war economy.

This first principle is subject to an important reservation: exportation is required to aid allies or to carry on war abroad. We maintained exports at a very high level through private and foreign loans in World War I; and primarily through foreign assistance in World War II. In the years 1941–45 this country exported almost $40 billion of goods under government aegis through lend-lease, these accounting for more than two-thirds of the exports of this country.[1] In addition, lend-lease included several billion dollars of aid not reflected in these figures. The large exports on account of the United States military forces are, of course, not included in these figures.

Despite the demands of the mobilization and war, then, and despite the relevance of the principle of minimum exports, United States exports have been at record heights in wartime. The $17 billion of exports in 1944 (exclusive of U.S. military exports) is still a record figure—even when compared with the $16 billion for the year 1947. Prices of exports were at least 50 per cent higher in 1947 than in 1944. At equal prices the exports (inclusive of lend-lease but exclusive of U.S. military) in 1944 were still about 50 per cent above the 1947 peak.

Just because the export drain is so great in wartime, it becomes imperative to scrutinize exports, both with a view to obtaining the most effective distribution of commodities between domestic and foreign uses and the best possible allocations according to destinations and uses, given the needs of the war economy. These objectives raise the problem of export controls, one that the Board of Economic Warfare and the Foreign Economic Administration were responsible for during the war, and, more recently, the Department of Commerce.[2]

Just as in World War II, continuance of tensions in the postwar period makes necessary large amounts of public assistance and export controls. In the mobilization of the fifties, the United States will have to continue large exports as aid to our allies and to scrutinize the exports. The important question will be: What proportion of total output should be diverted to exports, private and public? What proportion of the allotment should be financed through normal trade channels? To what extent should exports be divided between civilian and military goods? Between goods for consumption and development? What proportion of the total should go to Western Europe, to Asia, and to other friendly nations, for example?

An import policy is another facet of mobilization and war policy. Hitler was one of the first to see that a mobilized or war economy should import as much as possible and export as little as possible. In World War II, the U.S. Government made heroic attempts to procure supplies abroad. The government sent delegations abroad, spent money on development abroad with a view to expanding output and exports from foreign countries to this country, and lowered tariff barriers.

The Foreign Economic Administration summarized the activities of the government as follows:

Purchases have been made with government funds generally when war-time needs for strategic commodities were urgent or unpredictable or the military deadline for delivery stringent; when it was difficult or impossible for private importers to buy materials in a country when there was inflation and to bring them in and sell them under the Office of Price Administration ceilings; when shipping and insurance rates were up; when the output of sub-marginal mines and high-cost plantations was needed; when new aggregations of labor had to be recruited and housed; when it was necessary to pay high prices to keep strategic materials in neutral countries out of Axis hands; when it was necessary to build insurance stock piles both in the country and in foreign parts; and when problems arising out of the liberation of Axis-dominated areas created situations which private trade could not meet.[3]

In 1941–45, government imports amounted to $11½ billion; and from 1942 to 1945, they exceeded private imports. About two-fifths of these government imports consisted of reverse lend-lease; two-fifths, non-military purchases; and one-fifth, military purchases.[4]

INTEGRATION OF PRICE AND SUPPLY POLICIES

In order to maximize imports, it is necessary to offer prices adequate to elicit supplies. Prices consistent with this supply policy may, however, be too high to be consistent with price ceilings. The alternatives then become: (*a*) maintenance of ceilings and exclusion of high-priced items; (*b*) an increase in ceiling prices when the foreign sources of supplies are substantial; (*c*) government purchase at high prices and sales at prices consistent with ceilings.

The problem of reconciling price and supply policies is often beset with difficulties. By operating as a monopoly buyer, however, the government can frequently depress foreign selling prices sufficiently to avert substantial price increases. In the markets for antimony, chromite, copper, lead, platinum, tin, tungsten, and zinc, the government's record of stabilizing prices was remarkable in 1939–43, as compared with 1914–18.[5] Effectiveness of monopoly purchases indeed may be neutralized by monopoly behavior on the part of the sellers.

In determining the concessions to be made pricewise (i.e., rises in price ceilings), the authorities have to weigh the importance of the additional supplies to be obtained against the damage caused by higher prices.

The problem of controls is not merely one of integrating price and supply controls. It is also important to assure the maximum effectiveness of use of imports. That means import licenses through rationing of shipping space, and also agreements on the part of importers to dispose of essential imports according to regulations issued by the supply authorities.

In the export field, similar problems of integrating price and supply controls arise. As is noted in Chapter 20, excessive prices for exports stimulate excessive diversions to export markets. It is, therefore, necessary to control prices of exports, although the difficulties of achieving control all along the line mean that the ultimate foreign purchasers may not benefit at all from United States export price control. With a much more thoroughgoing control of the volume and direction of exports than in World War II, the country might dispense with export price control. The result would then be that the amount of exports would be determined by authority, and any gains to be associated with scarcities would accrue to United States exporters, not foreign importers. With heavy taxes, the government could drain off part of the extra profits. Despite high per unit profits, however, total profits of export merchants may not be large, if exports through private channels are greatly reduced.

PROBLEMS OF FOREIGN AID

An economist can say very little concerning the distribution of foreign aid among Europe, Asia, and other areas; or between military and nonmilitary aid. These are to a considerable degree problems of political policy. I can do little more than dwell on the record and suggest the nature of some of the problems.

Foreign aid is an old problem with this country. Over the last thirty-five years, inclusive of useless gold absorbed, this country has given away or loaned much more than $100 billion. In the postwar years 1946–50, this country financed an export surplus of about $25 billion: about one-half came from United States Government aid, 30 per cent from United States Government loans, 10 per cent in exchange for gold and dollar assets given up by the foreign countries, and 10 per cent by private investment on the part of Americans.[6]

The occasion for this aid has been war and its after-effects; the accompanying loss of foreign assets and markets by Europe and some parts of Asia; the continued competitive gains of the United States in the reduction of costs and development of new products and markets; the increased protectionism here, though not since 1934; the effects of weak fiscal policies and inflation upon exports and imports in Europe, related in turn to some of the factors mentioned above.

Economists are divided into two camps on the issue of dollar shortage. Few dissent from the view that the dollar shortage is genuine. The difference largely relates to the possibility of curing the disease, should appropriate measures be taken by the countries suffering from dollar shortage: e.g., reduction of government expenditures; increased taxation; pruning of investments not contributing to increased productivity; reducing consumption to the extent that it is not required as an incentive; readjusting exchange rates to a level conforming to relative costs and prices. The adherents to the "shortage school" have been inclined to emphasize the point that, given the institutional setup, the required financial monetary and real measures would not be forthcoming; and there were some doubts that the market response to price changes would be adequate.

Thus, could an unstable French Government survive which would increase taxes substantially, reduce imports and increase exports and restrain wage increases, with accompanying reductions in standards of living? Could a British Government survive which abandoned the housing, health and other social welfare programs as a means of reducing taxes and prices and improving Britain's competitive position? And if prices declined by 25 per cent, would British exports to dollar areas or to nondollar areas at the expense of the United States rise sufficiently to provide the British with the required supply of additional dollars?

These questions are of more than academic interest even in the midst of mobilization. We do not know that the dollar problem has been solved. Even in the midst of mobilization and war, we may have to provide dollars merely to cover the "normal" deficit of Western Europe and other parts of the world.

We do know that there has been a substantial improvement since 1947. From 1947 to 1949, Western Europe's dollar deficit was reduced from 7 to 3 billion dollars; and in 1950, there was a further improvement. Undoubtedly, the devaluation of 1949 was helpful, not so much in piercing the United States market but rather in squeezing United States exporters out of third markets, and making imports from dollar countries more expensive. With Western European output 20 per cent higher than in prewar, it became easier to impose adequate fiscal policies, control inflation, maintain an adequate investment program and minimum standards of consumption and defense. All of these are suggestive of improvement. Yet we are not ready to say that Europe and the rest of the world have solved their dollar problem and that in the mobilization or war economy the United States can disregard the dollar-scarcity problem.[7]

That the dollar-shortage problem is not as yet solved is suggested by the fact that since 1947 Europe gained primarily not in an expansion of exports but rather in a reduction of imports, and this reduction reflected largely discrimination against United States exports.

U.S. TRADE WITH ERP COUNTRIES ($ MILLION)

	1947	*1950 (first half at annual rate)*	*Change*
Exports of goods and services from the U.S. to ERP countries	7,217	4,344	−2,873
Imports of goods and services of the U.S. from ERP countries ..	1,789	2,492	+703

Source: *Report to the President on Foreign Economic Policies*, 1950, p. 107.

Of Western Europe's improvement in her balance of trade vis-à-vis the United States, approximately 80 per cent was in a reduction of imports, and only 20 per cent in a rise of exports. Similar correctives are evident in the plans of the countries participating in the ERP. Their plans were to improve their balance of payments by $6,000 million, visible exports by 93 per cent and invisible exports by 19 per cent, and to offset these gains by a rise of imports by 12 per cent. Imports from the United States and Canada were to fall from 35 per cent of total imports in 1947 to 16 per cent in 1951–52; and exports to these dollar countries, to rise from 7.2 per cent to 8.3 per cent.

PLANNED MOVEMENTS IN BALANCE OF PAYMENTS OF ECA COUNTRIES, 1947 TO 1951–52 ($ MILLION)

Rise of imports	704
Rise of exports	5,575
Rise of invisible exports (net) (shipping, interest, etc.)	1,116

Source: OEEC, European Recovery Program, *Second Report of the OEEC,* 1950, pp. 85–86.

ISSUES IN A MOBILIZED ECONOMY

We can safely conclude that the dollar problem has not been solved, though it may temporarily be shelved. The large gains of reserves by European countries since the Korean difficulties, reflecting especially higher prices and increased demands for raw materials sold by members of the British Commonwealth and other dependencies, emphasize the fact that dollar shortage was certainly less acute in 1950 than it was even in 1949. But this is far from saying that the problem is solved. There will no longer be dollar shortages when, with normal capital movements, the Western European countries can discard exchange control, introduce free convertibility of their currencies into dollars, end discrimination against the dollar, and discontinue special favors for the export trade and particularly for exporters selling in dollar markets.

Whatever the state of the dollar market in the pre-Korean situation, Western Europe is going to suffer from a serious dollar shortage as a result of the rearmament program. For rearmament means larger public deficits, rising prices, increased resources going into armaments and, therefore, reduced resources for exports and increased demands for imports. In one sense, the rise of prices will not be serious; for in international economic relations, the relative rise of prices is what counts. Should prices rise more rapidly in Europe than elsewhere, exports would suffer and imports rise. With the United States rearming, the pressure on prices is likely to be felt here as well as elsewhere; and it is not clear that prices will rise more rapidly in Western Europe than in the dollar countries. Starting from a more highly employed economy than the average of Western Europe and more reluctant to rely on controls than some of them, the price rise may be greater in the United States than in Western Europe.

Yet in these days of controlled economies, price movements are not so important as in the prewar days. The real issues are how much Western Europe is prepared to spend on defense and where these resources are to come from. A large rise of prices following substantial increases in military outlays would underline the point that the military expenditures are additional and are not being offset by increased output, reduced investment, consumption or nondefense outlays. To assure the required offsets, the governments would have to increase taxes, reduce nondefense outlays, stimulate savings adequately, and prune private investment, thus releasing resources from consumption and investment through measures which curtail demand (e.g., increased taxes), or which divert resources from nonmilitary uses (e.g., allocations).

How much aid Western Europe would receive depends in part upon how much she spends on defense; the sacrifices the nations make in reduced consumption and nonessential investment in meeting these demands; and how much help Western Europe will receive as a result of the increased purchases in dollar countries from the British Commonwealth and other dependent nations.

It is difficult to estimate the military outlays of Western European countries. Much depends upon their willingness to defend themselves and the sacrifices they are prepared to make. Even on the pre-Korean estimates for the Atlantic countries, the program involved a doubling of military expenditure for the United Kingdom and France in the years

1951–55, with these countries averaging outlays of about $7 billion, or 10 per cent of their gross national product (GNP). In the August plans (1950), after President Truman had recommended a three-year program of annual expenditures for military aid of $4 billion supplementary to all foreign aid, inclusive of the Mutual Defense Assistance Program, France and the United Kingdom, which accounted for about 75 per cent of the military outlays of the European Atlantic Pact nations, announced plans for outlays averaging $5.5 billion in 1951–53, or about 8½ per cent of their GNP.[8]

Before the Korean War, the Western European countries were spending about twice as large a proportion of their GNP on military outlays as the United States. A good guess would be that by early 1952 the United States would be spending about 20 per cent of her GNP on military outlays. Similar outlays for Western Europe would require at least $20 billion of military expenditures. (I leave out of account incomes of several countries not able to participate in the program and assume that *all* of Western Europe would spend 1½ times as much as the United Kingdom and France.) At this point, the proportion of gross income spent on military would be 20 per cent in the United States and somewhat less in Western Europe, since military outlays of substantial amounts are out of the question for some countries. From spending twice as large a proportion of income as the United States in early 1950, Western Europe would be spending less than the proportion spent in this country by (say) early 1952. The *relative* rise for the United States is explained in part by higher income, larger potential rises of output, and greater commitments in Europe.

For purposes of analysis, let us assume $20 billion of military outlays in Europe by early 1952 and $60 billion by the United States. Then the question is how much aid should the United States provide? Obviously, the more aid provided by the United States, the less Western Europe will have to depend upon reductions in investment and consumption (through private and public channels). According to the best estimates available for 1949, consumption per head was 10 per cent less in Western Europe than in 1938, and 40 per cent higher in the United States; and per capita income about one-third as high in Western Europe as in this country in 1949, as compared with one-half in 1938.[9]

These figures suggest that sacrifices can be made more easily here than in Western Europe, though to some extent the cut in consumption associated with a $60 billion military program would reduce these differences. At any rate, with the United States proposing a contribution of $4 billion toward military spending of Western Europe of about $7 billion, the United States share would rise with outlays of $20 billion. The Budget for the fiscal year 1952 provided $7.46 billion for international security and foreign relations ($4.73 billion in 1951). Most of this sum would be spent for military aid.

THE RELEVANCE OF AID TO UNDERDEVELOPED AREAS

Much depends also upon how much the United States spends on help to underdeveloped areas. Estimates of appropriate aid to these areas have been as high as $1,000 billion. Actually, in the pre-Korean days, annual outlays within (say) five years of about 4 to 5 billion dollars, as European aid was cut, seemed practical and desirable. These were to be investments to improve the standard of living of the underprivileged people as part of a fight against communism and avoidance of war. They seemed like small outlays as compared to the sacrifices made by the American people for foreign aid, or war in the years 1914–49, and small relative to what they might contribute toward averting a war which could easily cost three times the $350 billion cost of World War II. These large outlays, however, awaited increased absorptive powers by the beneficiary nations (e.g., improved administration, better fiscal system). It was clearly necessary to finance these programs by government or long-term loans with low rates of interest and generally without amortization features. Only in this way could a long-range program be effected without raising serious trade and financing problems. The required change-over from a lending (exporting) to a borrowing nation (receiving repayments and importing net) should be a gradual one. In fact, the program could be defended as one which makes possible a continued high level of exports and one which would not concentrate the burden of adjustment in a short period upon export industries. These industries would be unable to sell adequately without aid of some kind. The need of long-run arrangements, as suggested above, is clarified by the following:

NEW FINANCING REQUIRED TO MAINTAIN $1-BILLION EXCESS OF EXPORTS

2 per cent loan without amortization (in 25 years)	$1.64 billion
2 per cent loan with 20-year amortization (in 25 years)	4.41 billion
8 per cent loan without amortization (in 50 years)	46.9 billion

These are not the only serious problems that arise. Many are discouraged by the fact that the first gains of a development program would be a reduction of death rates and an intensification of the population pressure. Here the problem is largely one of generous aid in the early years which would yield an improvement in the standards of living, education, and the like. In this manner, the United States and others might induce a frontal attack on the population problem. A favorable factor would be the rise of the working population; and we receive some encouragement from British, Japanese, and other experiences with industrialization.

In the mobilized or war economy, these grants or assistance must be related to the prior demands of the military. Few would dispute the need of aggressive measures in Asia to contend with the communist threat. Hence, even in a mobilized economy, some aid will be necessary. That the help to the underdeveloped areas will contribute toward an acquisition of raw materials badly needed and that the dollars received will help solve Western Europe's problems, also suggest the relation of aid to underdeveloped areas and the military program.[10]

CONCLUSION

In the international sphere, the major problems confronting the mobilized or war economy will be the allocation of resources between domestic and foreign use; the division of military supplies between use by the American and foreign forces; the allocation of exportable goods and services between civilian and military, among regions, between private and public disposal, among use for foreign recovery, military aid, and developmental purposes. The government will also have to maximize imports, both by keeping prices down and assuring their most effective use. It is hoped that supply and demand and price policies will be better integrated than they were in 1941–45.

It is clear that, though the problem of dollar shortage is not solved, United States dollars and what they buy will be used much more for supporting the military and development programs and much less to maintain Western European consumption and investment standards. How much military aid will be provided will depend upon the extent of European rearmament, the sacrifices that the European governments can impose on their people, the attitude of the American people toward making available resources for this purpose in a period when their standard of living is certain to fall.[11]

Part Three

MONEY AND INFLATION

7. THE MONETARY PROBLEM

THE INCREASED NEED OF MONEY

OUR PRESENT experience of one major emergency closely following another is unique in our modern history. With only part of the debris of one disaster removed, another disaster is upon us. This unfortunate timing is reflected in our monetary situation.

In the past, this country has experienced vast expansions in her monetary supplies which the country ultimately absorbed without great damage. Thus, in the last quarter of the nineteenth century, despite the inflationary expansion during the Civil War, our problem was monetary poverty, not excess; and similarly during a large part of the interwar period following World War I. In fact, throughout most of our history monetary supplies have tended to rise much more than income. As a people become more affluent, they seem to put an increased part of their rising income in cash and bank deposits. Thus, in the years 1800 to 1940, the amount of money and deposits rose by 1,750 times, the national income by but 110 times. Yet the net change of prices was not substantial. In the absence of another great crisis, this country easily would have grown up to the large supplies of money bequeathed by the last war. In fact, experiences of the past suggest that the supply of money may well not have been excessive even in 1950.

MONETARY EXPERIENCE IN WORLD WAR II

In the World War II period, the banking system created vast supplies of additional money, largely as part of the process of absorbing government securities which could not be purchased by the public or savings institutions. Thus the Committee on Public Debt Policy (*Our National Debt,* p. 54) estimated that out of $383 billion expended by the government from July 1, 1941, to June 30, 1946, taxation provided $169 billion (46 per cent) and borrowing the remainder. Nonbank investors purchased $128 billion of securities, Federal Reserve banks $22 billion, and commercial banks $64 billion.

Perhaps a better way of putting the problem is to compare not taxes and total government expenditures but *additional* taxes (over prewar) and war outlays. Such calculation would yield a ratio of taxes to government outlays for war lower than that given in the above survey.

In the war years, there was a large expansion of monetary supplies. This was made possible by an expansion of Federal Reserve credit outstanding which, *ceteris paribus,* increases the reserves of banks correspondingly.

INCREASE OF VARIOUS MONETARY VARIABLES, END OF 1939 TO END OF 1945 ($ BILLION)

Federal Reserve credit	22.5
Monetary gold stock	2.5
Money in circulation	20.9
Member bank reserves	4.3
Excess reserves	—3.7

Source: *Federal Reserve Bulletin.*

The main factors involved are shown in this table. A combined expansion of federal reserve credit and monetary gold stock of $25 billion made possible a rise of money in circulation of $21 billion and of member bank reserve balances of $4 billion. (With an expansion of reserve credit or an inflow of gold, the reserves of member banks rise correspondingly and with an expansion of money in circulation, reserves decline: banks pay for cash required by the public with their reserves.) This expansion of reserve balances would not have been adequate to support an expansion of demand deposits of $73 billion (32 to 105) without the availability of large excess reserves. By obtaining $4.3 billion of additional reserves and reducing excess reserves by $3.7 billion, the banks were able to expand demand deposits by $73 billion, a ratio of 9 to 1.

This growth in demand deposits was much greater than that in income. For the former, the expansion was about 2⅓ times; for the latter but 1½ times. The supply of money was indeed high in relation to the growth of income; and in relation to the rise of prices it was even more excessive. The increase of money had been 7 to 8 times that in prices of consumer goods.

EXCESS OF MONEY IN THE FORTIES

This excess of money in relation to income and a fortiori in relation to prices was largely corrected in the postwar period. Price control and rationing, together with the related high level of savings in the war period, explained in part the abnormally high monetary supplies in relation to prices. The removal of controls in 1945–46 was a signal for the money to begin to chase the limited supply of goods available and raise prices, thus bringing monetary supplies into a more normal relationship with prices.

Obviously the high purchasing power of the dollar in 1945, with the dollar still worth 77 cents in 1939 dollars, was in large part fictitious. Multiply 0.77 by 3⅓ (the ratio of monetary supplies in 1945 to those in 1939) and the product, 2.56, is the apparent increase of purchasing power of money. The public's money was not really worth 2.56 times as much as in 1939. This might be inferred from the fact that the output of consumption goods (in 1939 dollars) was but one-half more than in 1939. Each dollar was worth 77 cents only on the condition that an unusually large proportion of these dollars were to be hoarded. Once the signal was given for free spending, prices were bound to rise.

By the end of 1949, the orgy of spending had largely corrected the distortion between money and prices. Money was much less plentiful, relative to income and prices, than in 1945. Removal of controls and release of pent-up demand tended to raise prices. A modest reduction of national debt also contributed to the relative reduction of money and, therefore, to a more normal relationship of money and prices. But the table below reveals that the supply of money was still large relative to income. The excess was not great, however, and from 1945 to 1949, the supply of money rose by 16 per cent and GNP by 34 per cent. The less than 15 per cent excess in money vis-à-vis GNP, relative to 1939, may well be explained away as the increased ratio of money to income expected at the high income levels of 1949.

RISE OF MONEY, PRICES, AND INCOME, FROM 1939 TO 1945 AND 1949 (PER CENT)

	1939 to 1945	*1939 to 1949*
Demand deposits and currency in circulation	178	206
Consumer prices	29	70
Gross national product (GNP)	136	182

Source: *Survey of Current Business,* February, 1950.

Even the rise of prices is not greatly out of line. Indeed, in 1949, the supply of money was 206 per cent in excess of 1939 and prices had risen by but 70 per cent. But allowance should be made for an increase in output of about 60 per cent relative to 1939: a rise of output offsets an expansion of monetary supplies, thus reducing the inflationary pressures.

With prices up 70 per cent and output up 60 per cent, the relative excess of money in 1949 was only of the order of 10 to 20 per cent. Hence the monetary excess was not so large as was generally assumed. For the professional economist, I add that this old-fashioned quantity theory approach oversimplifies the problem.

INFLATIONARY PRESSURES, 1946–49

In view of our capacity to absorb additional supplies of money at a greater rate than indicated by the rise of income, even the supplies of money in 1945 need not have been excessive. If they seemed to be, the explanation lies largely in the low level of private investment and consumption in the years 1942–45. Even when allowance is made for the rise of taxation, these outlays had been small. Once controls were removed, consumption and private investment rose in a spectacular fashion.

What happened is clear from the following figures:

	Four Years, 1942–45	*Four Years, 1946–49*
GNP ($ Billion)	785	959
Consumption expenditure ($ Billion)	428	668
Percentage consumption to GNP	55	70
Gross private domestic investment ($ Billion)	35	135
Percentage private investment to GNP	5	14

Source: Calculated from *Midyear Economic Report of the President,* July, 1950, p. 115.

What is especially striking is the relation of the rise of GNP and that of consumption (rise, 1946–49 over 1942–45):

	$ Billion
Rise of GNP	174
Rise of consumption	240
Rise of gross private investment	100

Consumption expanded by $66 billion more than the increase of total GNP and consumption and private investment by almost twice as much as that of GNP. It is not surprising then that inflationary pressures developed and that, on top of a full-employment economy in 1945, gross national product rose further and that from 1945 to 1949 consumer prices rose by 32 per cent.

These statistics point to the pitfalls in concentrating merely on money, price and output relationships. It is imperative to consider the growth of income and its allocation.

POSTWAR INFLATION AND GOVERNMENT POLICY

With inflationary pressures dominant in the years 1946–50 (with a brief interlude), attention once more was focused on monetary supplies and monetary policy. In view of the large programs superimposed on a full-employment program, only in part offset by a decline of governmental activity, some restrictive policies were in order. In fact by 1948, the national debt had fallen from the 1945 level of $278 billion to $252 billion, a decline of $26 billion. But it would be wrong to assume that this reduction reflects a corresponding contraction of spending. For the government paid off a *substantial* part of this debt by drawing on highly inflated wartime cash balances. Idle balances were exchanged for government securities now withdrawn by the Treasury. Yet there was some restraint put upon the banks; for in part the securities redeemed were held by reserve banks; and repayment meant a loss of reserves for member banks. Tax funds were thus transferred by member banks to the government at the reserve banks. A resulting hardening of rates occurred in 1947–48.

Demand deposits (adjusted), however, tended to rise—and despite the redemption of public securities held by the banks. The explanation was largely the continued expansion of bank loans, which, of course, accounted for the creation of new bank deposits.

In these years, prices rose more than might be explained by the expansion of monetary supplies. This might well be expected in view of the stampede to purchase consumers' goods long unavailable and to renovate and expand plant. The high level of spending called for corrective measures, the most obvious of which was high taxes and postponement of nonessential government expenditures for a more propitious time. But the government and particularly Congress did not have the courage to raise taxes and twice yielded to pressure to reduce them. The government could easily have collected $30 billion more in taxes in the years 1946–50 and reduced expenditures to some extent. Large economies should have been forthcoming in 1946–48 and 1950, though a reversal of these policies might have been called for in 1949.

OBSTACLES TO EFFECTIVE MONETARY POLICY

With inflationary pressure strong and with fiscal policy in default, those concerned with the inflation problem naturally looked in the direction of monetary policy. But here they met a road block. Indeed, the reserve banks held $24 billion of government securities at the end of 1945. With member bank reserves of but $16 billion, the reserve banks, by selling part of these securities to the market, could have reduced drastically the reserves of member banks. Actually, member bank reserves continued to rise in the next three years.

The reserve banks were powerless to control the situation. First, because it was necessary to support the government bond market. Member banks short of cash either because of increased demands or because of sales of government securities by the reserve banks, could replenish their reserves by selling government securities to the reserve banks. This was virtually an automatic process. Second, because business and the public were more independent than usual. That is to say, cash reserves supplemented by other liquid assets were larger than usual (though as I have argued elsewhere this may not be so important as is generally assumed). The second point means simply that large increases of outlays were possible without recourse to the banks. A comparison of the rise of consumption and investment in the years 1946–49 over 1942–45 surely underlines the point that the public could increase their outlays much more than any expansion of bank loans would suggest. The annual average rise of consumption and investment in 1946–49 over 1942–45 was $87 billion; that in bank loans, only $17 billion.

Again, total consumer credit rose from $6.6 billion in 1946 to $18.8 billion in 1949. The rise in consumer installment loans by commercial banks was much less. Thus consumer installment credit of commercial banks rose only from 1.4 to 4.6 billion dollars, or an amount equal to about one-fourth of the total rise of consumer credit. These statistics also point to some independence from the banks.

Those supporting stronger monetary measures urged large sales of government securities to the public and smaller sales to the banks—that is, a reduction of bank deposits as banks disposed of government securities. But obviously this would mean higher rates of interest required to attract the private investors. The Treasury was not receptive to this policy. Others were prepared to accept higher rates of interest, but they insisted that the government bond market be protected —e.g., by forcing banks to hold designated amounts in relation to deposits.

THE CASE FOR MONETARY POLICY

This brings us to the crises of 1950–51 and later years. In the thirties and forties, it became fashionable to concentrate on fiscal policy and regard monetary policy as outmoded. This change of emphasis stemmed from the appeal of the new fiscal weapon, from the failures of monetary policy, and also from the great strains put upon monetary policy in an economy saddled with a large government debt.

But recently it has become fashionable once more to pay attention to monetary policy. One reason for this is some dissatisfaction with fiscal policy: the failure of the Congress to make the most effective use of it; and the necessary delays in making it effective.

In the crisis of the summer of 1950, for example, it was clear that a serious inflationary situation was developing. The obvious attack was a rise of taxes and an encouragement of savings. But these take much time even on the assumption that the government and the public are prepared to take the necessary action. In response to the increased purchase of assets of all kinds and the widespread demands for large wage increases and the resulting activation of money, prices react almost instantaneously. Even a heroic fiscal policy, aside from delays, may not be able to carry the burden of anti-inflationary policies in the face of these unusual inflationary pressures. Hence every possible weapon should be enlisted.

In short, then, there is a strong case for monetary restraints as the quickest and most effective short-run anti-inflationary therapy. As anti-inflationary fiscal policy develops and as demands for higher pay increases are curbed, then the dependence on monetary policy may be reduced. The danger of monetary policy is that it operates like an axe and not as a scalpel. Not only may restraining influences weaken inflationary pressures but they may also increase the cost of national debt more than justified by the inflationwise gains, and may unnecessarily curtail output.

CONCLUSION

In summary, the war left a legacy of excess money and latent inflation. Given a freedom from a great emergency, the country might well have grown up to this excess supply of money without any serious inflationary results. Actually even in 1945, the excess may not have been substantial; and from 1946 to 1949, the unusual increase in spending for consumption and investment, not exactly explicable by excess monetary supplies nor by bank lending, contributed toward a more normal relationship of money income and prices.

The crisis of 1950 showed clearly that in the midst of a fear of war and an incipient wage inflation the supplies of money were more than sufficient to fuel an inflation. At this juncture, the authorities once more looked toward monetary policy as the quickest, if also the crudest, attack on this problem. Fiscal policy was too slow and indecisive. But here the Federal Reserve ran into the vested interests of the Treasury.

In 1951, the Federal Reserve tightened the monetary screw. A flattening out of the price rise in the middle of the year reflects overbuying earlier, the effects of controls, the monetary policy and delays in defense buying.

8. THE INFLATION PROBLEM

WARS AND INFLATION

MOBILIZATION and wars breed inflation. The rise of prices varies with the damage done to the economy and the measures taken to deal with the problem. In the French Revolution even the guillotine could not stop an inflation which ultimately was measured by a rise of prices of about 200 times, although the supply of money rose by but 20 times. World War I established new records with German domestic prices rising by 1,000 million times as much as prices in the United States in the years 1914–1923. In the Civil War, World War I, and World War II, the United States suffered serious inflation, but relative to the effort involved the rise of price was less with each succeeding effort. An improved tax program, better techniques for stimulating savings and the use of controls account for the gains of the later conflagrations. Indeed, other countries were not as fortunate. In Hungary, prices after World War II rose by 100,000,000,000,000,000 times, undoubtedly a world's record.

THE COSTS OF INFLATION

It is scarcely necessary to suggest why we must shun inflation. The resulting injustices breed discontent and interfere with production—e.g., consider the labor strife which follows. In 1950–51, there were special reasons for fighting inflation. Since 1939, prices had risen by 70 per cent; but hourly wages in bituminous mining and manufacturing were up by about 130 per cent, income of farm proprietors by 200 per cent (1949, but less in 1950), corporate profits after taxes about 270 per cent. Yet millions had received a rise of income less than that in prices. Their standard of living had deteriorated in a period during which the national product had grown by about two-thirds. Included in this unfortunate group are those living on fixed incomes (annuities) and large numbers of white-collar workers. To cite an example close to home: the average professor's income was down by 25 per cent in 1939 dollars. Since the average American's income was up 50 per cent (in stable dollars), the relative position of the professor had deteriorated by one-half ($75 \div 150 = \frac{1}{2}$).

A second dose of inflation superimposed on the 70 per cent rise of 1939–50 would be very costly indeed. Not alone because of the injustices; but also because of the distortions wrought on the economic system by the inflationary process—e.g., the encouragement of inefficiency.

SPECIAL THREATS IN THE FIFTIES

It is unfortunate that when the damage that may be inflicted is unusually great, the threat is serious. We are not so fortunate as in 1940. We do not have the 10 million unemployed, the 10 million potentially new members of the labor market, the excess capacity, the large reserves of raw materials. Ten years of war and quasi-war, ten years of full employment, and ten years of plundering our national resources—these have had an effect. The pressure of war demand superimposed upon unprecedented civilian demand will be confronted by bottlenecks much sooner and in larger numbers than in 1940–42. Hence we conclude that from the side of supply, the situation is precarious.

Despite improved records in the later major wars (i.e., price relative to magnitude of effort), there is one disconcerting aspect of the trends. The wage-price inflation spiral seems to become more threatening as trade unionism becomes more powerful. This is suggested by the relative rise of wage rates and prices in three successive crises. In the Civil War, labor suffered a serious decline in real wage rates, that is, endured much sacrifice as might be expected in a major war; but in World War I, the rise of wage rates greatly exceeded that in the cost of living and, a fortiori, in World War II. (It is scarcely necessary to add that a comparison of changes in the hourly earnings and the cost of living is not an adequate measure of the sacrifices made.)

PERCENTAGE RISE IN AVERAGE HOURLY EARNINGS AND COST OF LIVING, DURING THREE WAR PERIODS

	Average Hourly Earnings	*Cost of Living*
Civil War, 1861–65	54.4	149.3
World War I, 1914–20	142.0	100.0
World War II, 1941–45	40.2	22.5

Source: U.S. Department of Labor, *Problems and Policies of Dispute Settlement and Wage Stabilization During World War II,* 1951, pp. 169–70.

We take the above position subject to one reservation, namely, that business has expanded its capital plant at an unprecedented rate. This is suggested by outlays of 80–90 billion dollars in the years 1946–50 for plant and equipment. This is an amount which at 1950 prices comes close to equaling the prewar plant. The new dollars of investment are more efficient dollars than the old even when allowance is made for the rise of prices.

THE RELEVANCE OF HIGHER OUTPUT AND DIVERSIONS

This reservation is not, however, as important as it at first seems. Indeed, the more we produce, the lower prices will fall *ceteris paribus*. But the fact is that however helpful it is to turn out more goods (and we insist our great problem now is that we shall have to depend less on *expansions* of output), more production aggravates the inflationary problem.

The common view that the way to fight inflation is to increase production is correct only in the sense that *with a given demand,* inflation will be less with more output. Unfortunately demand does not stay put. More output means more income and hence more demand. What brings the inflationary pressure is the rise of income not accompanied by a corresponding flow of consumers' goods, or at least not equal to the amounts the public wishes to spend at current prices. That is why prices tend upward, not when production is low, as in the thirties, but when it is high, as in the forties.

What makes the inflationary threat especially great now is the fact that we shall have to rely so much on *diversions* from the civilian population in order to provide the military with the resources required. This means not only that the public must eventually yield any additional income associated with any rise of output but also part of current (1950) income. This is in contrast with World War II.

Thus, compare 1944 and 1939:

Change, 1939 to 1944	*$ Billion*
Rise of gross national product	120
Rise of expenditures for war	84
Rise of consumption	43

We had more guns *and* more butter.

Now compare 1950 and (say) early 1952. Assume war outlays of $65 billion. This equals about one-half (at current prices) of the 1940 level, and about $50 billion in excess of 1950 levels. Here is a guess of what ought to happen. (*I assume stable prices.*)

		$ Billion
1. Rise of war outlays		50
2. Rise of output		30
3. Reduction of private spending		20
a. Investment	10	
b. Consumption	10	

In other words, what is required is that the government arrogate to itself $30 billion out of additional output and $20 billion from diversions. When the public earns $30 billion more, they are asked to do with $20 billion less. This is entirely different from World War II—i.e., a rise of private consumption and investment of more than $40 billion accompanying an expansion of output of $120 billion. The inflationary threat is much greater today just because it is difficult to *cut* incomes in a period of expanding output.

This goal is a tough one in part because the current situation stimulates outlays not only from current income but also from past and future income. A greater general awareness of the inflationary threat and the possibility of restricted supplies induces the public to spend out of *past, present,* and *future* income. The vast accumulation of liquid assets, now about 100 per cent of personal income after taxes as compared with 80 per cent in prewar, the growth of demand deposits adjusted (from $30 billion in 1939 to $86 billion in 1950), the growth of currency outside the banks (6 to 24 billion dollars)—all of these engender the movement from cash into goods. They reflect largely the growth of cash which has accompanied the rise of income.

9. THE INFLATIONARY GAP

THE CONCEPT AND ITS USE

In World War II, the world of economists found the inflationary gap a convenient over-all measure of the inflationary pressures. For example, the analyst estimates the income available to be spent on consumers' goods; the amount likely to be siphoned off through taxes and savings; the value of consumers' goods likely to be available at unchanged prices. The inflationary gap measures the excess of this income minus taxes and savings over consumption goods to be available in this period.

President Roosevelt put the problem well in his 1944 budget speech.[1]

> Financing total war involves two main fiscal problems. One problem is to supply the funds currently required to pay for the war and to keep the increase in Federal debt within bounds. The second problem is caused by the disbursement of $100 billion a year to contractors, war workers, farmers, soldiers and their families, thus adding many billions to the people's buying power at a time when the amount of goods to be bought is declining steadily. A large portion of this excess buying power must be recovered into the Treasury to prevent the excess from being used to bid up the price of scarce goods and thus undermine the stabilization program by breaking price ceilings, creating black markets, and increasing the cost of living. . . .
>
> We cannot hope to increase tax collections as fast as we step up war expenditures or to absorb by fiscal measures alone all excess

purchasing power created by these expenditures. We must, therefore, provide a substantial portion of the funds needed by additional borrowing, and we must also use direct controls. . . . Each increase in taxes and each increase in savings will lessen the upward pressure on prices and reduce the amount of rationing and other direct controls we shall need.

As Director of the War Mobilization and Reconversion, Mr. James Byrnes, as of November, 1942, estimated the inflationary gap for 1943. The expected gap of $15 billion suggested a strong inflationary pressure and a likely rise of prices. But actually looking back (ex post facto) the gap was eliminated. The truth is that the gap always disappears: e.g., it is absorbed in rising prices and hence larger value of consumption goods made available, or reduced in response to higher taxes and savings. In this particular instance, Byrnes' estimates proved to be rather bad. Income payments to individuals exceeded the anticipated amounts by $11 billion, a rise tending to increase the gap. The supply of consumption goods available rose by $21 billion, a factor reducing the anticipated gap. Of course the gap disappeared, as is evident from the table below.

ESTIMATES OF INFLATIONARY GAP FOR 1943 (IN $ BILLION)

	Byrnes' Estimates of November 1942	*Ex Post Facto Values*
1. Income payments to individuals	125	142
2. Personal taxes	15	18
3. Individual savings	25	33
Net	85	91
4. Consumers' goods available	70	91
5. Gap	15	0

Source: *Survey of Current Business*, September, 1943, Table 5; *First Report of Director of War Mobilization and Reconversion*, pp. 18–19.

Byrnes had underestimated income by $17 billion, or 12 per cent, taxes by $3 billion, or 17 per cent, savings by $8 billion, or 24 per cent, and consumers' goods available by $21 billion, or 23 per cent. The inflationary factors rose by $17 billion (Item 1), the anti-inflationary (Items 2–4) by $32 billion, the excess of the latter ($15 billion) wiping out the anticipated gap. But it should be noted that the gap was wiped out, in part, because the cost of living rose by 3 per cent in this year.

SOME FURTHER COMPLICATIONS

Our World War II experience underlines both the usefulness and the limits of the concept of the inflationary gap. It is very helpful to look forward and compare the amount of money likely to be spent and the amount of goods available at unchanged prices. From these estimates the policy-maker can determine the appropriate income policies (should wages be frozen?), the required rise of taxes and savings, the residual excess of purchasing power and, therefore, the appropriate control policies. Our attention is focused on the relation of total demand and total supply. Monetary supply is only one aspect of demand, and not, as in the discussion of World War I, the exclusive factor from the demand side. Now we concentrate on income as the principle determinant of demand.

We also learned that our estimates may be way off the mark. This may result merely from a failure to estimate income or any of the other relevant variables accurately. Even if the variables were independent, it would not be easy to estimate accurately; but they are not. The government may expect an inflationary gap of $15 billion and, therefore, decide to raise $10 billion additional in taxes, and through a vigorous bond-selling campaign, increase savings by $5 billion. Having made these decisions, the authorities should then examine the various interrelationships.

Thus a $10-billion rise of taxes may have the following effects:

1. *Increase the gap*

   (*a*) By reducing savings by $3 billion. The taxpayer pays his taxes in part by drawing on savings.

   (*b*) By reducing the output of consumption goods by $2 billion.

2. *Reduce the gap*

   (*a*) By withdrawing $10 billion from potential spenders.

   (*b*) Through effects on incentives by reducing output (income) by $3 billion. Hence, the net effect would be a reduction of the gap not by $10 billion, but by $8 billion (10 + 3 — 3 — 2).

Increases Gap		*Reduces Gap*	
Savings decline	3	Rise of taxes	10
Decline of output of consumption goods	2	Decline of output	3
	5		13

Net reduction = 8

Even these are the crudest of estimates. It is necessary to consider the lag between any change of income and change in outlays on consumption: the secondary effects of a rise of taxes upon income and savings, etc.

It is scarcely necessary to add that the government will have to weigh the advantages of reducing the gap, that is, moderating inflationary pressures against the unfavorable effects upon output of a rise in taxes.

Or better, the issue is to weigh the unfavorable distributive and output effects of the additional dose of inflation against the adverse effects on output of the new taxes. In war, it is imperative that as much as possible be produced; and this explains to some extent why government compromises between an all-out tax program to finance a war and a mixed program, partly higher taxes and a rise of genuine savings, and partly inflation. A wholly tax-financed war would impair incentives and output too much. Government can obtain more for war by supporting financial policies consistent with a high output and diverting supplies to the war economy through the inflationary process as well as through the tax and savings process (cf. Chapters 12–15).

THE GAP IN THE IMMEDIATE FUTURE

In the current emergency, the errors of estimation of the inflationary gap may well be even greater than in earlier years. One important reason for this is that consumption is not closely related to current income. Another reason is (and this is related to the first) that the public is much more conscious of the inflationary dangers and the denuding of markets than they were in the early forties. Hence sudden changes in the proportion of income spent are likely to plague the forecasters. Insofar as the policy-makers stabilize the value of a currency and the flow of goods, this factor will become less important.

Here is an application of the inflationary gap to the expectations for 1951. (May I emphasize the fact that the figures below are for illustrative purposes to bring out principles, and, though they are not too far from reality, they should not be considered forecasts.)

We *assume:*

1. That national income would rise by 8 per cent over 1950 (2nd quarter), that is by $17 billion. (GNP would rise by $19 billion.)

2. That the government would increase military outlays (average) by $20 billion.

3. That the percentage of consumption expenditures to GNP would decline from 69 per cent (1948 and 1949) to 68

per cent in 1951. (The percentage was 68 in 1950.) Against the excess of buying related to the fear of inflation and imposition of controls, we put the tendency to save more as incomes rise, controls proliferate, and scarcities begin to prevail.

4. That the government would obtain the additional war goods by simple priorities, preference given to defense contracts, etc., with the result that the output of investment goods would remain unchanged (over the middle of 1950) instead of rising as might be expected. (In 1950, private gross investment amounted to $48 billion; and the annual rate in the last quarter of 1950 was $57 billion.)

5. That the tax program of 1950 would provide $5 billion additional *personal* taxes over the rate of the second half of 1950.

On these assumptions we estimate the following for 1951 (1950 prices):

	$ Billion *	
Gross national product	292	(300)
Less Government purchase of goods and services ($40 billion in second quarter of 1950 + $22 billion additional in 1951)	62	(63)
Equals Total goods and services available for private investment and personal consumption	230	(237)
Investment	40	(40)
Available for consumption	190	(197)

* Figures in parentheses are from the Harvard Business School Study, *Harvard Business Review*, 1951. Their estimates of income and amounts available for consumption are somewhat higher than mine.

Hence the inflationary gap would be indicated as follows (at 1950 prices):

	$ Billion *	
1. Personal income	232	(237)
2. Personal taxes	25	(23)
3. Disposable income (1 — 2)	207	(214)
4. Personal savings	7	(10)
5. Projected outlays for consumption (3 — 4)	200	(204)
6. Consumption goods available	190	(197)
7. Inflationary gap (5 — 6)	10	(7)

* Figures in parentheses from Harvard Business School Study.

An inflationary gap of about $10 billion for 1951 is the crude estimate presented here. A rise of taxes and savings adequate to cut demand by $10 billion would then solve the problem of inflation. But the amounts of new taxes alone required to balance the federal budget would be substantially more than $10 billion. (The President suggested in January, 1951, that $16 billion would be required for 1951–52 [fiscal year ending June 30].) It would be well if the authorities counted on a gap of at least $15 billion, which is well within the range of possibilities. If, for example, output should rise by $10 billion (more than assumed here) without an offset of additional consumption goods, or if personal savings should disappear (in response to great inflationary pressures not treated adequately by controls) and/or should investment drop only to $50 billion (from the $57-billion rate in the last quarter of 1950), then the gap may well rise to $15 billion. Certainly, our experience with the gap in 1942–44 should be warning that we may underestimate by at least $10 billion.

If we have possibly overestimated the dangers, they are genuine nevertheless. The bolder the government policy in pruning production of consumption goods, the greater the inflationary dangers. As the crisis advances, such pruning will become imperative. What this table suggests is a severe tax policy and a stimulation of savings. Surely an additional personal tax program of $5 billion is not enough. This may not yield more than $3 billion toward cutting the gap. (I assume here that the $5-billion tax bill would provide $3 billion in the fight against inflation and that $2 billion additional would come as a result of the increase in taxes associated with higher incomes.) Despite this $5-billion tax increase, an excess of spending of $10 billion or substantially more is promised, and unless something were done to stop it, the effects would be a cumulative price rise of 5 to 10 per cent $\left(\frac{190 \text{ (consumption)}}{10 \text{ (gap)}} = 5\%\right)$. For a price rise once started will tend to engender further rises in prices.

Moreover, in one particular we have been too optimistic. We do not take into account the possibility of inflationary income policies. An epidemic of inflationary wage increases may increase national income (not real output) by 10 to 15 billion dollars additional and thus raise the gap by 7 to 10 billion dollars additional—we allow here for the secondary effects on savings and taxes.

The reader should observe that this analysis for 1951 assumes that the major contribution to the increased military, etc., outlays is to come from a rise of output and the other large contribution from a cut of investment ($7 billion). Consumption would remain at the 1950 level.

The price history of 1951 would reflect the history of output, investment, taxes, savings, and consumption as revealed in the demand for consumption goods in relation to the supply (at 1950 prices). Should the gap remain large, then it will be gradually absorbed in higher prices. A gap of even $5 billion may not be serious if accompanied by effective wage and price stabilization controls which might sterilize the small excess. Unfortunately, the early history of these controls is not too promising.

10. HOW TO STOP INFLATION

MAGNITUDE OF WAR EFFORT AND INFLATION

OF ONE thing we may be sure. Neither on the battlefield nor on Capitol Hill nor in the Executive Offices will World War III be fought like the recent war. Just as each succeeding war requires new methods of warfare, so it calls for new techniques to assure the military the required supplies with the minimum disturbance and the best possible distribution.

Institutions, the scale of war and moral standards all change, and with them the economic management of war. Leaders in the three great revolutions, French, American and Russian, relied primarily on great inflations and commandeering of supplies. The result was expropriation of large segments of the population and chaotic economic conditions for years. The French Assignat and the American Continental Currency ("not worth a continental") have long been symbols of the way not to carry through war mobilization.

In our three great wars of the last 100 years, we have tried to shun the crude techniques used on the earlier occasions. Although each succeeding war was a bigger one, the price inflation was less.

Our Civil War was a $3-billion war; World War I a $30-billion war; and World War II a $300-billion war. Note the geometrical progression in the rise of costs.

In relation to national output, the Civil War used up 15

per cent, World War I, 20 per cent, and World War II, 41 per cent.

Inflationary effects varied not with the amounts spent nor with the proportion of national income used up. During the Civil War period, the costs were least and the inflation a maximum; in World War II, the cost the greatest, the inflation the least. In fact, as the table below shows, had prices risen in World Wars I and II as much as is suggested by the ratio of price rise and proportion of income going to war in 1861–65, the rise of prices in World War I would have been 3 times the actual increase, and in World War II, 14 times. Surely our techniques seem to improve with each succeeding war.

	Rise of Prices (Per Cent)	
	As Experienced	*To Be Expected* *
Civil War	108	—
World War I	57	144
World War II	21	290

* Rise of prices to be expected on the basis of Civil War experience as given by proportion of income taken for war and the rise of prices.

COSTS OF ANOTHER WAR

So much for history. We do not know how much World War III will cost. On reasonable assumptions (e.g., bombing in this country on the German scale in World War II), I can easily envisage a prospect for a $1 trillion ($1,000 billion) war. Should costs rise in the manner of the last three wars (a progression of 10 times the cost of the preceding war), then this war might cost $3,000 billion (10 times the cost of World War II). A less frightening prospect is to estimate the cost at $300 billion (last war) and raise this amount by the percentage excess of prices in World War III over the level when these $300 billion were spent. This gives a figure of

$576 billion (300 + 180 for 60 per cent present excess of prices over those [average] when $300 billion were spent and $96 billion additional to cover the estimated 20 per cent average rise of prices in World War III). An all-out war may cost then 576 or 1,000 or 3,000 or *x* billion dollars depending on the assumptions made. Obviously since our total wealth is less than $1,000 billion, a cost of $3,000 billion could be incurred only by allowing for adverse effects on postwar income.

Indeed we do not assume that an all-out war is inevitable. We pray for a better outcome. But we would be foolish not to consider the possibility. Our analysis relates to both partial and full mobilization.

THE EARLY 1950'S ARE NOT THE EARLY FORTIES

So far we have found some cause for optimism in the improved inflationary record; but also some cause for concern in the geometric rise of war costs. Now our problem is to show why the early 1950's are not the early 1940's, and the relevance of these considerations for economic mobilization.

First, we start this mobilization with a full-employment economy. That means we cannot count on a 70 per cent rise of output as in World War II. In 1941–45, we could add 11 million to the military and 7 million to the employed members of the labor market by drawing on new entrants to the labor market and reducing unemployment by 8 million. In 1950 (June) these reserves were not available: unemployment was but 3 million and our labor force was 10 million above the 1940 total. We shall be fortunate to add 6 million to the military and civilian employed labor force, and 10 per cent to our output (cf. Chapter 3). A rise in output of 25 per cent would be a most unlikely achievement especially if allowance is made for the possibility of bombardment and the high unit costs in a full-employment economy. In World War II large rises of man-hour output were forthcoming as unused plant and reserve labor of good quality were put to work. At best we can expect a small improvement in man-hour output; at worst, a substantial decline. Technological and managerial gains will be offset by the pressure on limited resources and facilities and (later) effects of bombing. It is not easy to keep man-hour output from declining when on top of full employment we introduce a full mobilization program.

Our second point derives from the first. Whereas in World War II the country obtained more guns and more butter, this is not a likely outcome in World War III. This means that, whereas in World War II workers, farmers, and management could arrogate to themselves part of the fruits of increased output, in the current mobilization the public will have to work *more* and receive *less*. *Here is our most important point: In World War II, we depended primarily on a rise of output; now we shall have to depend primarily on a reduction of private spending, on consumption and on investment.*

In 1944 relative to 1940 the country could provide *both* $85 billion additional for war and $44 billion more for consumption. Even at 1940 prices this represented a gain of almost 25 per cent in total consumption.

We cannot count on such good fortune in the years to come. Assume an effort of but one-half our 1944 rate—namely, $42 billion plus an allowance for the expected rise in the price level in 1950 (20 per cent in excess of 1950 and 72 per cent in excess of that of World War II), that is $70 billion. The excess of these expenditures over 1950 outlays would then be $55 billion. Additional output ($25 billion), reduction of private investment ($15 billion), and reduction of consumption ($15 billion) would account for the $55 billion needed.

Should war outlays equal those of 1944, then at World War III prices the amounts required (in excess of 1950 outlays) would be $125 billion:

	$ Billion
Increase of output	25
Reduction of private investment	30
Reduction of consumption	70

That is to say, at the peak of World War II, output was up 50 to 70 per cent and consumption 20 to 25 per cent; but in 195?, output would be up by 10 per cent (actually in stable dollars, there might be a decline, as might well be expected in a bombing war and with a mobilization program superimposed upon a fully-employed economy), and consumption would decline by about 40 per cent. At stable prices, the reduction would be almost one-half.

Here is a summary in tabular form (cf. Chapter 2, where a more optimistic presentation is made which involves smaller cuts in consumption):

	Change, 1944 from 1940	*Planned Mobilization over 1950 (Summer, 1950)*	*Substantial Mobilization (Change, 195? from 1950)*	*Advanced Mobilization (at World War II Level) (Change from 1950)*
GNP, $ billion	+112	+10	+25	+ 25
Expenditures for war, $ billion	+ 84	+20	+55	+125
Expenditures for consumer goods, $ billion	+ 40	— 5	—10	— 70
Private investment, $ billion	— 6	— 5	—20	— 30
Percentage change of consumption, current dollars	+ 54	— 3	— 6	— 38
Percentage change of consumption, stable dollars	+ 24	— 8	—14	— 48

The crux of the matter is that we shall have to put more people to work. They will have to work harder. We shall strain our capacity. We shall face the possibility of bombing. If we are fortunate, we shall produce more although this is a most unlikely outcome with advanced mobilization. We shall to some extent live on fat: the $20 billion of plant built by the government in World War II, the $183 billion of private investment in 1946–50, inclusive of $109 billion of expenditures for nonfarm producers' plant and equipment (in 1940 our entire plant was probably not worth $60 billion in 1940 prices), the record $40 billion spent for residential construction (nonfarm), the $114 billion spent for consumer durables ($40 billion for automobiles alone), the $55 billion of inventories in factories and trade available in 1950 (about $20 billion in excess of prewar after allowing for price changes).

THE CASE FOR VIGOROUS FISCAL POLICY

What does all of this mean in terms of current policy? It means, above all, drastic fiscal policy. Even in the 1951 phase, it means taking away and/or immobilizing more billions than the rise of income. As the program accelerates, the government will have to rely increasingly on cuts in current spending by the private economy. Thus in 1951–52, we ought to have a *rise* of taxes of more than $30 billion. We shall be fortunate indeed if tax receipts rise as much as is required. It is estimated that, as a result of new taxes voted in 1950 and the expected gain of income and spending, tax receipts will rise in the fiscal year 1951–52 by $11 billion over the receipts of 1950–51. In order to balance the budget, additional taxes of about $16 billion would be required. This amount could be set against the 10- to 20-billion-dollar gap which we should be prepared to treat for 1951 (calendar year). Taxes will not rise by the required amounts in 1951, though failure to spend for the military as fast as is anticipated (or hoped) may reduce the need for new taxes for 1951–52 below $16 billion. A failure to obtain $16 billion would, however, be unfortunate, for in 1952 the deficit would then be so much larger. A rise of savings would also be helpful. But we emphasize the point that savings may merely postpone the problem of excess spending.

The case for heavy taxes is much greater than has been so far suggested—even for 1951. Our whole fiscal policy in World War II was premised on the theory that there would not be another major war for a long time. We raised close to two-thirds of the excess expenditures over prewar by borrowing, and a large part out of genuine savings. We cannot count on such good fortune now. In the midst of the crisis the Treasury is confronted with the problem of redeeming securities issued in the earlier emergency. Even my barber tells me how disappointed he is in the loss of purchasing power of his government bond. (The value of our national debt in goods is about two-thirds of the value at time of issue.) The public is not likely to subscribe to government bonds in amounts commensurate with those of the last war, in part because of the loss of purchasing power of these securities; and in part because the market is more nearly saturated. It should be said, however, that insofar as the people saved more in response to appeals, they are not necessarily worse off. They merely have not gained as much from their savings as they otherwise might have.

There is still another reason why severe taxes are needed. Not only is it necessary to cut spending out of current income; but also out of past income. This is an especially serious problem because of the large expansion of money and liquid assets (the residue of past income) resulting from the past war. With another emergency confronting us, there has not been an opportunity to absorb the excess money through growth. The excess amount of cash is another threat to price stability.

Taxes will have to offset rises of income, cut into present incomes and offset outlays out of past incomes.

Unless we want a large dose of inflation, we shall also have to use taxes (e.g., excess profits) both to moderate demands of trade unions and to offset the unwise demands now being made. Surely there is little justification for demands for substantially higher wage rates in the midst of a great emergency with gross weekly wages in railroads, building construction, manufacturing and mining up 103, 143, 145, and 194 per cent, respectively, over 1939 levels—and prices up but 71 per cent. But until the government stabilizes prices, no improvement can be expected. Taxes and more taxes are needed now; and still more as mobilization proceeds. The time will of course come when controls will have to play an important part, but it will come much sooner and be less effective with a feeble tax effort.

The problem of the contribution of taxes and savings is discussed in greater detail in Part IV; and the relevance of controls, which was discussed briefly in Chapter 1, receives fuller treatment in Part VI.

Part Four

TAXATION, EXPENDITURE, AND SAVINGS

11. ECONOMIES OF PUBLIC OUTLAYS

In Part IV, we are interested in the manner in which the government pays for the large costs of the military effort, and the contribution of taxes and additional sales of public securities both to the financing and to the containment of inflation. Insofar as the government reduces outlays in the nondefense categories, it also contributes toward a solution of the financing and inflation problem. Economies are the first problem to be treated here.

FEDERAL ECONOMIES [1]

Part of the large bill required for the military might be paid through a reduction of public expenditures. But in view of the large part of federal expenditures (about 83 per cent in 1951–52) committed to war, interest, veterans, and international aid, and in view of the rise of prices and resultant increased cost of the budget, the savings on these outlays are not likely to be large.

According to the 1952 budget, the federal dollar is to be allocated as follows:

Military services	58¢
International	10¢
Veterans	7¢
Interest	8¢
Other	17¢

Large economies are not possible here.

In a memorandum prepared by the Executive Office of the President (February 12, 1951), entitled *Controllability of 1952 Budget Expenditures,* the Budget Bureau attacks the problem of economy in a new manner.

> This analysis of expenditures in the Federal Budget for the fiscal year 1952 is intended to clarify the extent to which these expenditures are controllable and the extent to which they are not controllable—that is, fixed as a result of prior government commitments.
>
> The analysis divides the total expenditures into two main categories—those which are "relatively fixed" and those which are "relatively controllable." The word "relatively" is employed because of the wide variation in the legal provisions and administrative processes which determine whether an expenditure must be made. These range from completely binding commitments, such as the payment of interest on government bonds, to what may be termed "moral commitments" that have been created by administrative action based on statute. Essentially, items classified as "controllable" are subject to review by the Congress through the appropriation process, while those classified as fixed either cannot be affected by the Congress at all, or can only be affected through legislation or rescission action.

For 1951–52, expenditures, relatively fixed, amounted to $43.2 billion, or 60 per cent of the total; relatively controllable, $28.4 billion, or 40 per cent. These totals might suggest large possible economies. But the major items in the relatively controllable category are military services and international security and foreign relations (total of $21.95 billion of $27.15 billion of controllable expenditures). Incidentally, more than half of these two categories of outlays are "relatively fixed." We cannot find large potential economies as a result of this analysis.

Let us turn to another approach.

Federal grants to state and local government amount to nearly $3 billion. These governments largely determine the costs to the federal government, for they are on a matching basis. As the war effort expands, however, large economies may be expected in construction aids to state and local governments.

Another item which should yield economies should be the $990 million estimated for the 1951 budget for purchases of private mortgages. The 1952 budget re-estimates 1951 net expenditures at $189 million and shows for 1952 net receipts at $530 million. (The ultimate results depend on extent of sales of mortgages now held by the government.) As the construction boom abates, the need for these investments declines. This saving, however, is not a genuine one, for though classified as an expenditure, the government obtains in exchange assets probably of equal value.

With rising prices, the government should be able to save on funds allocated to support farm prices. Indeed, the outlays for 1951–52 should be small compared to 1948–50; but since in 1950–51 there was an actual excess of receipts, the 1951–52 budget registers a rise for this item. Here again, though, the outlays are not expenditures in the usual sense.

Possible economies lie primarily in the following categories:

VARIOUS CATEGORIES OF OUTLAYS, 1950–51

	$ Million
Aid to state and local governments	3,000 *
Purchase of private mortgages	990
Aids to private and public housing, slum clearance, etc.	473 †
Rural electrification and communication	436

Source: Bureau of the Budget, *The Federal Budget in Brief, Fiscal Year 1951.*

* Includes $574 million counted in other items—especially highways.

† Exclusive of $134 million of HOLC receipts.

VARIOUS CATEGORIES OF OUTLAYS, 1950–51 (*cont.*)

	$ Million
Transportation and communication (highways, $530 million; navigation aids and facilities, $452 million)	1,680
Natural resources (but atomic energy $817 million) ..	2,220
Veterans' services and benefits	6,100
	14,899

A most optimistic estimate of possible savings on these items would be about $3 to 4 billion. These estimates leave out of account, however, the additional outlays in these categories related to the military effort. A large part of the economies lies in a reduction of investments—e.g., housing mortgages. These are economies in cash outlays, not in budgetary savings.

These estimates of possible savings were made in the autumn of 1950. Since then, the President's Budget for 1951–52 has appeared. The economies for 1951–52 in re 1950–51 amounted to $1.6 billion, the major reductions (in order) were in veterans' services and benefits, housing and community development, and transportation and communication. There were, on the other hand, increases in broad categories not associated *generally* with defense of about $2.5 billion. These reductions are from the revised budget estimates, not from the amounts shown in the preceding table.

In comparison with the original budget for 1950–51, the major declines for 1951–52 were $1,878 million and major increases, $2.7 billion—increases notably were $1,156 million for finance, commerce and industry, $443 million for agriculture and agricultural resources, $402 million for natural resources, $340 million for education and general research, $175 million for interest, $105 million for social security, etc., and $99 million for general government. The decline of

$1,878 million includes $247 million for unemployment insurance, an item that properly belongs to the consolidated cash budget, not to the budget proper. Similarly, a rise of $549 million for old-age insurance, etc., belongs properly to the cash budget, not to the budget proper. It should be noted, however, that the outlays, which in fact involve borrowing from the contributions of the present young—since a large part are payments in excess of contributions plus earnings of annuitants—represent substantial deficits.

When compared with the revised budget of 1950–51, the economies for 1952 are larger. There were, of course, many rises and declines in other categories. For example, the overall rise for natural resources for 1951–52 over revised 1950–51 was $402 million, but estimated expenditures for flood control and reclamation decreased by $147 million. The major changes were:

	$ Million
Purchases of private mortgages	−1,930
Veterans' services and benefits	−1,189
Natural resources	+299
Rural electrification and telephones	−167
Aids to private and public housing	−45
	−3,032

Source: *Memorandum from Budget Bureau,* February, 1951.

Why are the results so disappointing? Note that for 1951–52 the President estimated the rise of *all* expenditures at $24.4 billion and for military service and international security and foreign relations at $23.2 billion, that is to say, all expenditures were to rise by about $1 billion more than the military and related (i.e., foreign aid) outlays. One explanation of the failure to cut outlays in the broad categories exclusive of those most directly related to defense is that important military outlays are classified elsewhere—e.g., the $1,092 million for defense production and economic stabilization included under *Finance, Commerce,* etc.; the rise of $164 million for merchant marine included under *Transportation and Communication;* a rise of $405 million for civil defense and defense housing under *Housing and Community Development* and RFC loans for civil defense; an increase of $158 million for dispersal of Washington offices under *General Government;* an increase of $459 million for atomic energy under *Natural Resources.* These items, which are not by any means all inclusive, amount to $2.2 billion. For example, we have not mentioned a rise of outlays for TVA of $65 million or an increase of $67 million for education of children on federal property and in emergency areas.

Another difficulty stems from increases in outlays related to earlier legislation. Thus the rise of outlay for old-age insurance, survivors' benefits, and retirement was $549 million over fiscal year 1951–52 and about $1.1 billion over the year 1949–50. Here again the problem is one of cash outlays rather than the budgetary problem. These rises are the result largely of the Social Security Amendments of 1950, which were long overdue.

In relation to legislation of the past, it should also be said that the large savings on veterans is primarily related to the reduction of readjustment benefits—e.g., for students eligible for GI benefits. Obviously, these are economies for which the Administration should not receive any credit.

Still another aspect of the problem is that in some instances when the gains over 1950–51 do not seem to be large, they are much greater when compared with 1949–50. Thus, the successive outlays for unemployment insurance in these three fiscal years are estimated at 2,013, at 962, and at 715 million dollars. Again the outlays for the Commodity Credit Corporation were 1,606, −296 (excess of receipts over expenditures), and 238 million dollars.

Finally, a relevant point is that the President, aware of the need of postponing his major social objectives, nevertheless is determined to push ahead in some directions, where the need is great and where the gains over years of mobilization would be important—e.g., federal aid to public schools and medical schools.

A few general remarks should be made here. The apparent economies seem to be small. The explanation in part is the large outlays related to the military effort but not included in the two major categories; a substantial rise of prices which increases the cost of government; increased outlays related to commitments made under earlier legislation; declines concealed by the unusually favorable position in 1950–51 (e.g., outlays for farm price support); the pushing ahead of the welfare state on shortened lines. The result is a reduction of outlays on the nonmilitary front which are disappointing; and even insofar as savings are made, they are largely in cash outlays (reductions of investments rather than genuine budgetary savings) or the automatic result of earlier legislation (GI Bill) and do not reflect the use of the axe. At 1950–51 prices, the nonmilitary (and related) part of the federal budget for 1951–52 has been cut. But experience shows again how difficult it is to retrench.

STATE AND LOCAL GOVERNMENT

Finally, a word about state and local government finance. As has been suggested, federal finance is tied to state and local finance. As state and local governments respond to high employment and shortages by raising taxes and reducing outlays, the federal budget will profit. The most important contribution of state and local government would lie in curtailed outlays in a period of inflation.

In the years since the depths of the depression, state and local governments increased their outlays by only two times as against a rise of total public and private spending of four times. In the war years, these governments underspent by $8 billion. That is to say, they would have spent $8 billion more had they spent in each war year as much as the amount spent in 1939 corrected for prices. Had they increased their spendings *pari passu* with the rise of national income, their deficiency of spending would have been much greater.

In the five years, 1941–45, state and local governments, despite the rise of prices, spent but $8.75 billion yearly as compared with $9.3 billion in 1939. In these five years, their receipts amounted to $54.1 billion, their expenditures only $43.7 billion, or an excess of $10.4 billion of receipts. In spending less than receipts the state and local governments made an important contribution toward restraining inflation during the war.

In the four years, 1946–49, however, average annual expenditures rose to $16.1 billion, and the excess of receipts over expenditures for the four years was but $1.4 billion. In fact, in the two years 1948 and 1949, these governments spent $1.6 billion more than they received. The growing deficit and promised shortages point to more economical policies for these governments in the future.[2]

CONCLUSION

A comparison of estimated outlays for 1951–52 with the revised budget of 1950–51 points to economies of $3 billion as presented by the President. Against these economies are substantial increases in various categories, the explanation being in large part the repercussions of mobilization programs. I have included changes in receipts and outlays of the trust funds when important, not because these should strictly be included in the budget, but rather because they are of some significance as part of the anti-inflationary picture—e.g., a rise of receipts cuts private spending.

It is possible that Congress might cut nonessential expenditures by a few billion dollars additional. But the rise of prices reduces the possible economies; and many of the economies are on a cash basis, involving no savings on the budget —e.g., a reduction of mortgage financing. Certainly every effort should be made to curtail nonessential expenditures.

12. TAX POLICY

THE CASE FOR TAXATION

A MILITARY effort costs money. Taxes are an obvious way of obtaining the cash to pay for the armament program.

The case for heavy taxes rests on the following:

1. *Pay the bill and keep the debt down.* The larger the taxes, the smaller the rise in national debt. Since we start our preparations with a large debt bequeathed by the last war, this argument carries special weight in the current emergency.

2. *Make the present generation pay.* Many insist that a war should be paid for by those who participate directly or indirectly. This argument also carries much more weight than it used to, in part because the old theory of making future generations share the cost because the current generation has "saved the world for democracy" seems less convincing in a world of continued strains. For each generation will have its own problems. Those who held that future generations share the cost generally supported financing largely by loans.

But the case for taxes and putting the burden on the present generation is all the stronger just because it is generally recognized that the major costs are borne by those who fight and die and those who work harder and consume less in the war period. Taxation is in large part a technique for inducing reductions of consumption.

To some extent, however, the future generations do pay for the war. Capital may be allowed to run down; mental and physical deterioration sets in as a result of war; all kinds of strains bring dissensions and internal conflicts; the war bequeaths financial problems which impair incentives—in these ways and others, the war affects future generations. Nevertheless, we still insist that the major burdens are put upon the current generation.

3. *Heavy taxation satisfies the canon of equity.* In a modern war, it may be necessary to mobilize 10 to 15 per cent of the adult population for military services; and millions additional for ancillary services. Even in 1950–51 a program for universal military service for the young was in prospect. Under these circumstances with lives being lost, there is strong sentiment for taxation severe enough to pay the costs of the war. Even in World War I many orthodox economists urged a war financed wholly by taxation.

4. *Stop inflation.* The contention that heavy taxes will stop or at least moderate the rate of inflation weighs more heavily than in earlier wars. This is in part the result of the spread of Keynesian economics with its stress on anti-inflationary measures in periods of excessive demand. The almost universal awareness of the inflation potential and of the damage done by inflation has contributed to the great emphasis put upon the anti-inflationary aspects of taxation. Heavy taxation in war is premised largely on the theory that taxes cut funds available for private spending and therefore keep buying and prices down.

THE DIFFICULTIES—POLITICAL AND ADMINISTRATIVE

The most obvious obstacle to an adequate tax program is the almost universal dislike of taxes; and the resulting delays and inadequacy of taxes. Under our political system, the gestation period of a tax program from the original proposals to the collection may well be 1 to 2 years, although, as a result of the payroll-deduction plan, that period has been shortened.

Reluctance to pay taxes on the part of the citizens under a political system, where each member of the legislative body exercises independent influence, results in less vigorous taxation than under a system like the British, where party responsibility is much greater and individual authority much less.

Yet the historical trends are encouraging. In World War I, this country raised but 25 per cent of war outlays by taxation and in World War II about 40 per cent. A rise in tax receipts from 5 to 45 billion dollars in four years was a remarkable achievement in World War II. Yet with expenditures up from 9 to 100 billion dollars, the rise of taxation could account for much less than one-half of the increase in expenditures. Even an acceptance of President Roosevelt's strong recommendations would have raised revenue by but 5 to 10 billion dollars yearly additional.

NEW TAXES SUPERIMPOSED ON A HIGH TAX STRUCTURE

It is not easy to raise taxes *pari passu* with expenditures. Since rates of taxation are much higher now than they were in prewar, this problem is even more serious than in World War II.

Here, for example, is an indication of direct tax burdens in 1938 and in 1947.

EFFECTIVE RATES OF INDIVIDUAL TAX UNDER REVENUE ACTS, 1938 AND 1947—MARRIED PERSON, TWO DEPENDENTS

	Effective Rate (Per Cent)	
Net Income	*Revenue Act of 1938*	*Revenue Act of 1947*
$5,000,000	75.8	85.5
100,000	32.0	62.3
25,000	9.3	34.1

10,000	3.4	18.6
5,000	1.0	11.8

Source: Adapted from *Treasury Bulletin,* February, 1947, p. A7; and Senate Committee on Finance, Hearings on *Income Tax Reduction,* April, 1947, p. 22.

Indeed, Congress reduced tax rates in 1948, and tax rates were somewhat lower in the next two years. But the differences in rates between 1947 and 1949 were not large. The 1948 act provided as follows:

These changes affect the tax liabilities of taxpayers, according to their marital status. For single persons with no dependents, taxes are reduced 100 per cent for net incomes between $500 and $600, 17 per cent at the $2,500 level, 12 per cent at $5,000 and less than 10 per cent above $10,000. For married persons with no dependents (where the spouse has no income), the tax reduction is 100 per cent for net incomes between $1,000 and $1,200, 24 per cent at the $2,500 level, 21 per cent at $5,000, 26 per cent at $10,000, 35 per cent at $25,000, 26½ per cent at $100,000, and less than 10 per cent above $500,000.

Hence at $5,000, the effective rate would be about 10.4 per cent (instead of 11.8 at the 1947 rate); at $10,000, 15 per cent (instead of 18.6 per cent); at $100,000, 47 per cent (instead of 34.1 per cent); at $25,000 at 22 per cent (instead of 62.3 per cent). Under the 1950 Act, individual tax rates were about 3 per cent lower than peak wartime rates all along the line (e.g., 26 per cent as compared with 29 per cent in 1944 for incomes of $4,000 to $6,000). In February, 1951, Secretary Snyder demanded rates 1 per cent above peak war rates.[1] As usual, Congress was not equally enthusiastic.

It is clear from these figures that, even before the mobilization, taxes were high. Rates were clearly much higher than they were in 1939. On top of that, marginal rates were often high enough to impair incentives. It follows, therefore, that a rise of rates would encounter more opposition and result in greater interference with production than in 1939.

Not only were rates higher, but, as might be expected, taxes absorbed a larger part of all income than in 1939. This fact is evident from the figures below. They are explained primarily by the continuing high level of outlays related to the war and secondarily by an expansion of state and local outlays. In 1949, federal receipts were less than in 1945 by $4 billion, or 9 per cent; but in the meanwhile state receipts had risen by $8 billion, or 69 per cent. The large rise of these taxes of state and local governments is related to the growth of their outlays, in turn explicable by underspending of $8 billion in the war period (cf. pp. 125–26).

INCOME AND RECEIPTS
FEDERAL, STATE, AND LOCAL GOVERNMENT

	1939	*1945*	*1949*
1. Gross National Product ($ billion)	91.3	215.2	255.2
2. Personal income ($ billion)	72.6	171.0	206.1
3. All government receipts ($ billion) *	15.4	53.6	56.2
4. Federal receipts ($ billion) *	6.7	43.1	39.2
5. State and local receipts ($ billion) *	9.6	11.4	19.3
6. All personal tax and non-tax receipts ($ billion)	2.4	20.9	18.7
7. *Percentage* of all receipts to GNP	16.9	24.5	22.0
8. Percentage of personal taxes, etc., to personal income	3.4	12.2	9.1

Source: *Survey of Current Business*, National Income Numbers (my calculations).

* Rows 4 + 5 exceed Row 3 because state and local receipts are in part transfers from federal government and hence involve double counting.

In general, then, we start from a higher tax burden and higher tax rates. But we should note that as a percentage of GNP government receipts have risen but from 17 to 22 per cent. Furthermore, with a reduction of rates and a rise of income, the burden was less severe than in 1945. But personal taxes as a percentage of national income increased substantially: 3.4 to 9.1 per cent. Even here, observe that the public is left, after paying personal taxes, with $187 billion in 1949 as compared with $70 billion in 1939. At 1939 prices, the gain after taxes is about $67 billion, or almost 100 per cent.

TAXES AND THE STATE OF THE ECONOMY

The rate at which taxes should rise in the midst of a military effort depends on many factors. One, the existing tax structure, has already been mentioned. Another is the supply of civilian goods available. A drastic rise in taxation while large supplies of consumption goods were being turned out might jolt the economy more than is necessary. In the early part of our World War II effort, President Roosevelt, with this problem in mind, tailored his tax demands accordingly.

Still another factor is the effect of a drastic rise of taxes on output. It is conceivable that the adverse effects on output might outweigh the favorable effects on prices and on revenue. Here again, the government in World War II kept this consideration in mind. Even in the current emergency, many are concerned lest a large rise in taxes should interfere with output. For example, Professor Slichter has emphasized the greater importance of raising output than of preventing a moderate inflation.[2]

In the present emergency, it does not seem necessary to moderate the advance of taxes in order to assure adequate demand. We start with a full-employment economy, whereas in the earlier effort there were 8 to 10 million unemployed. At the outset, the danger is civilian shortages and excess demand—especially in view of the monetary situation in 1950–51. The correct policy seems to be to raise taxes as much as is politically possible. With demand much in excess of available supplies at current prices, taxes will serve primarily to reduce excess demand.

We do not mean that the military effort can be financed exclusively out of taxes. We should finance the first phase, say, the $23.2 billion additional required for military services and international security and foreign relations (*Budget,* 1952, p. M7) exclusively out of taxes. The rise of total expenditures for fiscal year 1952 over fiscal year 1951, suggested in the *President's Budget Message* of January, 1951, was $24.4 billion. But as the program expands, and especially if it expands rapidly, nontax sources and even inflationary finance may have to play a part. Resistance to taxes, with accompanying unfavorable effects on output, may make this necessary. But at least through the second phase ($50 billion additional outlays, say, in 1952–53) the objective should be pay-as-you-go.

To some extent inflation brings its own cure since as prices and money income rise, taxes and savings also increase. The greater the inflation, the greater the yield of taxes and savings. Inflation provides the government with the goods and services needed not only because, as prices rise, buyers competing with public procurement agencies are gradually squeezed out of the market, but also because higher money incomes yield more taxes and savings. (An offset would be increases of expenditures resulting from higher prices. But controls might correct this tendency.)

I am not writing in defense of inflation. I am merely suggesting a partial offset to the damage done by inflation, and once outlays advance beyond phase two, some inflationary finance is almost certain. The remarkable achievement of World War II was that the yield of taxes in 1945 rose to 8 to 9 times that of 1940, with the result that prices rose but 30 per cent. All government receipts increased by $38 billion, or more than 30 per cent of the rise of GNP; and the rise of federal personal taxes of $18 billion equaled close to 20 per cent of the rise in personal income. Of course, we could have done even better.

In the new emergency, the growth of tax receipts will have to be financed at least in part out of existing income. I show later (p. 153) that on the average we may expect a rise of $100 billion in GNP for the years 1951–54 over GNP in 1946–49. Should we increase taxes by $30 billion, as in the last war, the rise of receipts would roughly equal the expected rise of output. The other $70-billion growth of GNP would be the result of price increases, and not reflect expansion of output. Then the public would give up the gains of increased output to the tax collector. But we should go further and will have to go further. Thus, with a war effort of $100 billion, we should increase taxes by at least $60 billion. Then $30 billion, or one half the rise, would contribute toward a large reduction of consumption—the other half would siphon off the rise of the income associated with higher output.

We can expect much opposition to rising taxes. Current rates, the proportion to national income, and total taxes are all above the prewar level. Furthermore, additional taxes will come substantially out of income, not out of *rises* of income. But on the other side of the canvas, the amounts left after taxation are much larger than in 1940, and, though the tax bill in 1949 exceeded that of 1945, in 1948 dollars the bill was 18 per cent less than in 1945.

The result of this reluctance to impose or accept much larger taxes may well be greater inflationary pressures. Then prices would have to rise sufficiently so that out of the higher income associated primarily with inflation, not higher output, sufficient taxes and savings may be squeezed to finance the war—over and above what is made available through the inflationary pressures.

TAXES AND CONSUMPTION

In its anti-inflationary aspects, what taxation achieves depends largely upon its effects upon consumption. In the last war, it was possible to wage a strenuous war and yet to allow consumption to rise by 25 per cent. The accompaniment of a large war effort now will have to be a substantial decline of consumption. Hence we are even more interested than we were in World War II in the effects of increased taxes on consumption.

Determined to cut consumption, the government will try to impose severe taxes on the low income groups which account for a large part of total consumption. For example, the OPA estimated in 1943 that spending units with incomes of $5,000 or less accounted for 68 per cent of the money income, 78.8 per cent of the total consumption, and only 15.6 per cent of the taxes. In 1951, the Treasury estimated that the $5,000 or less group received 83 per cent of total income.[3] Obviously, to cut consumption substantially, it was necessary *inter alia* to raise taxes on those with incomes of $5,000 or less. The higher income group with more excess income could more easily allow increased taxes to impinge on savings than the low income group. That is why *x* dollars raised by an increase in income tax rates was likely to cut consumption much less than, say, an equal amount of revenue raised by a reduction of exemptions for income tax or by excise taxes. That the major rises in taxes, as we shall see, were in direct taxes, tended to reduce the anti-inflationary effects of a given increase of tax revenues. In his budget message of January, 1942, President Roosevelt answered those who contended that higher taxation should be concentrated on the mass of consumers.

> There are those who suggest that the policy of progressive taxation should be abandoned for the duration of the war because these taxes do not curtail consumers' demand. The emergency

does require measures of a restrictive nature which impose sacrifices on all of us. But such sacrifices are themselves the most compelling arguments for making progressive taxes more effective. The anti-inflationary aspects of taxation should supplement, not supplant, its revenue and equity aspects.

This statement by President Roosevelt suggests that he had not as yet absorbed the modern compensatory theories of public finance. In the current emergency, the case for imposing taxes which discourage consumption is much greater than in World War II. First, because a substantial part of the resources for war will have to come at the expense of current consumption standards; and, second, because a reduction of consumption from the high current levels would do less damage than a decline from the low standards of 1939.

According to the latest income figures available, the distribution of income among the nation's 38½ million families in 1948 was as follows:

	Millions of Families
Under $1,000	4.1
$1,000–$1,999	5.6
$2,000–$2,999	7.9
$3,000–$4,999	13.0
$5,000–$9,999	6.9
$10,000 and over	1.1

Source: Bureau of the Census, *Consumer Income,* Series P-60, No. 60, Feb. 14, 1950, p. 1.

It is obvious that the 4.1 million families with incomes of $1,000 or less should be spared as much as possible; and the sacrifices for the 5 to 6 million families with incomes of $1,000 to $2,000 should not be large. Reduction of consumption will have to be concentrated largely on the families in the higher income groups; but, because of their numbers and their large share in total consumption, especially on those with incomes from $2,000 to $10,000. That is to say, insofar as taxation is used to reduce consumption, the tax system should be oriented toward curtailing the consumption of those with incomes of $2,000 to $10,000. As the crisis deepens, any resulting injustices will be corrected through price control and rationing.

CHANGES IN THE TAX STRUCTURE

One of the significant changes in the American economy has been a large shift from indirect to direct taxes. Our tax system is certainly not so regressive as it was in prewar.[3] As a result of the war, the part played by income and corporation taxes has increased greatly. Elsewhere, I estimated that direct taxes (exclusive of property taxes) accounted for one-fourth of all taxes in 1940 and three-fourths in 1944. Consumption taxes had fallen from 45 to 20 per cent in these years. This decline continued a steady reduction in the relative importance of consumption taxes, which had been increased in the thirties.[4]

The table below summarizes the main trends since 1939. Direct taxes on firms and corporations were twice as important relatively in 1949 as in 1939, and indirect business taxes, largely sales, excise, and property taxes, were but three-fifths as important relatively. Notable was the decline of property taxes from 28 to 11 per cent.

In the years since the war's end, however, taxes once more tended to become more regressive (i.e., larger relative burden on low than on high income groups), with consumption taxes increasing in importance.

These changes, as the earlier ones in the years 1939–45, stem from the varying parts played by state and local governments, which on the whole rely much more on indirect than on direct taxes. Whereas federal receipts were 44 per cent of all governmental receipts in 1939, they rose to 80 per cent by 1945 and declined to 70 per cent by 1949. With the rise of federal participation, the direct taxes became increasingly important; with the recouping of lost ground by state and local governments the indirect taxes once more tended to become more important. From 1945 to 1949, federal receipts dropped by $4 billion; and those of state and local governments rose by $8 billion.

PERCENTAGE OF RECEIPTS FROM VARIOUS TAXES BY ALL GOVERNMENTS IN THE UNITED STATES *

Main Classes of Taxes	*1939*	*1945*	*1949*
1. Personal taxes and nontax receipts before refunds	16	39	33
2. Corporate tax accruals	9	21	19
3. Indirect taxes and tax accruals before refunds	61	29	38
4. Property taxes (included in Row 3)	28	8	11

Source: Calculated from *Survey of Current Business,* July, 1947 and July, 1950.

* Most important items included.

A TAX PROGRAM

It is essential that as military expenditures rise, taxes increase also. These taxes should be levied on all groups, with the joint objectives of raising revenue and keeping down inflationary pressures. In the early stages of the effort, we might expect almost full coverage of outlays by taxes. But as the war effort progresses, it will not be possible to finance exclusively by a tax program. We should, however, greatly improve our record of World War II, in which taxes accounted for 40 per cent of our war outlays.

We have already noted that our tax system is much less indirect and regressive than in 1939, but more so than in 1945. In the midst of a great military effort, it will undoubtedly be necessary, in order to reduce consumption, to put an increased burden on the low-income group. On this score, it is interesting that in the United Kingdom, indirect taxes in 1949 accounted for 45 per cent of total taxes of 3.719 million. This compares with 38 per cent in the United States. In other words, the United Kingdom depends more than the United States on consumption taxes. In view of the pressure on resources and dollar shortage, the need for reducing consumption was much greater in Britain than here—hence one reason for the greater burden of consumption taxes. But relevant to this comparison is the fact that taxes were 33 per cent of the national product as compared to 22 per cent in the United States. Hence the pressure to tap consumption taxes was greater than in the United States. Transfer payments (e.g., social security, subsidies, war payments) were roughly 20 per cent of all outlays in both countries.[5]

TAX POTENTIAL

In this section, I estimate the tax potential, tax by tax.

Income Tax

From 1945 to 1950, income rose by $50.5 billion and all personal taxes declined by $0.5 billion.

Assume personal income of $244 billion in 1951. ($222 billion estimate for 1950, plus a 5 per cent rise of output in 1951, plus a 5 per cent increase in prices.)

Apply the yield of 1945 (12 per cent of income) to this estimated 1951 income. The result is a yield of $29 billion, or $10 billion in excess of the $19 billion yield (annual rate) of the first half of 1950. *This gain of $10 billion includes the additional amounts assessed in the 1950 post-Korean tax bill.*[6]

Corporation Income Tax

From 1945 to 1950, corporate profits rose by $20.5 billion and taxes by 7.1 billion. After taxes, corporate profits rose from 8.5 to 21.9 billion dollars.

Corporate profits before taxes in 1950 rose to $40 billion and should rise to $50 billion in 1951.[7] (The annual rate was $48 billion in the last quarter of 1950.)

A tax of 50 per cent (yield) assessed on $50 billion would provide $25 billion, and of 60 per cent, $30 billion. To achieve these objectives, the tax rate would have to be somewhat higher than 50 and 60 per cent. *The excess of receipts over those in the first half of 1950 (annual rate) would be 11.4 and 16.4 billion dollars.*

Excess Profits Tax

Here I use the estimated yield of the 1950 excess profits tax, inflated somewhat to $4 billion for the next year. I shall discuss the excess profits tax issue separately in another chapter. As we shall see later, on reasonable assumptions, the annual yield for the years 1951–54 might well average $13 billion. (This is a gross figure, and when deflated for the loss in other tax receipts should not yield in excess of $6 billion.)

Excise Taxes

In periods of great strain, there is much to be said for substantial rises in excise taxes on luxury items. In this manner, the government arrogates to itself part of the difference between costs and prices; and insofar as prices in response to higher taxes are raised, the government discourages buying. In this manner, excise taxes supplement or reduce the need of controls.

It will require political courage to impose a selective excise tax, the counterpart of the famous British purchase tax. Strong pressure groups, particularly those representing the producers and sellers of items subject to such tax, will make their weight felt. Yet though there is much to be said against such taxes when consumption tends to be too low, the case is strong in the midst of a mobilization. The argument that the automobile, the radio, expensive entertainment are necessities in American life, whatever they are in the British, does not carry conviction. Dollar for dollar, this kind of tax will cut consumption and save resources much more than adjustments in the income tax. Excises should not be limited largely to tobacco and alcoholic drinks, both because these are highly regressive in their effects and because in competition for scarce resources, industries producing these products are not especially significant.

This does not mean that I would go so far as to support a general sales tax—not even a general expenditure tax, which exempts, say, $250 per capita of outlays. This might be an effective way of discriminating between outlays on luxuries and necessities. Neither this point nor the point that a general sales tax would solve the problem of evasion by millions of taxpayers are adequate offsets to the point that a general sales tax is a most inequitable kind of tax, especially in view of the fact that state and local governments rely heavily on sales and excise taxes. Moreover, a sales tax would hit all the people, and not only the minority of evaders. Why burn the house to roast the pig?

In 1949, the American public spent $40 billion out of $179 billion on consumption of luxury items. These include primarily jewelry and watches ($1.2 billion), personal care ($2.2 billion), some items included under "house operations" ($7.8 billion), recreation, and notably admissions, player participation, gambling, toys and sporting equipment, radios, foreign travel ($9.5 billion), and transportation ($19.3 billion). I do not include purchased meals and beverages, which accounted for $11.5 billion and might be given consideration. *An additional tax of 10 per cent on the $40 billion included here would yield $4 billion; of 20 per cent, $8 billion.* I would recommend a 20 per cent tax. Indeed, there would be some reduction of demand; and as the war effort progresses, less luxuries would be made available, and hence revenues would suffer. But as at least a partial offset, prices would rise; and with shortages more prevalent, rates should rise further.

Payroll Taxes

The case for an increase in payroll taxes is strong indeed. A rise is in fact a compulsory loan and contributes toward a reduction of consumption. Large accumulations now will also make it easier to finance unemployment and old-age insurance later. These are the most important contributory programs.

In general, payroll taxes collected rose from $1.9 billion in 1939 to $4.9 billion in 1949, and wages and salaries from $45.7 to $134 billion dollars—the rise in these variables was roughly of the same proportions.

In 1949, the contributions under old-age insurance and survivors' insurance amounted to $1,670 million. Add 30 per cent for rise of coverage under Social Security Act Amendments of 1950; then add 15 per cent for the rise of money wages in 1951 over 1949 (the excess of 1950 over 1949 was 7 per cent); and increase the payroll tax rate from 2 per cent to 4 per cent. (The 1950 Amendments provide for an increase to 3 per cent for 1951 and to 4 per cent by 1954.) The net result would be an increase of taxes by $3,300 million. But the 1951–52 budget estimates receipts at only $1,731 million in excess of the $2,106 million received in 1949–50.

In 1949, the contributions under unemployment insurance were about $1,200 million. This was less than 1 per cent of all wages and salaries, a low figure explained partly by non-coverage and partly by the widespread use of merit rating which kept the tax down to about 2 per cent on covered wages. I would strongly recommend the abolition of merit rating which in practice is a subterfuge for reducing contributions. Fluctuations in employment are primarily due to the nature of the industry and economic fluctuations generally, not, as the merit rating system assumes, to the behavior of the entrepreneur.

On the assumption that the rate would be raised, then, to 3 per cent, that coverage would rise from $32.6 million of 1948 to $40 million (as recommended by the Advisory Council on Social Security to the Senate Committee on Finance) and that wages and salaries would rise by 15 per cent over the 1949 level, the taxes would rise to $2.3 billion, or more than $1 billion in excess of the amounts raised in 1949.[8] (The 1951–52 budget anticipates receipts of but $1,296 million or $183 million in excess of 1949–50.)

Summary of possible Tax Increases at 1951 Incomes

Tax	*Total Increase (\$ Billion)*
Income taxes	10
Corporation	11.4–16.4
Excess profits tax	4
Payroll taxes	4.3
Excise taxes	8
	37.7–42.7

Aside from the part contributed by the masses of consumers under income taxes, the payroll taxes and consumption taxes would account for about one-third of the low estimate of $37.7 billion. It is clear, even when allowance is made for the interdependence of these taxes—e.g., a rise of excess profits tax reduces the yield of income tax—the wherewithal to raise taxes is there.[9] As revenue needs increase, it will be more difficult to finance entirely out of taxes. But even if we assume a rise of output of 10 per cent and an inflation of 25 per cent, large additional revenues could be found without increasing the burden greatly.

In the summary table, we estimate a possible rise of taxes of around $40 billion. Obviously, only about one-half would be necessary for 1951, inclusive of the amount provided under the 1950 amendments. A program for 1951 might well be the following (actually, about $5 billion of these $20 billion would come out of the rise of tax yield associated with higher incomes):

	$ Billion
Income taxes	5
Corporation	3
Excess profits tax	4
Payroll taxes	4
Excise taxes	4
	20

In the future, tax potential will be greater. Even at 1951 incomes, it is possible to raise $40 billion additional. This amount would exceed the increase of income over 1949.

At average GNP in 1951–54 of $100 billion above the 1946–49 level (see Chapter 13), it would be necessary to raise much more in taxes. An appropriate figure might well be at least $60 billion. My table reveals potential rises of $40 billion at 1951 incomes. In addition, the excess profits tax at 1951–54 incomes could yield $13 billion gross, or $2 billion annually (*net*) in excess of the amount listed in the table. Additional amounts should come from increased yields from income, payroll, and excise taxes as incomes rise, and tax rates are increased. Obviously the $60 billion additional is an average figure: the appropriate figure for 1951 might be $30 billion over 1949, and for 1954, when incomes would be much higher, $90 billion.

It will not be easy to arrogate 60 per cent of the increase of GNP for the use of the tax collectors. Here are some interesting figures of World War II:

1941–45

Average rise of GNP over 1940 GNP, $ billion	80
Average rise of federal receipts over 1940 receipts, $ billion	32
Percentage of rise of federal receipts to rise of GNP	40

Results in World War II would seem to suggest an increase of additional taxes to additional GNP of only 40 per cent. (The earlier figure of 30 per cent relates to the years 1940 and 1945.) We shall have to perform much better than in World War II, and especially since the relative (*real*) gain in GNP will be much less. A minimum goal should be 60 per cent.

CONCLUSION

In this chapter, I have tried to state the case for heavy taxation, as well as difficulties confronting the government in imposing an adequate tax program. We shall have to raise a much larger proportion of taxes relative to the increase of GNP than in World War II. In the early stages, all additional outlays should be covered by increased taxes. Should the effort require an additional outlay of $100 billion, then taxes will undoubtedly fail to do the entire job. To achieve a high average level of taxes, it would be necessary for the rise of taxes to outstrip the increase of public outlays in 1951, for as the program gains in 1952, outlays would probably rise much more rapidly than taxes. A rise of taxes of $20 billion over the receipts expected late in 1950 *and* additional savings of 5 to 10 billion dollars might well check the inflation in 1951–52. To deal with the inflationary problem adequately, an excess of tax receipts over federal outlays in 1951 should offset the inflationary pressures (excess of investments over savings) in the private economy. The rise in 1950 of incomes of $16.3 billion and of personal taxes of but $1.7 billion is not a good omen. Should taxes rise as proposed by President Truman (and this is a practical goal), then the Treasury would absorb roughly one-half of the rise of GNP in 1951 over 1949. (I estimate GNP at $310 billion [in current dollar rate, not in stable dollars as in earlier chapters], an increase of $55 billion, and tax receipts at $70 billion, a rise of $30 billion.) It is, however, extremely doubtful that $70 billion would be collected in 1951. In order to average 60 per cent of the rise of GNP (40 per cent in World War II), the government would have to increase taxes by an average of $60 billion in 1951–54 over 1949 (with a $100-billion rise of GNP I assume a defense or war effort in the years 1951–54 averaging less than $100 billion); and taxes would have to rise by about $90 billion by 1954. To achieve these results, the government would have to make courageous use of all kinds of taxes, inclusive of payroll and consumption taxes and possibly new taxes.

The objectives of the proposed tax program are to contend with the inflation, to provide the government with required revenue, to depend as little as possible on sales of Treasury bonds, which to some extent really postpone sacrifices, and to impose the additional burden as equitably as possible. Indeed, the need of reducing consumption explains the heavy demands to be made on low-income groups.

NOTE: OTHER TAX PROGRAMS

In "A Tax Program to Support the Policy of Containment," six Harvard economists, late in 1950, presented a tax plan to the House Ways and Means Committee in which they preferred to omit the excess profits tax and to impose a sales tax with some exemptions. The National Association of Manufacturers (*A Federal Tax Program for the Period of Defense and Partial Mobilization,* October, 1950) also urged a pay-as-you-go policy; but the emphasis here was almost exclusively on adequacy and incentives, with minimum attention to equity. A sales tax received the maximum attention; and the NAM approved the statement of Secretary Snyder:

> Moreover, a relatively small increase in the rate in the lowest brackets contributes more revenue than a larger increase at the higher income levels. For example, a 1 percentage point increase in the first bracket rate is equivalent in revenue to a 3 percentage point increase for all brackets together.

The program of November 16, 1950 (*Paying for Defense*) of the Committee for Economic Development sponsored a rise in the corporation tax rather than the enactment of an excess profits tax. But the over-all program paid much more attention to the equity criterion than the NAM Report. Concerned also with incentives and, therefore, fearful of high marginal rates, the CED objected not only to an excess profits tax but preferred under the income tax a rise of x per cent on net income above exemptions and present tax to an x per cent rise of rates for all—the latter raised marginal rates too much.

Finally, the Treasury tax program of January, 1951, which proposed $10 billion of additional tax (a "quickie" program) with a second bill to come later, is relevant. Of the $10.15 billion to be obtained, $3.03 billion were to come from excise taxes, $3.08 billion from an 8-point rise in the corporation income tax, and $3.60 billion from individual income taxes.

(Taxes on capital gains were to provide the remainder.)

The weakness of this program (possibly to be corrected by later proposals) is the failure to increase payroll taxes and the inadequate coverage of consumption items to be taxed. Ultimately there will also have to be further rises in income and corporation taxes and excess profits taxes.

In his February 5, 1951, statement, Secretary Snyder allowed that only 22.7 per cent of all consumption expenditures were subject to tax. Why not tax more than 6.8 per cent subject to tax of the $22.6 billion spent on clothing, accessories and jewelry, or the 21.8 per cent subject to taxes of the $23.5 billion spent on household operation? Surely the $19.3 billion spent on transportation should yield more than $1.265 billion additional (6 per cent) as proposed by the Treasury. Even the tax on passenger automobiles to rise from 7 to 20 per cent of manufacturers' price equals but 12 per cent of the consumers' price. Why not a further rise in taxes on recreation and railroad travels? Other consumer durables (e.g., television sets) are to rise only from 7 to 15 per cent of the consumers' prices.

Even an increase of $16 billion is easily attainable. My estimate of 37.7 to 42.7 billion dollars may be high, as the Treasury experts on examining this chapter suggested to me. Yet my estimate of the increased yield of the corporate income tax (over 1949) with a 10 per cent rise of rates corresponds with the Treasury estimate. My excise potential is much higher, both because I assume wider coverage and higher rates. But even if the potential increase were cut to $30 billion (from my estimate of 38 to 43 billion dollars), inclusive of about $8 billion to be had from taxes voted in 1950 and early 1951, the President's goal of $16 billion is not by any means chimerical. This is a must to prevent serious inflation unless savings rise greatly and private investments are curbed substantially. One way to cut excess spending is to tax more; another is to increase savings and reduce private investment.

13. THE EXCESS PROFITS TAX

INTRODUCTION

IN WARTIME, the excess profits tax is an accepted part of a war finance program. It provides needed revenue and supports a popular demand that when the war requires large sacrifices, business should not make large gains out of the war. Moreover, the imposition of an excess profits tax facilitates the introduction of a wage-stabilization program. Workers are not disposed to submit to a wage freeze so long as profits rise excessively. In practice, the excess profits tax has been both a tax on war profits and a tax on high profits. The taxpayer may pay on the basis of the excess of profits over those of a base period (war profits concept); or on the basis of the excess over a normal return on capital investment (high profits concept).

In 1950, business groups organized in a vigorous manner to stop the enactment of an excess profits tax. The issues are important and should be discussed.

SOME ARGUMENTS FOR AN EXCESS PROFITS TAX

The case for the excess profits tax rests largely on the following grounds.

1. An excess profits tax is a necessary financial measure in wartime. We were in fact at war in 1950. Hence the argument that this was not the time to enact an excess profits

tax because we were not at war seems untenable. We were surely more at war than we were in 1940, when the excess profits tax was enacted in the last emergency. Our outlays for war and foreign assistance (the latter related to the war threat) even in 1950 equaled twice the total of all federal outlays on goods and services in 1940; and the program of the summer of 1950 was one for *total annual* outlays for military purposes exceeding *all* the costs of World War I. Indeed we were at war.

2. Raising an equal amount of revenue through a rise of, say, 12 per cent in the corporate income tax, as suggested by some groups, does not solve the problem of differentiating between those whose profits are high because of war and those whose profits are high irrespective of war.

3. A related issue is that in the emergency, every possible source of taxation must be tapped. The resistance to taxation will be great, especially since taxes would come partly out of existing income, not as in the last war, out of additions to income. We started this mobilization with taxes 22 per cent of gross national product (GNP), as compared with 17 per cent before World War II, and with total taxes about four times as high as before World War II.

THE ADEQUACY OF REVENUE

One of the most popular arguments against the excess profits tax is that with income so high in the base period (1946–49) and hence with excess profits relatively small, the yield of the tax would not be great. This argument loses its potency with examination.

Here are some estimates of the future GNP, corporate profits and excess profits tax on the basis of the experiences of the last war.

In the years 1941–45, the excess of GNP over 1936–39 was $95 billion. This sum yielded an average yearly excess of $22 billion in corporate profits for the period 1941–45 over that of 1936–39. Furthermore, the average yield (gross) of the excess profits tax was $7 billion over these five years.

In his statement of November 15, 1950, before the Ways and Means Committee, the Secretary of the Treasury revealed that in 1940–45 $35 billion were collected under the excess profits tax, and that the corporation tax would have accounted for 16 to 17 billion dollars of these $35 billion. The net contribution of the excess profits tax was but $16 billion.

NET INCOME, CORPORATE INCOME, AND EXCESS PROFITS TAXES, 1940–45

1. Net income after renegotiation, $ billion	120.9
2. Corporate income taxes, $ billion	23.2
3. Excess profits tax, $ billion	35.1
4. All taxes as per cent of net income	48.5
5. Estimated yield of corporate tax is applied to *all* corporate net income, $ billion	40.2
6. Estimated net yield of excess profits tax, $ billion	16.2

The estimated net yield of excess profits is computed thus:

	$ Billion
1. Excess profits tax	35.1
2. Deduct yield of additional corporate income if income not taxed under excess profits tax	16.7
3. Yield of excess profits tax before adjustments for various refunds	18.4
4. Deduct these refunds	2.2
5. Estimated net yield of excess profits tax	16.2

For the future, we make the following estimates of gross national output and compare them with 1946–49 results: [1]

Period	GNP (*$ Billion*)
1946–49, average	240
1950, estimate	276 *
1951, estimate	304
1952, estimate	334
1953, estimate	350
1954, estimate	370
Average 1951–54, estimate	340

* The official estimate early in 1951 was $279 billion.

From the table below, we draw the conclusion that the Treasury may obtain $54 billion in revenue from the excess profits tax in the years 1951–54. These results are based on the assumption of (*a*) a 10 per cent rise of output by 1954 over 1950 and a price increase somewhat in excess of 20 per cent; (*b*) a percentage rise of corporate profits relative to that in GNP in 1951–54 given by the ratio of the increases of GNP and of corporate profits in 1941–45 relative to 1936–39; (*c*) the yield of excess profits tax given by the percentage of excess profits tax to corporate profits in 1940–45.

1. Annual average excess of GNP over 1946–49, $ billion	100
2. Annual average excess of GNP, 1941–45 over 1936–39, $ billion	95
3. Annual rise of corporate profits, 1941–45 over 1936–39, $ billion	16
4. Percentage of (3) to (2)	17
5. Expected *rise* of corporate profits, 1951–54 over 1946–49, $ billion (apply 17 per cent to $100 billion rise of GNP)	17
6. Expected annual corporate profits, 1951–54, $ billion ($28 billion average in 1946–49 plus $17 billion)	45

7. Annual yield of excess profits tax in 1951–54, $ billion (apply 30 per cent to corporate profits, the percentage of excess profits tax to corporate income in 1940–45) 13.5
8. Yield of excess profits tax for four years, 1951–54, $ billion 54

Source: GNP from *President's Economic Report,* July, 1950. Corporate profits and excess profits tax yield, Exhibit I to accompany *Statement of Secretary Snyder before the Ways and Means Committee,* November 15, 1950. Estimates 1951–54 are mine.

This potential yield should be compared with that of $35 billion in 1941–45. In these five years the federal government raised $163 billion in taxes of which the excess profits tax accounted for about 22 per cent, and the corporate income tax 15 per cent.[2] The amounts to be obtained in 1951–54 exceed somewhat those in 1941–45 corrected for price changes.

Can we afford to give up revenues of these proportions? The net yield (allowing for losses in yields of other taxes) would be less than one-half the $54 billion.

THE BURDEN ON SMALL ENTERPRISE

In the discussions of the excess profits tax, much is made of the point that the tax discriminates against the small and growing enterprise. Undoubtedly the charge has some substance. But here again the critics of the tax make too much of this point.

Some statistical material is relevant here. The first shows that *in the years of the excess profits tax* the unincorporated business firm, the sole proprietorship and partnership, that is the smaller business units, gained on the average relatively both in the amount of business done and in the profits earned.

Thus from 1940 to 1945, income originating in corporate business enterprises rose by 105 per cent, income from sole-proprietorship and partnership enterprises by 112 per cent; income earned (before taxes) rose by 117 per cent and 138 per cent, respectively. (After taxes, *corporate* profits rose by but 41 per cent.) The reader will also observe that corporate business recouped its losses in the years 1946–49, when there was no excess profits tax. (A small amount was collected in 1946.)

INCOME ORIGINATED AND PROFITS, CORPORATE AND SOLE-PROPRIETORSHIP AND PARTNERSHIP BUSINESS ($ BILLION)

	1940	*1945*	*1949*
Income originated:			
Corporations	42.2	87.0	117.6
Sole proprietorships and partnerships	20.9	44.2	58.5
Profits:			
Corporate (before taxes)	9.3	20.2	27.6
(after taxes)	6.4	9.0	17.0
Unincorporated	12.7	30.2	33.7

Source: *Survey of Current Business,* Annual Income Number, July, 1950.

The second relevant point here is that the small firms seem to be treated much more generously under the excess profits tax than the large firms. We know that many concessions were made to the small firms and especially to allow for the growth in such a way as to reduce the burden on growing firms.

The support of this point is suggested by the relation of the excess profits net income (roughly corporate net income minus income in base period, or excess over "normal" returns on capital) and the *adjusted* excess profits net income. (The latter is excess profits net income minus various allowances for reducing the tax burden.) In the year 1945, the totals were $14.2 billion and $8.37 billion, respectively, that is, the *adjusted* excess profits net income was almost 60 per cent of the excess profits net income. But note the small percentages of income liable to tax for small firms, the steady rise in this ratio as income increases, and the substantial percentages for the larger firms.

Adjusted Excess Profits Net Income Classes	*Percentage of Adjusted Excess Profits Net Income to Excess Profits Credit*
Under $5,000	9
$5,000–$10,000	22
$10,000–$15,000	31
$15,000–$20,000	35
$20,000–$25,000	39
$25,000 and over	66

Source: Calculations from *Statistics of Income for 1945*, Part II.

Finally, the small-business units pay much less relatively than the larger-business units, and a much smaller proportion is subject to the excess profits tax.

CORPORATIONS SUBJECT TO EXCESS PROFITS TAX AND EFFECTIVE RATES BY SIZE OF CORPORATIONS, 1944

Corporation Net Assets	*Percentage of Corporations Subject to Tax*	*Percentage of Net Income Subject to Excess Profits Tax*	*Effective Tax Rate*	
			All Corporations with Net Income	*Corporations Subject to Excess Profits Tax*
Less than $50,000	5	4	28	42
$50,000 to $100,000	24	18	37	49
$100,000 and over	75	47	57	60
All	27	50	59	63

Source: *Statement of Secretary Snyder before the Ways and Means Committee*, November 15, 1950, Exhibit I, pp. 10, 11.

RESULTING DISSIPATION OF RESOURCES

Another source of attack on the excess profits tax is the wastage involved in the levy of this tax—e.g., it encourages wasteful advertising outlays since the government pays the major part of the bill as a deduction from taxes; and with its imposition, opposition of business men to wage increases weakens: the employer weighs the gains of good will on the part of employees against the small additional cost to him of the wage rise.

The reader who is overly impressed by these claims of wastage should consider the following: In providing additional tax revenue and in facilitating wage stabilization, the Treasury in imposing an excess profits tax contributes importantly to the attack on inflation. And inflation induces uneconomic use of resources. I suggest the gains here greatly outweigh the losses adumbrated above. Moreover, the government can control advertising outlays both by limiting deductible amounts and through other controls. In fact, advertising outlays, relative to income, declined in World War II, when the excess profits tax was in vogue, and rose in the years 1946–49, when it was not. From 1936–40 to 1941–44 gross national product rose by 93 per cent; and advertising in the three major media by only 25 per cent.[3] Finally, the rise of output of 50 to 70 per cent in World War II, despite a heavy excess profits tax, is not without significance. Incidentally, the case for the excess profits tax is greatly strengthened in a period when the country is confronted with strong inflationary pressures, and yet is reluctant to accept genuine controls. An excess profits tax, as part of a general high tax policy, would contribute toward reducing spending and hence toward checking inflation and thus reduce the need of controls.

Much has been made of the point that in World War II, employers were disposed to grant wage increases because at the high corporate rates in effect the cost to them was small. Though high taxes may have contributed to high wage policies, one could argue with as much validity that because the Treasury siphoned off so much, relatively, the employer would resist any further drains whether the occasion be gifts or a rise of taxes. The reader should also recall that the major factors in the rise of wage bills in World War II were the increase of employment, in overtime, and in up-grading, and not the increase in basic wage rates.[4]

Indeed the argument has been used that an excess profits tax without price and wage control is highly inflationary, since the business man passes the tax on to the consumer.[5] But this argument rests on the assumption that business men do not already charge what the traffic will bear. The generally accepted theory is that a tax on profits is not passed on, though there are indeed many instances when, because of the pressure of public opinion or ignorance, the business man does not charge what the traffic will bear.

ALLEVIATIONS

Few will contend that the excess profits tax is an ideal tax. It has many defects, among which are its discriminatory aspects, and interference with growth. Yet on grounds of equity and need of revenue, I would support its use in wartime.

It is, however, imperative that the legislation and administration be sufficiently flexible. The fact is that the government was reasonably generous in World War II in dealing with injustices: the special privileges for personal corporations, the alternative methods of estimating excess profits, the privilege of changing base periods when injustices otherwise result, the right to carry backward and forward unused base period credits, the special adjustment for a bad year in the base period, the privilege of reallocating profits not properly related to the years of receipt, the limit of 80 per cent on all corporate taxes, the 10 per cent refund, the special relief to corporations with rising incomes in 1936–39—all of these reduced the sting of the excess profits tax.[6]

The fact that in 1945 excess profits credits were $5.18 billion, or 40 per cent of excess profits net incomes, shows that the government's provisions for making the tax bearable were not merely paper provisions. Moreover, the failure to deal with specific difficulties was not so harmful as it otherwise would have been because the government could allow for efficient operations in administering contract renegotiations. No one would insist that contract renegotiation was a great success. But it served a useful purpose in reducing excess profits by 6 to 7 billion dollars ($1.7 billion, if allowance is made on the loss of tax receipts on these 6 to 7 billion dollars).[7] That it could not be a substitute for the excess profits tax is implied by the fact that renegotiations relate only to war contracts, not to rising profits resulting indirectly from war. The excess profits tax supplemented the renegotiation in that the failure to renegotiate effectively from the government's viewpoint could largely be corrected by excess profits tax.[8]

Not only were the alleviations important in World War II, they will be even more important under any excess profits tax enacted in the fifties. Among the liberalizing features are the inclusion of only the three *best* years of 1946–49 as the base for past earnings (thus substantially reducing the base period earnings and hence the excess profits tax): a much higher return on capital as a base than in 1940–45 for those who use the "earnings" standard; a larger allowance for invested capital (again thus reducing the tax liability); a minimum credit of $25,000 against an exemption of $10,000 in World War II; special treatment of growing concerns.

In this discussion of the excess profits tax, I do not mean to minimize the serious limitations of it. There are inequities. They have to be weighed against the revenue and anti-inflationary gains to be had from the excess profits tax. Professor Dan Smith, for example, argues with some cogency that the new firm is at a great disadvantage against the older firm because the latter's securities frequently sell at 4 to 8 times their annual earnings. Investors are not inclined, therefore, to put their money in new enterprises. "A rate of prospective allowed rates of return of even 7 to 12 per cent would not even be adequate if the rate of tax applied to income above these levels were substantially confiscatory." The solution, according to Professor Smith, is to allow a large percentage deduction on capital invested by the new concerns.[9] Undoubtedly there is much merit in this proposal. Perhaps also the problem is not so serious, because a relatively small percentage of the small firms are subject to excess profits tax and when subject, the tax is a relatively small part of total income. The restrictions on growth are probably more important.

CAN INDUSTRY AFFORD AN EXCESS PROFITS TAX?

Finally, we should emphasize the point that business is in an excellent position to endure heavy taxes in wartime. It has gone through 10 years of unparalleled prosperity. Their tax capacity is much greater than in 1940, a year following 10 years of depression. Their average corporate profits in 1946–49 were $28 billion ($5 billion before the war) and are estimated at $40 billion in 1950; and after taxes, the respective figures were $4 billion (1936–39), $8.5 billion (1945), $22 billion (1950).

Industry's plant is in excellent shape, and the liquidity position satisfactory. In the years 1946–50, they spent $109 billion on plant and equipment, or five times as much *per year* as in the thirties. Indeed, prices are much higher; but on the other hand the increased effectiveness of each dollar spent (aside from the rise of prices) probably largely offsets the increase of prices.

In summary, the case for an adequate excess profits tax in 1950–51 is strong. The high level of corporate profits is one important reason—at the level of $40 billion in 1950, profits *after* taxes were $22 billion as compared with $4 billion in 1936–39 and $8.5 billion at the end of the war. Among other relevant factors is the large contribution that an excess profits tax can make toward stabilization, especially if used as the first move toward a well-integrated tax system, and as a condition for wage stabilization. So long as the country forgoes advanced controls, increased taxes are especially important as a guard against inflation. Finally, the impairment by the excess profits tax of incentives and contributions to waste is not so great as is frequently claimed.

In the light of this analysis, we should comment briefly on Public Law 909 (81st Congress, the Excess Profits Tax), enacted in January, 1951. The Congress was greatly concerned over the inequities involved in the excess profits tax. As a result, many alleviations were introduced: the excess profits tax of 1950 was a much less oppressive one than the World War II version. In the treatment of growing concerns, in the 62 per cent ceiling on all corporate income taxation, in the allowance of the three *best* years, 1946–49, as a base, in the $25,000 exemption, in the more liberal provisions for including capital as a base for deductions from total profits, in the higher returns on capital for those using the alternative (capital base) method of computing profits than in World War II, in the allowance of a five-year carry forward and a one-year carry back of unused excess profits credit, in the generous and specific (as compared with World War II) relief provisions, and in many other respects—the 1951 Act was generous in its treatment of the taxpayers and reflected an earnest effort to meet the critics of the excess profits tax.[10]

In a gray mobilization, the Act might well be supported. Should the crisis deepen, an excess profits tax with more teeth in it will be required.

14. SAVINGS

INTRODUCTION

As THE government increases its military outlays, savings tend to increase. The expansion of savings is related to the growth of income in periods of mobilization and/or war; to the unavailability of civilian goods or to the restrictions on private spending; and, finally, to the pressures put upon citizens to purchase war securities.

The rise of savings is a weapon in the anti-inflationary arsenal: the more that is saved, the less is spent on consumption goods. In order to achieve the maximum in anti-inflationary effectiveness, it is necessary that the savings be channeled into investment for purposes directly associated with the war. That means the application of savings either to the purchase of government securities or to the expansion of private investment for furthering the mobilization or war effort. Should the increased savings be hoarded, then the government could sell securities to the banks for a corresponding amount with no net inflationary effects: the new money would be a substitute for the cash or deposits now added to hoards.

In order to understand the net effects of savings, three additional considerations require attention. First, the contribution of additional savings and taxation are not additive. A rise of taxes tends to reduce savings. Second, the anti-inflationary effects of additional savings may prevail only during the war effort. Once the emergency is over, consumers and business may dissave, thus increasing the demands for consumption and investment goods. This tendency to draw on past savings accounts in part for the inflationary pressures of the years 1946–50. Third, a continued rise of prices with an increased awareness of the reduced real values of securities tends to accelerate the dissaving process; and the more so if the rate of interest is kept at a low level.

EXPERIENCE, 1936–49

A useful over-all picture is given by the table below:

VARIOUS ASPECTS OF SAVINGS, PREWAR, WAR, AND POSTWAR
(EACH IN FOUR-YEAR PERIODS)

	1936–39	*1942–45*	*1946–49*
1. Gross private savings, $ billion	42.6	194.7	127.7
2. Gross private savings (per cent of GNP)	12.2	24.8	16.2
3. Personal savings, $ billion	11.1	119.2	35.5
4. Personal savings (per cent of personal income)	3.9	19.5	4.5
5. Undistributed corporate profits, $ billion	0.4	21.2	42.7
6. Business depreciation charges, $ billion	26.7	38.9	51.0
7. Capital outlays charged to individual account, $ billion	3.0	3.6	9.3
8. Gross private investment, $ billion	37.0	29.0	150.9
9. Government deficit, $ billion	5.6	165.4	—23.1

Source: Calculated from *Survey of Current Business,* National Income Numbers, July, 1947 and July, 1950.

In the war period, gross private savings rose to almost $200 billion, or close to five times that of the prewar years; and the rise was twice as great relatively as in GNP. In the four postwar years, these savings declined to $128 billion, a reduction from 25 per cent of GNP in World War I to 16 per cent in 1946–49.

The most volatile changes occurred in personal savings. The increase was from $11 billion, or 3.9 per cent of personal income, in 1936–39 to $119.2 billion, or 19.5 per cent of personal income in World War II. In the years 1946–49, personal savings sank to $35.5 billion, or to only 4.5 per cent of personal income. In these postwar years, with personal incomes two and two-thirds times as high as in 1936–39, savings were roughly the same percentage of personal income as in 1936–39. The inference is that savings were at a surprisingly low level relative to the high incomes; and the explanation is largely the large outlays associated with the use of savings accumulated in World War II.

This table also reveals that in the war period gross private investment amounted to but $29 billion, although gross private savings amounted to $195 billion. The $29 billion were but two-thirds of the business depreciation charges. In other words, the country was living on capital. By using only a small part of gross private savings, business thus enabled government to finance $165 billion of deficits out of private and business savings that otherwise would have been used primarily for private investment. (We are aware, of course, that the savings would have been less than $195 billion in the years 1942–45 in the absence of war and large public deficits.)

In 1946–49, the picture was entirely different. Gross private investment at $151 billion exceeded gross private savings by $23 billion, and was three times as great as business depreciation charges. Personal savings accounted for an even smaller percentage of private investment than in 1936–39; and around $23 billion of the private investment were offset by savings (surpluses) of government.[1]

THE ORIGIN OF SAVINGS

From the preceding table, the reader will note that savings derive from business and from individuals. In prewar (1936–39) personal savings were about one-quarter of all savings; during the war, more than three-fifths; and in the postwar, a little more than one-quarter.

In war periods, business savings available for government use rise both because profits increase and because outlets to private investment are closed. In the postwar, the dissaving results from investments exceeding business profits: earlier savings are spent and business increases its loans.

In response to rising incomes and restrictions on output and sales of consumption goods, personal savings rise. The following figures clarify the relation of income and savings. They show an increased tendency to save as the war proceeds, and also a tendency through 1942 for the percentage increases of consumption to those in income payments to decline.

CONSUMPTION AND SAVINGS IN RELATION TO INCOME

	1939	*1940*	*1941*	*1942*	*1943*	*1944*
Percentage of disposable income saved by individuals	9	10	16	25	27	29
Ratio of consumption expenditures to income payments	87	86	82	71	64	63
Rise of consumption as per cent of rise of income payments	—	85	63	37	50	77

Source: *Survey of Current Business,* various issues, 1944–45; House Hearings on *Revenue Revision of 1943,* pp. 36, 40; Bureau of the Budget, *Budget, 1946,* p. xxv.

THE ALLOCATION OF SAVINGS

As we have noted, even in wartime, all savings are not invested in government securities. Thus from the end of 1941 to the end of 1944, liquid assets of individuals and corporations rose by $106.5 billion; but deposits and currency increased by $54 billion and public securities held increased by $62 billion.[2] This distribution suggests that in wartime, as the government finances in part by borrowing from banks, monetary supplies rise, and part of the savings are held in the form of cash and deposits. This expansion of monetary supplies is a condition for the ensuing rise of demand for securities; but it also offers competition to the government in the sale of assets to savers.

Another approach is suggested by a comparison of liquid savings of the public and deficits of the federal government, first presented in the U.S. Treasury *Annual Report on the State of the Finances* (1944, pp. 82–93). Thus, in 1944, after payments of taxes and outlays on consumption goods, the public was left with $52 billion of liquid savings, an amount equal to the government deficits, i.e., the difference between government expenditures and tax receipts ($93 billion — $41 billion = $52 billion).

For the period, July 1, 1940, to June 30, 1945, the relation of private surpluses and federal deficits was as follows:

	$ Billion
Federal government:	
Federal expenditures	323
Taxes	133
Deficit	190
Private economy:	
Income after taxes	651
Expenditures	469
Surplus	182
Add surplus of state and local government	8
	190

Source: *Treasury Bulletin,* December, 1945, pp. A-1 to A-2.

Finally, note the table below. The interesting aspects are the following:

1. Even in 1936–39 and 1946–49 the proportion of liquid savings embodied in currency and demand deposits was roughly the same (40–50) percentage as in the war inflationary years.

2. But the rise in *total* liquid savings was much greater in war: ten times that of prewar and five to six times that of postwar.

3. In the war years, about one-third of all liquid savings went into securities; in prewar the amount of securities held was reduced; in postwar the public invested about two-fifths of their savings in securities. The large liquid savings put into insurance and pension reserves and into savings and loan associations are also relevant. These investments in turn, and especially during the war, are put into government securities. Roughly one-half of the $67 billion invested in insurance and pension reserves were in public programs, an important outlet for federal issues.

4. Whereas in the war period debts were liquidated, in the postwar period the accumulation of new debts roughly exceeded one-half of gross liquid savings and almost equaled all *net* liquid savings.

LIQUID SAVINGS, PREWAR, WAR, AND POSTWAR *
(FOUR-YEAR PERIODS)

	1936–39	*1942–45*	*1946–49*
All	15.3	148.2	27.6
Currency and bank deposits	7.1	63.7	10.2
Savings and loan associations	.03	2.7	5.1
Insurance and pension reserves	11.0	28.6	26.9
Securities	—.49	49.4	11.9
Debt liquidation (mortgage and not otherwise classified)	—2.45 †	3.8	—26.3 †

Source: Adapted from *Survey Current Business,* National Income Numbers, July, 1947, and July, 1950.

* Small items omitted.

† = Rise of debt.

15. THE RELATION OF INCOME, TAXES, AND SAVINGS

In World War II, the rise of taxes was not so large as that in gross savings. The inference may be drawn that savings contributed more to the fight against inflation than did taxation. But it is necessary to allow for the greater effectiveness of taxes in that savings in war may account for larger outlays in the postwar.

The World War II experience also reveals that in the early period of the war additional personal savings contributed much more than additional taxes. Thus, from 1939 to 1942, the rise of net individual savings was $23 billion, of federal taxes only $4 billion; from 1942 to 1944, the increases were 11 billion and 13 billion dollars, respectively. For the whole period, income payments rose by $87 billion, all *individual* savings by $34 billion and personal taxes by $17 billion.[1] It is interesting that in the four years, 1941–44, net individual savings of $114 billion roughly corresponded to $100 billion of noninflationary purchases of public securities. *Gross* private savings in these years amounted to $179 billion.[2] In successive years, the inflationary sales of federal issues were 3, 14, 24, and 21 billion dollars, equaling approximately 14, 24, 26, and 23 per cent of federal outlays in 1941, 1942, 1943, and 1944. The proportion of taxes to federal outlays amounted to 53, 33, 38, and 45 per cent of federal outlays.[3]

SAVINGS IN THE FUTURE

On the basis of World War II experience, we can make some estimates of the savings potential of the next four years.

These estimates are made on the following three assumptions:

1. GNP will average $340 billion in the years 1951–54, or $100 billion in excess of GNP in 1946–49. This gross product will be obtained on the assumption of a rise of output of 10 per cent over the four years and a yearly increase of 5 per cent in prices. The likely rise in dollar income is greater.

2. Gross savings will rise to 25 per cent of GNP as in 1942–45; and personal savings, 20 per cent of *personal income,* as in 1942–45.

3. Gross private investment will amount to 4 per cent of GNP. (The figure was 3.7 per cent in 1942–45.)

The net result would then be:

Expectation, 1951–54	*$ Billion*
1. Annual amount of gross private savings *	85
2. Annual amount of personal savings	55
3. Annual amount of gross private investment	14
4. Savings available for defense or war use (line 1 — line 3)	71

* Note that for 1951, gross private savings would be $76 billion and for 1954, $92.5 billion.

RESERVATIONS

Heroic measures would be necessary, however, to obtain gross private savings of $85 billion and savings available to the federal government of $71 billion. And for the six following reasons:

1. In 1949, gross private savings were but $36.8 billion and 14.4 per cent of GNP.

2. In 1949, personal savings were but $8.6 billion and 4.2 per cent of personal income.

3. Taxes will have to rise to a much larger percentage of GNP than in World War II—with adverse effects on savings.

In fact, all government receipts in 1942–45 were 24 per cent of GNP and in 1949 they were already 22 per cent.

4. Large savings for the use of the war economy are the product not only of high incomes but also of restrictions on output and sales of consumption and investment goods. In the first half of 1950, gross private investment was running at the rate of $44 billion, or 16 per cent of GNP. Almost half of the investment was other than on nonfarm producers' plant and equipment: private construction (residential, religious, educational, etc.) alone amounted to $12.7 billion (annual rate). Obviously, most of these outlays and a large part of the business outlays are not essential from the viewpoint of the war economy. In other words, a must for channeling adequate private savings into public security markets is a vigorous check on private investment. (By the second half of 1950, gross private investments had risen to $53 billion.)

5. A related problem is that of restraints on consumption. These may stem from control of output and imports and from control of distribution.

In 1949, personal consumption expenditures amounted to $179 billion, or 70 per cent of GNP. In 1942–45, consumption had averaged $107 billion, or only 55 per cent of GNP.

At a $340 billion GNP, consumption at the 1949 rate would yield $238 billion of personal consumption expenditures. At the 1942–45 ratio to GNP, the figure would be $187 billion, or only $8 billion more than in 1949, and in *real* value a decline of 15 to 20 per cent. The result would be that with an expansion of GNP of $100 billion, consumption in dollar value would rise by but $8 billion; and in relation to an expansion of personal income of $80 billion, consumption would rise by $8 billion. The result would be an additional $72 billion for the war economy to be obtained through savings and (or) taxation.

It is obvious that this outcome would be possible only if serious checks are put upon the output and distribution of consumption goods.

6. Finally, there is the issue of the inclination to save. In view of the continued rise of prices, the average investor in public securities over the last 10 to 15 years has received less in goods equivalent than expected.

The average value of government securities in 1949 relative to their value at time of purchase was down by $75 billion or close to 30 per cent.

Americans will be less disposed to save than in the last war. It will, therefore, be necessary to depend more heavily on taxation and possibly forced savings. Denying consumers' goods will contribute toward a diversion of savings to the government. But with a reduced propensity to save, the pressure to buy consumers' goods may be great nevertheless—with a resultant rise of prices on free, and to some extent, on controlled markets.

The only way out may well be much heavier recourse to taxation, and possibly forced savings. The latter are, in fact, a kind of taxation. The citizen is forced to purchase public securities equal (say) to 25 per cent of incomes from $5,000 to $10,000, 50 per cent of incomes from $10,000 to $20,000, 75 per cent of incomes from $20,000 to $100,000, etc. (all after taxation), at a rate of interest (say) of 2 per cent. Insofar as the rate is less than what is required to elicit these savings on a voluntary basis, the forced loan is equal to a corresponding tax.

POTENTIAL TAXES AND SAVINGS

Gross savings, it will be recalled, on the basis of the relation of savings to GNP in 1942–45, are estimated at $85 billion per year in the years 1951–54.

In the years 1942–45 about 30 per cent of the savings were put into cash and deposits. On the assumption that inflationary pressures would be less than in World War II, we assume here that only 20 per cent would be put into cash and deposits. (With less inflation, the rise of money would be less than in World War II.) It follows then that $54 billion of savings would be available to the Treasury.

	$ Billion
Gross savings	85
Deduct (20 per cent of total savings) to be put into cash and deposits	17
	68
Deduct (4 per cent of GNP) for private gross investment	14
Available for Treasury	54

I assume that 25 per cent of GNP would be taken by taxes and other government receipts (24 per cent in 1942–45). Therefore:

	$ Billion
Taxes, etc.	85
Deduct federal, state, and local receipts (1949)	56
Additional taxes	29

It follows that on these assumptions a $340-billion GNP would yield $83 billion of additional savings and taxation for the use of the federal government. The proportion of taxes to all additional receipts (36 per cent) is substantially less than the percentage of war outlays provided by taxes in

World War II; and the amount clearly is not adequate. In this war, we need a better tax record. And especially since the public would not voluntarily put $54 billion of savings (as is assumed above) at the disposal of the Treasury.

Here is another goal:

1. Taxes = 30 per cent of GNP = $102 billion, or $46 billion in excess of 1949 receipts. This should be a minimum goal. Our objective should be a rise of taxes of $60 billion and hence financing 60 per cent of a $100-billion program through taxation. (Perhaps in part through forced savings.)

2. Savings = $40 billion (voluntary or forced). The rise of taxes, it is assumed, would reduce savings; and in the absence of comprehensive controls, private investment would not be cut as drastically as in World War II. In the absence of global war, private investments would continue at a higher rate than in World War II. Perhaps a $100-billion effort would require $15 billion of savings for industry and $40 billion for government. With new taxes at $60 billion, only $26 billion of savings for government would be required.

3. Sales of securities to banks; with the expansion of deposits, as adumbrated above, would equal $17 billion.

4. Total resources available to finance the war on the assumption of a GNP of $340 billion would amount to $103 billion. The proportion of taxes is somewhat higher than in World War II and of inflationary finance less.

Part Five

THE RATE OF INTEREST AND THE NATIONAL DEBT

16. THE RATE OF INTEREST

INTRODUCTION

IN MODERN economic life, the rate of interest is a crucial matter—in part because economic activity is influenced substantially by the relation of what has to be paid for the use of money and what the money will earn. In part this holds because in these days of increased activities by government and rising public debts, the rate of interest is a matter of considerable importance to the government, and public policy decisions are frequently influenced by the cost of money.

DECLINE IN THE INTEREST RATE

One of the unexpected developments in the last 20 years has been the downward movement in the rate of interest. In particular the experience in World War II was unexpected. As a general rule, under the stress of war demands and rising prices, the rate of interest tends to increase. In the Civil War, interest was payable in gold and therefore the expected rise in rates is not to be found. Compare, however, World War I and World War II. From 1916 to 1919, the computed rate of interest on the government debt rose from 2.376 to 4.178, an increase of one-third; but from 1941 to 1945, this rate declined from 2.52 to 1.92, or a reduction of close to one-quarter. Yet World War I was a $30-billion war and World War II a $300-billion war. It seemed as though the more securities issued by the government in World War II, the higher (lower rate of interest) not the lower the price of these securities.

Note also that the computed rate on Federal debt averaged 4.11 per cent in the twenties, 3.04 per cent in the thirties, and 2.17 per cent in the forties (figures from *Annual Report of the Secretary of the Treasury on the State of Finances,* 1945, p. 600, and *Treasury Bulletin,* May, 1950, p. 19).

AN ANALYSIS OF THE DECLINE IN RATES

Why this marked drop of rates? An obvious explanation may well be the special privileges accorded to government bonds, and especially in wartime. Government agencies and trust funds offer special outlets; and financial institutions and the public are under special pressure to buy federal issues. That these are relevant considerations is evident from the fact that from 1940 to 1945 the computed rate on all federal issues declined by 25 per cent, on U.S. Treasury long-term issues by 27 per cent, and on Moody's corporate bonds by but 19 per cent. These variables are all the more significant if we consider the rise of the national debt from 42 to 256 billion dollars and of corporate debt from but 89 to 100 billion dollars.

A second factor is undoubtedly the change in the types of issues outstanding. In recent years, and notably in the war period, it has become fashionable for government to finance itself increasingly by short-term issues. This means simply that the reduction in rates is in part fictitious; for short-term securities are floated at lower rates than long-term issues. The basket of securities now includes a larger proportion of short-term securities. In issuing these the Treasury pays less but is confronted with more difficult problems of refinancing, for large short-term issues outstanding may be embarrassing.

Thus in 1940 (end of fiscal year), outstanding Treasury bills and certificates, the lowest yielding securities, amounted to

$1.3 billion, or 3 per cent of the gross debt, and in 1945, $51.2 billion, or 20 per cent. Obviously, even if rates on each issue remained unchanged, the average rate on all issues would decline with a *rise* in the proportion of short-term, that is, low-yielding, securities. Indeed, part of the explanation of lower rates is the increased recourse to short-term issues. Additional proof is to be found in the relative stability of rates for identical issues during the war years. The rate on Treasury bills actually rose in 1941–42, and that on longer-term issues did not decline substantially until 1945.

One other explanation of the reduction in the computed rate and of the general tendency of rates to decline is undoubtedly the control system. First, because prices were fairly well stabilized from 1942 to 1945, and government securities appeal more in periods of stable prices than in those of rising prices. Second, because with large increases in employment and thus income and restrictions on spending, both for consumption and investment, the government security was bound to become a favored market. Where else could the money be put?

DISTRIBUTION OF OWNERSHIP AND RATES

In the years since the war ended, the government has maintained the prices of its securities reasonably well. Thus in June, 1945, the computed rate of interest was 1.936 per cent; in March, 1950, 2.199 per cent, or a rise of about 14 per cent. The debt outstanding was but $3 billion less in the later period. The maximum rise from 1944 was about 16 per cent.

It has not been easy to keep the rate from rising. Business and institutional savers were inclined to desert the government security market in order either to obtain cash for investment purposes (e.g., expansion of plant) or to replace government securities with assets yielding higher returns.

In the five years ending June 30, 1950, the following changes in holdings of Federal issues occurred:

	$ Billion
Rise:	
U.S. Government trust agency and trust funds	12.9
Individuals	10.7
State and local government	3.3
Mutual savings banks	2.0
Decline:	
Commercial banks	18.5
Other corporations	6.2
Federal Reserve banks	3.5
Insurance companies	2.5

Source: *Treasury Bulletin.*

In general, the financial institutions and business corporations liquidated part of their holdings; and government agencies and trust funds and individuals added to theirs. In these years, the proportion of issues held by financial institutions declined from 53 to 45 per cent and the proportion held by government agencies and trust funds and individuals rose from 33 to 42 per cent.

This tendency on the part of financial institutions to dispose of securities contributed to the hardening of rates—and especially since this was accompanied by a relative decline in short-term (i.e., low-yield) securities and an accompanying reduction in the supply of money. In these five years, Treasury bills and certificates outstanding declined by almost $20 billion, and as a proportion of total debt from 20 to 13 per cent.

The problems confronting the government can well be clarified by an examination of the proportion of savings put into government securities in the five war years and the five years since. In the war years, the American public put about 40 per cent of their savings in federal issues; in the five years 1946–50, only 13 per cent. Again in the war years, corporations invested twice their savings in federal issues; but in

1946–50, they actually liquidated (net) $9 billion of securities, though corporate savings were $53 billion. (The excess of investments over savings in 1941–45 is explained by the accumulation of depreciation, replacement, etc., funds not investable during the war.)

SAVINGS AND INVESTMENTS IN FEDERAL GOVERNMENT SECURITIES, INDIVIDUALS AND CORPORATIONS ($ BILLION)

	Individual Savings	*Personal Investments in Federal Securities*	*Corporate Savings* *	*Corporate Investment in Federal Securities* *
1941–45	129.2	53.9	26.1	52.8
1946–50 †	45.0	6.0	52.7	−9.0

* Not strictly comparable.
† 1950 estimated.

Source: *The Midyear Economic Report of the President Transmitted to the Congress,* July 1950.

THE FUTURE

Now what about the future?

The government will find it more difficult to keep interest rates down. In view of the large real losses suffered by investors in public securities in the last ten years as a result of the rise of prices, there will be much resistance to increased purchases. This is already evident. Whereas private investors absorbed an average of $2.65 billion in the fiscal years 1946–49, the net gain was but $1.3 billion in the fiscal year 1950, but $253 million from February to August, 1950, and a net reduction of $98 million in August. Moreover, the government faces large maturities in the years 1951–55.

As deficits rise, the Treasury will have to borrow from the banks with resultant expansion of monetary supplies. In turn the expansion of money will tend to raise prices and especially in a full-employment economy. In response to this rise of prices, potential buyers of federal issues will become even more reluctant to buy government securities. Their increased savings with rising incomes will move into commodity and capital markets: consumers' goods, inventories of all kinds, real estate, common stocks, new plant. It is significant that common stocks rose by 20 per cent in the year ending August, 1950, whereas in the ten years 1939–49 the rise was but 29 per cent. This suggests a flight from fixed-interest securities.

Is there an effective manner of dealing with this dilemma? Obviously as the prices of consumers' goods and other assets rise, the advantage of buying these assets will decrease. But the desertion of these markets may not be forthcoming for many years.

Another approach is to control prices of commodities and possibly even other assets. The first effect of this policy would, however, be an even greater movement into these commodities. We conclude from this that a comprehensive control system which restricts spending in areas competitive with government securities would be required to shunt adequate supplies of cash into the government-security markets.

There is one other way out, namely, a *much* higher return on government securities. This increase in yield would have to be high enough to offset losses associated with expected price rises. Should the government have to borrow 10 to 40 billion dollars annually, the costs of the high rate policy may be too great. A variant of this policy is one suggested by my colleague, Professor Slichter, and was one of the favorite themes of the late Irving Fisher: The lender is to be guaranteed against any losses resulting from rising prices. Unfortunately, this may prove to be a highly inflationary method of warding off the effects of inflation.

In short, there does not seem to be any simple solution. Surely an all-out control system is not a very happy solution. Nor is a large increase in the rate of interest. Perhaps the most helpful way out is a really vigorous tax system which will keep the expansion of marketable securities down to a minimum, coupled with restrictions, as war needs grow, on sales or production of many nonessential consumers' goods —and particularly those that use up scarce factors and attract money that otherwise might go into government securities.[1]

17. THE NATIONAL DEBT

HISTORY

THE RISE of national debt has been a matter of concern to most Americans. Another emergency following so soon after World War II focuses attention on the growing national debt. There is a great fear that another large jump in the debt on top of recent growth will bankrupt the nation.

Indeed the national debt has been growing at a rapid rate. In 1836, the federal debt of the United States was at the record low level figure of $38,000. The problem, then, was how to dispose of large surpluses. A century later (1937) the national debt had risen to $37 billion, or an increase of close to a million times. In the ten years following 1936, the debt rose by $235 billion, or roughly seven times. By June 30, 1946, the national debt was $269 billion. This expansion of seven times in ten years was much more serious than the rise of a million times in the preceding hundred years. In this decade the absolute rise was at an annual rate of approximately 64 times that of the preceding hundred years.

In per capita terms the rise of debt seems fantastic when the 25 cents burden of 1836 is compared with the $1,689 burden of 1950. The debt rises in periods of war and then declines. Note the reduction of debt as a percentage of income from 45 to 4 per cent in the period from the Civil War to 1914, and of 40 to 22 per cent from 1919 to 1930, and of 141 to 115 per cent in the period after World War II. In 1950, the burden of the debt incurred as a percentage of income was 2½ times that of 1866. But the interest cost was 2.22 per cent of income in 1866 and only 2.27 per cent in

1950, and yet the debt was 92 times as large in 1950. That suggests how both the rise of income and the reduction of interest tend to reduce the burden of debt.

DEBT, TOTAL, PER CAPITA, AND IN RELATION TO INCOME, FOR VARIOUS YEARS

Fiscal Year	*Total ($ Thousand)*	*Per Capita ($)*	*Total Debt, Percentage of Estimated Income*
1836, end of fiscal year	38	0.25	.00004
Civil War peak, 1866	2,755,000	75.42	45 *
1914, end of fiscal year	1,188,000	11.99	4
World War I peak, 1919	25,482,000	242.54	40
Minimum interwar period, 1930	16,185,000	131.51	22
Postwar peak, 1946	268,110,000	1,907.62	141
1950 estimated	253,377,000	1,689.00	115

Sources: National Debt—*Report of the Secretary of the Treasury,* 1948, pp. 444–445; my *National Debt and the New Economics,* p. 149.
Per Capita Debt Burden—*Report of the Secretary of the Treasury,* 1948, and my calculations.
National Income—N.I.C.B., *The Economic Almanac for 1945–46,* p. 71, and the *Mid-Year Economic Report of the President,* July, 1950, p. 118.
Percentage of Debt to National Income—my calculations.

* Income interpolated.

THE BURDEN OF DEBT

This debt is indeed a burden. It is more of a burden than it should be, because many suffer from a debt neurosis. Approximately $5 billion to $6 billion annually are taken from taxpayers to pay the interest charges. This is more than 2 per cent of the national output. Indeed the money is transferred from taxpayer to bondholder, and the two are often the same, but this does not mean that the taxpayer who holds the bonds accepts the additional taxes without some resentment. He expects interest on bonds, but dislikes the taxes levied to finance the interest. In disbursing these interest billions, the government does not drain the country of goods and services; for these are merely transfer payments. Clearly the costs to the economy are less than if the payment of the same number of dollars removed goods from the market—e.g., ships for military service.

From the discussion so far we conclude that the national debt is a burden; but perhaps not so much as is frequently assumed—not only for the reasons given above but also for two other reasons. First, it is well to relate the growth of debt with the accompanying rise of income. Government deficit financing guaranteed markets and provided additional income. That is to say, if the national debt is a burden, its expansion also contributed importantly to the rise of income which is the source of taxation. Thus, in the years 1940–45 the national income was $450 billion above prewar levels, a rise which made possible the absorption of $175 billion of federal securities by private interests. In these years government spending of $385 billion accounted for three-eighths of the $987 billion of total spending; and increased outlays mean more demand and employment.

Second, this rise of debt charges was accompanied by a large growth of income. In relation to income, the burden was much less than might be suggested by concentrating on the increase of the charge. Thus for the years 1880 to 1945 we set against an increase of national income (1935 dollars) from 12 to 120 billion dollars, an increase of the debt charge of less than $3 billion. Again, in dollars of current purchasing power, the rise of income from 1933 to 1950 was from $40 billion in 1933 to $220 in 1950 (estimated). The cost of the national debt in this period rose 4 to 5 billion dollars, or

2 to 3 per cent of the gain of income to which the debt expansion contributed in an important manner.

This satisfactory relationship of the debt burden and the national income is related not only to expansion of real output; but also to two other factors. One is the rise of prices. At 1950 prices, the financing of each dollar of debt in terms of goods costs 40 per cent less than at 1933 prices. What is more, the costs are about one-third less than the costs at prices at time of incurring debt. The second factor is the decline in the rate of interest. At the rate of interest of the twenties, the cost of financing the national debt would be 10 to 12 billion dollars, not 5 to 6 billion dollars. At the purchasing power of the dollar and rate of interest of the twenties, the burden of the financing charge of the national debt would be $14 billion in 1950 dollars or 2.4 times the actual cost.

In general, then, the current burden of the debt is not serious, and the movements in prices, incomes, and the rate of interest have tended to lighten the burden. Moreover, a sane tax and debt repayment policy would have reduced the national debt further by $100 billion, or 40 per cent. A courageous tax policy could have yielded $100 billion more in taxes in the forties. Both Presidents Roosevelt and Truman had supported much higher tax rates. Surely the tax reduction bills of 1946 and 1948 were unnecessary. Perhaps an average rise of taxes of $10 billion is visionary. But $5 billion is not. The $50 billion involved would have been but 3 per cent of the income of the period, or 4 per cent of the rise of income over the thirties.

But somehow we never have adequate tax policies in wartime and usually stupid policies of debt repayment. In the post-Civil War we repaid two-thirds of our debt, but by imposing a monetary strait jacket on the economy. In the twenties in the midst of an inflationary orgy we reduced tax rates and slowed up debt repayment, thus allowing the public to keep more money for spending and speculation and thus weakened the anti-inflationary process. In the early postwar (1946–48), we reduced taxes in the midst of inflation, and thus retarded the repayment of debt.

We should be clear on another point. As the nation grows, the debt burden is reduced. This is clear from history. It should also be clear from projections. Possibly President Truman's estimate of a $900-billion national income (at present prices) by the year 2000 seems overly optimistic, though it is far from being optimistic when comparison is made with past gains. Some relief is almost certain to be had from a further rise of population of 20 to 35 per cent; from continued increases of prices; from some gains in productivity; and possibly a further fall in the rate of interest. Should our income rise to $900 billion by 2000 in current prices, then servicing our present debt at current rates of interest would require but ⅓ of 1 per cent of our national income.

A good example of what can happen is suggested by British history in the century preceding World War II. Following the Napoleonic Wars, the national debt of Great Britain had risen greatly. The £840 billion debt of 1818 had been reduced only to £656 billion in 1913. Yet the debt had fallen from more than twice the national income in 1818 to but one-quarter in 1913; and the debt charge from 8 per cent to 1 per cent of national income. Large growth of population and of real income per capita contributed importantly to these gains.

THE CASE AGAINST FURTHER RISE OF DEBT

So far we have stressed the magnitude of the national debt and attempted to measure the burden. It is unfortunate that we should be confronted with a new emergency so soon after World War II. After earlier wars, the country had an opportunity to pay off a large part of the debt and grow up to the remainder. From the Civil War peak to 1914, the nation had reduced her debt by close to three-fifths and income had increased by four times; from 1919 to 1930, the debt had been reduced by one-sixth. But from 1946 to 1950, the national debt had declined by but 6 per cent and national income had increased by a little more than one-fifth. The national debt vis-à-vis income in 1950 was 30 times as heavy as in 1914 and 5 times as heavy as in 1930.

We conclude from this that the government will have to be more cautious in incurring debt than in earlier emergencies. Two other considerations strengthen this position. The first is that the public is likely to be less interested in government securities than in World War II. This follows from an increasing awareness of inflationary dangers and the losses suffered by investors in government securities in World War II. Hence a larger proportion of Treasury borrowing than in World War II will have to be from banks and hence be inflationary.

The second point is related to the first. In World War II, the government spent about $300 billion for war. But in the course of the war the inflation was only 25 per cent. This proved to be, however, only one-third of the total inflation in the years 1941–50. By controlling the economy in the years 1941–46, the government succeeded in moderating the inflation. But this was to prove to be a temporary relief once controls were removed. The country was not given a chance to grow up to the monetary supplies inflated by a rising debt.

The significance of this point for the future is that the inflationary pressures resulting from World War II are probably still extant. If, on top of these, we increase the debt further, then the pressures will be even greater. Hence to avoid an inflation, the need of exercising controls will be even greater than in World War II. Yet the public seems less disposed to accept controls than in World War II. Moreover, and more important, recent experience has taught us that unless the country is prepared to continue controls for many years after the war, the inflationary process will be merely halted or better concealed only to move ahead with the removal of controls. The fact that controls are not likely to be continued for many years even if introduced in the midst of the emergency, emphasizes the importance of restraining the growth of the national debt.

MAINTENANCE OF SECURITY PRICES AND CONTROLS

It must be clear to all that the monetary expansion resulting from the growth of debt will increase pressure on prices. In World War II, the expansion was consistent with declining rates of interest largely because outlets for money other than government securities were restricted. With expanding money and incomes, savings were shunted to the government bond market. Competitors for funds were silenced either because consumers' goods were not available or business could not obtain resources for private investment. Hence the stimulated demand for government securities raised their prices, that is, reduced the yield. One decline begot an expectation of further declines. Actual rates then fell with expected rates. But this was dependent upon continued expansion of money and control of alternative uses. Expansion of money in the future will be consistent with maintenance of prices of securities and even falling rates of interest and relative stability of commodity prices only if the process is accompanied by the use of controls and the more so since sales of securities are more likely to be accompanied by monetary expansion than in World War II. As money expands, the amounts disbursed on commodity markets in the absence of controls increases.

ALTERNATIVE CONTROLS

In concrete terms, we may discuss a mobilization program costing $30 billion yearly over the 1949 outlays; and then one costing $100 billion additional. These may be considered a 10-year program costing $300 billion or a 6-year program costing $600 billion.

A minimum goal for the first program should be as follows:

	$ Billion
Taxes	20
Noninflationary purchases of securities	5
Inflationary purchases	5

In World War I, the goal of 25 per cent of the war expenditures financed by taxation was considered an achievement. In World War II, this country financed 40 per cent of war expenditures by taxation. Even in World War I, Professor Sprague had demanded exclusive financing by taxation. This has not proved practicable. The effects on incentives and output would be disastrous. A rise of tax receipts from $5 billion in 1940 to $46 billion in 1945 was notable. But a rise to $100 billion required to cover all outlays was beyond the practical.

Our continued advance since the Civil War in the proportion of war outlays financed by taxation suggests, however, that our goal might well be two-thirds of war outlays by taxation. The resulting expansion of but $5 billion of money would scarcely be inflationary. It might offset the additional cash required by the annual rise of income of 2 per cent expected in the war. Actually, a $5-billion growth of income would require but $2½ billion of additional money. Hence the inflationary effects would be slight. Even if over these years national income did not rise as a result of the loss of manpower and other reasons, the inflationary effects would not be large. Actually, with this moderate program, income should rise at least 15 per cent by 1960.

The added burden also would not be serious. The additional interest cost would be but $2 billion, or 1 per cent of present income, and possibly substantially less in 1960. In fact, the amount may be 5 to 10 per cent of the usual growth of the period.

A $600-billion six-year war is another matter. Here is our goal.

	$ Billion
Additional taxes	400
Noninflationary sales of securities	100
Inflationary sales	100

Here the great problem would be the expansion of $100 billion of monetary supplies. Clearly the rate of interest would rise and prices would rise greatly unless strong control measures were taken. For here the supply of money would be doubled on top of a trebling in the forties.

Our debt would rise to $450 billion by 1956. With a mobilization program of these proportions, it would be foolish to expect a large rise of income and stable prices. A reasonable guess would be a 25 per cent price rise and no increase in output.

Hence the 1956 situation would be:

National income, $ billion	275
National debt, $ billion	450
Interest on debt, $ billion	9
Debt charge as percentage of national income	3.3

In this situation the crucial problem would be the timing of removal of controls. Even with this courageous fiscal policy—and better than I fear we are likely to get—there is a genuine danger of a doubling of the price level. Only if we maintain controls until the country has grown up to the excessive supplies of money, would the dangers be removed. The danger is not only the $100 billion of additional money.

It is also the possibility of unloading part of the $450-billion debt and also using excess supplies of money still remaining from World War II.

I have not forgotten about my goal of full coverage of military expenses by taxation at least until the additional amounts involved are less than $50 billion (cf. Chapter 12). The 10-year $300-billion program might well be financed exclusively by taxation. In this chapter, however, I have been inclined to discuss the kind of programs we are likely to get rather than those which we should have. The proposals for the 6-year $600-billion program, however, do not diverge greatly from the blueprints prescribed in Chapters 12 and 15. Full coverage by taxation of this program, however attractive on theoretical grounds, is out of the question in a modern democratic society.

Part Six

CONTROLS

18. THE RELATION BETWEEN DIRECT AND INDIRECT CONTROLS

MOST ECONOMISTS agree that a major war effort requires direct (e.g., price) controls. They also agree that the effectiveness of direct controls depends in part upon the indirect (e.g., tax policy) controls used. On the issue of the precise point in the expansion of military outlays where direct controls should be introduced as well as on the panorama to be covered by these controls—on these issues there is much disagreement.

Indirect controls reduce the pressure of excess incomes on the markets. A rise of taxes cuts the spending of civilians, inclusive of business. Restraints on monetary expansion result in reduced demands for materials and labor on the part of the nonwar economy. Control of consumer credit tends to reduce the demand for consumers' goods and especially automobiles, housing, and household goods; and with this reduction in demand, the inflationary pressure subsides and the incentive to produce consumer durables is reduced.

In World War II mobilization, the United States Government introduced a comprehensive price freeze at an early stage. Earlier the government had introduced priorities and other limited controls of supply and demand. But the price freeze came too early, in view of the limited efforts made to deal with monetary supplies and taxes. Apparently, the White House had given the price agencies assurances that the freeze would be supplemented by adequate fiscal and related (indirect controls) policies. The tax policy did not prove to be vigorous enough nor the rise prompt enough to prevent an excess of purchasing power from hampering the experiment of the price freeze. If, for example, there are $100 billion of potential demand for $60 billion of consumers' goods and controlled prices, then the pressure of excess purchasing power is bound to be felt in price violations.

VARIABLES RELEVANT FOR A STUDY OF INFLATION

	1940	*1941*	*1942*
Personal income, $ billion	78.3	95.3	122.1
Personal taxes, etc., $ billion	2.6	3.3	6.0
Personal savings, $ billion	3.7	9.8	25.4
Consumption expenditures, $ billion	72.0	82.3	90.8
Bank deposits and currency, $ billion	75.2	82.8	104.3
Bank loans, $ billion	18.8	21.7	19.2
Bank investments, $ billion	25.1	29.0	48.2
Consumer price index (1935–39 = 100)	100.2	105.2	116.5

Source: *Survey of Current Business,* National Income Number, July, 1947; and *Economic Report of the President,* 1950.

How inadequate the indirect control program was is suggested by the table just above. Under an indirect control program, the price authority was bound to encounter difficulties. For example, from 1940 to 1941, personal income rose by $17 billion; but personal taxes by only $690 million, or 4 per cent of the rise of incomes. Only a substantial rise of personal savings—by $6.1 billion—prevented even greater pressures on prices. Even in 1942, the rise of personal taxes was but $2.7 billion, or 10 per cent of the rise of $26.8 billion in personal income. In view of the large inflationary gap (i.e., excess of disposable income over consumers' goods available at stable prices) remaining despite the large rise of savings, the record of an increase of prices of 5 and 10 per cent in these two years was better than might have been expected. In the years 1942 to 1944, the government's fiscal policies improved: against a rise of personal income of $42.9 billion, personal taxes rose by $12.9, or 30 per cent, and taxes and private savings by $23.2 billion, or more than half the rise of income. There was still a large inflationary gap. A rise of prices of about 8 per cent in these two years reflects the unavailability of goods, improved administration of controls, and similar factors.

Our experience from 1940–42 should not go unheeded in 1951 and later years. It is premature to impose comprehensive controls inclusive of a price freeze unless we take drastic measures to deal with the excess of money and income. Once the country is spending $50 billion additional (over pre-Korean outlays) for military purposes, then the country may have to consider a comprehensive control system seriously. Within a year (say, the winter of 1951–52), additional expenditures of $50 billion (annual rate) should be matched by $35 billion of additional output (one-half accounted for by higher prices). A drastic saving and tax program then should remove most of the additional income. Insofar as the government curtails private investment, then taxes and savings might be increased somewhat less. Our main conclusion is that it is safe to spend at the rate of $50 billion additional without a general price freeze if the government siphons off most of the difference of the rise of income and the increase of output (assuming a 5 per cent annual rise of prices) through increased taxes and savings and offsets any remaining deficiency through curtailment of private investment.

These paragraphs were written before the general wage-price freeze of January, 1951. Prices were indeed rising at a disconcerting rate, and in part because, as might be expected, businessmen were charging what the traffic would bear. As a result of unfavorable war developments, large excesses of purchasing power, fear of higher prices (and ultimately of unavailabilities and rationing), frequent announcements of an impending freeze which encouraged business men to raise prices further—as a result of all of these, prices continued to soar. Purchases in January, 1951, were much above the seasonal level. With taxes and savings far too low, the conditions were ripe for a substantial rise of prices.

The freeze, a most inept administrative episode, might be justified as a temporary measure to contend with the unusual concatenation of inflationary forces operating early in 1951. But there is much to be said for scrapping it in favor of a vigorous tax and savings program supplemented by price controls of essentials (cf. Chapter 1, 20 and 21).

At substantially higher rates of military spending, the pressure for comprehensive controls becomes much greater. The problem becomes one of closing the gap of the rise of income and the supply of consumption goods available.

Assume an *additional* military program of $100 billion (annual rate). The sources of such a $100 billion of military outlay would be:

	$ Billion
Reduction of private investment	30
Increase of output (income)	30
Reduction of consumption	40

This might, for example, suggest the rate of military spending within two years. On these assumptions, the country, embarrassed by a rise of $30-billion income, will have to do with $40 billion less of consumption goods. This is a different situation than that in the years 1940–44, when a *rise* of personal income of $86 billion was accompanied by an increase of personal consumption of $38 billion.

Now with a need for *cutting* consumption, the government will have to increase taxes and savings by $70 billion. Even if this could be done, there might be inflationary pressures in some areas. A more likely program is a price freeze with military outlays at (say) $75 billion, and a tax and savings program which would absorb the *major part* of the difference between the *sum* of the rise of income and the amount by which the supply of consumption goods to be made available is reduced. (Part of the savings would be invested by private industry but they would also be channeled to the government.)

19. INTERRELATIONS OF DIRECT CONTROLS

THE PROBLEM OF COVERAGE IN PRICE CONTROL

A LESSON quickly learned from war economics is that controls are interrelated. It is, therefore, imperative that responsibility for controls be centralized as much as possible.

The interrelationships are clear: the imposition of price control in a limited number of markets soon affects other markets. In part, the effect is felt through the diversion of purchasing power to the uncontrolled markets. Since price control (if accompanied by rationing or allocations) reduces the amount of money spent on commodities controlled, the effect is to shunt excesses of purchasing power to other markets. Hence the inflationary pressures concentrate on smaller areas, with the free markets gradually being reduced. Because of these interrelationships of markets, the obvious attack is to impose comprehensive price control at the outset. That, in practice, this is not done is to be explained by the inadequacy of staff and plans at the early stages of a war effort, and to some extent, by a lack of understanding of the issues. It is of some interest that in World War II and also in the present emergency the attack on prices at first has been on a piecemeal basis.

An example of misunderstanding is the theory quite widely held in World War II that price control at one level would keep prices down at another. Thus it was assumed that a freeze at home would keep importers from bidding up prices of imports and then evading price regulations or pressuring authorities to raise ceilings. Actually, this assumption proved unfounded. This type of approach failed to allow for the increased excess of purchasing power associated with piecemeal control.

This mechanical connection between markets is not the only explanation of the spread of price control. Two other factors play a significant part: *The first is that the free markets become the more profitable markets, and, therefore, there is a tendency to apply scarce resources excessively to providing the less essential goods and services.* Control domestic prices and producers divert excessively to export markets; control the price of hamburgers and more resources go into steaks (?); control foods and the public will increase their outlays (and stimulate diversions) on gambling, jewelry, alcoholic drinks, etc.

Here, for example, is the rise of consumption expenditures from 1940 to 1944:

	Rise (Per cent)
All	53
Jewelry	149
Purchased meals and beverages	117
Clothing, accessories, and jewelry	104
Personal care	90

Source: Calculated from *Survey of Current Business*, July, 1947.

It is evident that with curtailment of supplies and with the introduction of limited price control, purchasing power tends to be shunted to free markets. In World War II, virtually all commodities were under control and yet in many markets both total expenditures and the rise of prices were greatly out of line with the increase of outlays and prices in the relatively well-controlled markets. The fact is that in many of the markets where outlays rose so much, the explanation was failure to restrict adequately the movement of manpower and other scarce resources to these markets, and the unenforceable type of price control used. In clothing, in services of all kinds, in restaurant food, price control was, and probably had to be, a formula type not easy to enforce; and especially since so much excess purchasing power tends to move into these areas.

What is said above is a partial answer to those who would restrict price controls to essentials. The country rightly pokes fun at a price administrator who issues a price regulation on fruit cake or Christmas holly.

Coverage of all items under a general freeze is another matter. In fact, the problem of drawing the line between essential and nonessential commodities is far more difficult than might be anticipated. It is dubious that it was worth the trouble in World War II to exempt pigeons, squabs, Eskimo art work, rum sold by the possessions of the U.S., sliced apples, and many other items, the listing of which required six pages (*Revised Supplementary Regulation 1* of April 16, 1943). In some instances there were special reasons for exemptions: difficulties of administration, newspapers (fear of control of the press), military supplies where discretion had to be left to the military.

I am not contending that the system used in the United States is necessarily preferable to that applied in the United Kingdom, where control was restricted to essential items. But in order to deal with the problem of the best allocation of resources, a program of selective price control is supportable only if the government in wartime controls allocation of manpower, raw materials, credit, and capital much more than the United States did in World War II; and if the authorities genuinely control profits. British control of the flow of resources and her extremely progressive tax system justified the limited range of price control in the United Kingdom.

We also can support selective price control in a great emergency, if we should follow the British example. Especially notable in the British war economy was the large excise taxes on luxury and semiluxury products. That is to say, allow the wealthy to pay $2,000 for a fur coat, but insist that the government collect (say) $1,500 in taxes. Thus the diversion of resources will be discouraged, extensive price control averted, and the purchaser of the coat will contribute toward the fight against inflation in more essential areas. In this manner, the government may allow prices generally to rise, but the increase would be concentrated on luxuries.

So much for the first reason for comprehensive price control—namely, the conservation of scarce resources for the more important uses. The second point relates to distributive justice. Control of prices in one market and freedom in another arouse the resentment of those who are subject to control. In World War II, the control of price of many domestic commodities inspired many vigorous protests by sellers in domestic markets at the freedom to sell abroad at exorbitant prices. This resentment contributed to the control of export prices.

PRICE AND RELATED CONTROLS

In Great Britain, the approach to controls was to concentrate all relevant controls for one segment of the economy in one ministry—e.g., food. In this manner, the government could achieve integration of price control, allocations, rationing, import control, etc., as they related to food. The problem of integrating food and (say) clothing controls was, however, an interagency problem.

In the United States, price control and rationing were the responsibility largely of one agency, the Office of Price Administration (OPA). The War Labor Board (WLB) was responsible for wage control, and the Office of Economic Stabilization (OES) was supposed to reconcile differences among the stabilization agencies. Allocations and priorities were largely entrusted to another agency, the War Production Board (WPB). But to some extent, the War Food Administration (WFA) shared in this responsibility. The control of exports (once the allocation was made) lay with the Board of Economic Warfare (BEW) and later with the Foreign Economic Administration (FEA). Manpower control lay with the War Manpower Commission (WMC). Ultimately the President established a Director of the Office of War Mobilization and Reconversion (OWMR), who was the final arbiter and integrator.

In World War II, the conflicts among agencies were partly the result of a poor administrative setup, ideological differences, and conflicts on technical grounds concerning the means of achieving objectives. It was probably a mistake to set up two independent agencies, one responsible for prices primarily, and the other responsible for control of supply and demand. In appointing a mobilization director in December, 1950, with authority over economic stabilization, President Truman seems to have learned something from World War II.

Examples of the conflicts among agencies follows: The OPA, largely manned by college professors, was much less concerned with the financial position of firms or with the accustomed manner of doing business than was the WPB, which was largely a businessman's organization. This conflict in approach is readily to be understood.

In concrete instances, the WPB would seek price adjustments as the means of achieving a rise of output. Aware of the limited availability of free resources, and hence opposed to the use of the price incentive to increase output, the OPA would seek an order of the WPB as a means of increasing the output of (say) a scarce type of lumber. Whereas the OPA would emphasize authority as the road to better allocation of resources, the WPB in many instances would stress the profit motive.

Another example of the conflicts lay in the simplification and concentration programs of World War II. There was much greater enthusiasm for these programs in the OPA than in the WPB. In simplification (e.g., reducing the number of shoe styles), the OPA envisaged a program for reducing unit costs and, therefore, keeping prices down; and in supporting the programs for concentrating output of civilian goods now greatly reduced in a limited number of plants, the OPA again sought reduced unit costs. The WPB was not so enthusiastic in support of these programs. Again, there was a reluctance on the part of the WPB to use governmental authority in order to achieve more economical output at the expense of established ways of producing and at the expense of particular firms. In the great debate on standardization of food products as a means of tying prices to quality, and thus improving price control, the OPA waged a losing fight.

THE LOW-END PROBLEM

Many other aspects of interagency differences or co-operation require brief consideration. One effect of price control is to stimulate the production of higher-priced types of goods. In part, this is the result of unavailability of raw materials and semifinished goods and the need of using substitutes; and in part the greater profitability of producing higher-priced goods. The explanation of the preference for higher-priced goods is the use of the percentage margin markup, whereas the explanation of the preference for price control under "new goods" categories was the greater latitude in setting prices.

In the program to encourage output of low-end products, the relevant agencies co-operated, though tardily and on an inadequate scale. The WPB agreed to release materials only on the agreement that a designated proportion would be used to produce low-end (low-priced) items. In this manner, the WPB blocked attempts at evasion of price control by upgrading output (e.g., selling a $4 pair of shoes for $5). That the price agency stabilizes the price of low-priced dresses at $5 does little good if the producers insist on manufacturing dresses exclusively in the $10 or higher class.

THE COMPLEMENTARITY OF CONTROLS

Controls are to a considerable degree complementary. Thus, the WPB established priorities in the use of scarce materials: limitation (L) orders which reduced the production of nonessential goods (e.g., automobiles); allocated scarce materials (M) orders; bestowed preferences and allocated materials to an industry on the basis of its importance to the war effort (Production Requirements Plan); allocated important and scarce materials (carbon steel, alloy steel, copper, copper-plate alloy, aluminum) to the various claimant agencies (Controlled Materials Plan, CMP), both as a means of conserving these materials and, in response to these denials, as a means of economizing on other scarce resources—manpower, electric power, transportation.

The main interest of the WPB was to conserve and use the limited supplies available in the most effective manner. But in pursuing this end, the WPB also facilitated the task of the Price Administrator. A rise of supply or the exclusion of nonessential demand tends to reduce inflationary pressures in the most vulnerable markets; and denial of essential commodities contracts demands for resources and commodities used in conjunction with these essential commodities. In the absence of priorities, CMP, etc., the competing firms and agencies would obtain their supplies through competitive bidding. Indeed, the OPA might set price ceilings but, in the absence of measures directed to excluding nonessential demand, the pressure to purchase essential supplies would greatly weaken the effectiveness of price control.

RATIONING AND PRICE CONTROL

In the area of rationing, the relation of supply and demand controls is especially relevant. First, the authorities control prices; and that generally means prices lower than those that would have prevailed in a free market. As a result of depressed prices in an economy with large excesses of purchasing power, demand becomes inordinate on these markets and authorities maintain price ceilings with difficulty. At any rate, what is almost certain to follow a price below the free market price is the denuding of markets. The explanation is partly the stimulus to demand associated with artificially low prices, and partly the discouragement of production with prices depressed. In order to contend with the enhanced pressures on essential consumers' goods markets, the government introduces a rationing program which tailors demand to available supplies.

Why is it necessary, then, to have both rationing and price control? By restricting demand to the 200 million pounds of meat available each week (say), there should be no upward pressure on prices. The fact is, however, that estimates of supply and demand under a rationing program can at best be crude, and it would be naive to assume that all consumers would abide by rationing regulations. Price controls reduce the incentive of the seller to conspire with the potential violator to sell him (her) in excess of the legal amount.

Rationing is largely a defensive instrument used to distribute scarce consumers' goods fairly. But it can be much more than that. In the British war economy, the rationing program (e.g., clothing) was an offensive tool directed toward conserving scarce resources, that is, reducing the supplies going into the manufacture of clothing.

PRICES, WAGES AND MANPOWER

In World War II, the government erred in introducing a price freeze without an adequate control of wages. Obviously, the businessman would resent a freeze of his prices not accompanied by a freeze of wages. That the price freeze, unaccompanied by vigorous control of wages, was not more harmful is to be explained by two facts.

1. Prices were not in fact frozen. In 1942, prices rose by 10 per cent; in 1943, by 6 per cent; in 1944, by 1½ per cent. Moreover, the genuine rise of price was greater than indicated by the price index, for inadequate allowance was made for deterioration, shifts to higher-priced items, readjustments in spending patterns (e.g., eating out) which did not receive adequate attention in index numbers, etc.

2. The businessman could frequently offset any rise of wages by reductions in overhead costs associated with the rising level of output relative to capacity.

By the fall of 1942, it was evident that control of wages was an ingredient of any comprehensive price control. We discuss elsewhere the magnitude of wage advances. It is clear that basic average rates rose by about 20 to 25 per cent in the course of the war. This rise was, however, small compared with the increase of hourly earnings from 60 cents in 1940 to $1.02 and of weekly earnings from $25.20 to $46.08, both in manufacturing, and of total salaries, wages and other labor income from $49.5 billion in 1940 to $116.2 billion in 1944.

Hourly earnings rose more than basic rates because of the upgrading, the increased importance of highly productive industries, and the increased significance of overtime. Weekly wages increased more than hourly earnings, largely because the number of weekly hours rose from 38 to 45. The much greater rise in total wages and salaries than in weekly earnings is associated with the vast expansion of numbers on the labor market—from 38 to 55 million.

Percentage Rise of Wages, Various Categories, and Number of Workers, 1940 to 1944

Category	Percentage
Basic wage rates	20
Gross hourly earnings, manufacturing	70
Gross weekly earnings, manufacturing	83
Total wages and salaries	135
Number of full-time equivalent workers	45

Sources: *Survey of Current Business,* July, 1947; *Economic Report of the President,* 1950; and S. E. Harris, *Inflation and the American Economy,* pp. 292–93 and 312–13.

Of what significance was the rise of wages for profits and for inflation? These figures reveal a substantial rise of wages, although the profit figures of business enterprise do not suggest that price freezes and limited control of wages had any serious effects on profits. Another conclusion to be drawn from these figures, which incidentally help explain the rise of profits, is that the largest part of the rise of wages and salaries was associated with increased output; more workers, more hours per worker (a rise of almost 20 per cent per week from 1940 to 1944), more workers in productive industry. To this extent, the rise of wage payments was justified by an expansion of output.

But from the demand side, the increase of wage payments was unfortunate. As incomes rise, the pressure on commodity and service markets increases, that is, unless the government diverts an adequate proportion of the additional incomes into purchases of securities and into the coffers of the tax collector. The greater the rise of income, the greater the burden put upon fiscal policy and, therefore, the less chance of achieving a stable economy. There is a point beyond which no feasible tax policy can neutralize the inflationary effects of rising incomes.

In the crisis of 1950–51, similar problems were troubling the stabilization director. The businessman demanded wage stabilization as a condition for price stabilization. In many respects, the problem was more difficult of solution. First, because trade unionism was stronger than in 1942 and trade unions dislike wage freezes. Their disapproval springs from the fact that the exclusion of wage increases deprives unions of one of their main fields of operation. Second, because many wage contracts were tied to cost-of-living indices. This is especially unfortunate, since in a major mobilization, what is required is a reduction of standards of living. As the supplies of consumption goods available for the civilian economy fall, the income recipient should receive incomes rising less than prices or else the government should take strong measures to sterilize part of the income. Tying wages to the cost of living aggravates the difficulty of reducing standards of living and equalizing burden. Third, the businessman is not likely to be able to offset any substantial wage increases, as in the last war, by economies resulting from a rise of output within ranges which yield lower unit costs. Fourth, since we started from a position of virtually full employment, the pressure to use wage increases as a means of attracting workers is likely to be even greater than in the last war, and employers short of workers will co-operate with workers who demand the wage incentive.

This conflict of wage and price policy is further complicated by the problem of manpower control. A flexible wage system is helpful both in increasing the total supply of workers and in inducing an improved distribution of workers as required by the war economy. As the economy mobilizes, the rise of wages attracts many to the labor market. Probably the more important magnet, however, is the increased number of openings. The time comes ultimately when the reserves of manpower dry up, and further rises of wages do not attract large additional numbers to the labor market. But wage increases for attracting workers to particular industries, occupations, and areas would still be necessary—at least until the country introduces a vigorous control of manpower.

In World War II, the country needed wage control as a part of a stabilization program. But in the absence of genuine manpower control, it became difficult to reallocate labor according to the needs of the war economy. A war industry could attract workers with seniority rights from a service industry only if it were allowed to raise wages significantly above those in the industries competing for these workers. Insofar as wages were stabilized, the wage incentive could not be used to move workers.

A fair criticism of the Roosevelt Administration would be that, having scrapped price (wage) incentive, they substituted a feeble manpower policy. The result was that the shortage of a few thousand workers in the copper mines and in the heavy-tire and foundry industries threatened to stifle our war economy. Had the wage-stabilization program been more rigid, the war economy might have suffered much more.

Manpower control consisted largely of increasing hours and seeking deferments for vital workers. In the latter part of the war, the WMC introduced a referral system under which it became more difficult to leave an industry or occupation, when serious shortages of manpower prevailed. But WMC never exercised its authority to compel workers to move from nonessential to essential industries, and even its referral system was not greatly effective. That the manpower problem did not become much more serious was the result of the effectiveness of other controls which denied vital materials to nonessential industries and thus released manpower indirectly.

20. EFFECTIVENESS OF PRICE CONTROL

THE MEASURES OF EFFECTIVENESS

OBVIOUSLY, the simplest measure is the extent of the price rise. To finance a war costing 300 to 350 billion dollars with a price increase of only 25 to 30 per cent is a major achievement. The price rise was much smaller relative to the magnitude of the effort or relative to the proportion of resources going to war than in the Civil War or World War I.[1] For example, in 52 months of war, the rise of prices in World War I was 64.6 per cent, and in World War II, 25.9 per cent. Yet World War II cost about 10 times as much. In these 52 months the rise of prices in World War I was many times as large as in World War II for many items: pig iron, 10 times; copper, 6 times; tin, 20 times; cement, 27 times; coke, 8 times; petroleum, 12 times. The World War II record was less favorable in other important products—e.g., lumber, rise of 67 per cent for World War I and 60 per cent for World War II; wool, 195 and 63; anthracite coal, 65 and 32.[2]

The rise of prices might have been even less if the Congress had followed the President's recommendations on taxes. We repeat, however, a point made elsewhere, namely, that insofar as the war economy through controls sterilized purchasing power, which was to be used later when controls had been removed, to that extent, the price controls provided only temporary relief. In fact, the averted inflation in 1942–45 to some extent became overt inflation in 1946–50.

This experience of the forties is germane for the price problem of the fifties. Price control moderates the rise of prices in the mobilization phase and, of course, in wartime. The gains pricewise are important in mobilization and war periods because it is especially important to obtain fair distribution and avert wage disputes in such times. But unless the government is prepared to maintain controls until the country has grown up to the expanded but sterilized purchasing power, then the gains in the mobilization periods become distortions in the postwar. In fact, part of the problem of inflation stems from the excess money, bequeathed by World War II, and not fully absorbed by 1950.

The rise of output in the face of the restraints imposed upon price control is another criterion of the success of price control. Above all, it is necessary to increase output. Should price control jeopardize this rise or substantially reduce output below the potential, then the price control might well be considered a failure. Actually the official figures point to a rise of GNP of about 50 to 70 per cent from 1940 to 1945. In part, the explanation is a rise of employed workers (34 per cent in 1945 over 1940) and, in part, a rise of productivity (14 per cent gain).

Dr. Kuznets, it should be noted, was less optimistic concerning the rise of output in World War II. The problem of measuring the rise of product when its composition changes greatly is difficult indeed. How are we to compare output of consumers' durables in 1940 and tanks and planes in 1944? In Kuznets' view, the price deflator used to convert GNP in current dollars to GNP in stable dollars was too low. The explanation of this fact is that the high prices paid for war supplies did not receive adequate weight in the index numbers used for deflation (related to the changed composition of output in wartime); and besides the high prices in these industries reflected competitive bidding for resources, not high efficiency. In Kuznets' views, efficiency in producing war goods even in 1943 was less than in producing civilian goods; and a fortiori in 1941.

Dr. Kuznets concluded:

> National product adjusted for changes in the prices of resources (i.e., input of resources at their 1939 efficiency and price levels) increased about 50 per cent from 1939 to 1943. In terms of final product and on the most plausible assumption concerning the relative efficiency of resource use in munitions and war construction, it increased somewhat less. . . . Estimates based on the Department's concept and price adjustments increased 75 per cent, those based on our concept but using the Department's price adjustments, 87 per cent.[3]

On the test of relative rises of prices and output, the price policy was indeed successful. In each year of mobilization and war (1940 to 1944), the expansion of GNP was from 2 to 20 times as much as the rise of wholesale prices; that of national income to the cost of living, from 2.4 (1942) to 12 times (1940). From 1940 to 1945, the expansion of GNP was about 4 times, that of national income 5 times that of prices. (This is subject to the reservations implied by Kuznets.)

In general, the large unemployment and the need of stimulating output justified significant price rises (5, 10, and 6 per cent in 1941, 1942, and 1943) in the first three years of mobilization and war. Attainment of close to peak employment and output levels by 1943 supported a policy of price stabilization in the latter part of the war—an increase of 1½ per cent in 1944 and 2½ per cent in 1945.

In the mobilization of the fifties the case for soft price measures or the use of the price incentive was much less than in World War II. Output was at a high level in 1950. The gains productionwise of higher prices would not be large, although price adjustments for particular products might help bring about a desired reallocation of resources. But we stress the fact that even in World War II the availability of orders and jobs contributed much more than prices to the rise of output; and that controls can be much more precise than price adjustments in achieving the desired redistribution of resources.

PROFITS AND PRICES

One measure of the effectiveness of price control is the amount of profits earned by business in the course of the war. Obviously, if the Price Administrator fails in his objective of stabilizing the economy, profits rise skyward.

It is necessary to understand that the Congressional directive to the OPA was that price regulations should be *generally fair and equitable,* that the OPA should seek *stabilization of the economy,* and that attention should be paid to *general increases or decreases in costs of production and profits during and subsequent to the year ended October 1, 1941.* But the OPA was warned that its task was not to fix profits, though how it was possible to control prices without influencing profits was never made clear by the Congress. In practice, the OPA tended to emphasize the equity and stabilization objectives and to neglect consideration of cost increases when the latter conflicted with the other two objectives.

An examination of business profits in the war period does not suggest any great success of the Price Administrator. Profits rose greatly over those of prewar—much in excess of the amount justified either by higher prices (that is, stabilization of profits in 1939 prices) and/or the increase of output. The later gains in 1946–49 suggest, however, that controls probably kept profits substantially below their likely level in a free economy.

PROFITS, 1936–39, 1942–45, AND 1946–49 ($ BILLION)

Years	*Corporate (Before Taxes)*	*Unincorporated*
1936–39	5.4	11.1
1942–45	22.6	26.8
1946–49	28.9	37.0

Source: *Survey of Current Business,* National Income Numbers.

Why, then, did profits rise so much in World War II, in an economy where price control of a reasonably firm type prevailed?

The first of three explanations is that prices rose to some extent, and also that output expanded. Even at stable prices, a large rise of profits was possible as output rose substantially. Not only are profits adjusted to prices and number of units sold, but as output expands toward full capacity, unit costs tend to fall within a fairly large range of output. Thus from 1939 to March, 1943, the quantity of freight rose by 120 per cent, and unit costs declined by 2 per cent; in steel, payrolls increased by more than 100 per cent, output by 70 per cent, and prices remained virtually stable.[4]

Second, OPA never succeeded in forcing business to absorb cost increases to an extent justified by the fall in unit costs associated with higher output per plant or firm and/or with the higher profits resulting from increased output. In interpreting the "equitable" objective, the OPA generally applied profits in the years 1936–39 as the guide. Hence under a price freeze, it was up to the business concern subjected to higher costs, resulting from (say) higher-priced imported raw materials, or an increase of local taxes, or a rise of wage rates, or an increase of transportation costs, to show that the result of these increases was a profit below the 1936–39 level. Insofar as the price freezes or formula type of price regulation excluded the automatic passing on of higher costs as higher prices, these regulations were in the anti-inflationary tradition. Unfortunately, many formula regulations allowed sellers automatically to pass on designated rises in costs. The effect was that the buyer did not profit adequately from the economies of increased production as offsets to specific higher costs.

Third, when it was necessary to increase supplies, the OPA frequently abandoned its guide of "generally equitable" profits, i.e., equal to or in excess of the 1936–39 level, and would allow coverage of costs if there were no alternative manner of obtaining the essential supplies. Again, in many instances, the OPA abandoned its principle of being guided by over-all profits. It might grant price increases to cover costs of individual items considered essential even though the over-all profit position was satisfactory. In this manner, the industry or firm would be encouraged to produce unprofitable but essential items.

TECHNIQUES OF PRICE CONTROL AND THE PROFIT POSITION

In part, the large profits stem from the difficulties of controlling prices. In the American economy, there are millions of different products. One of the first lessons a price official learns is the degree of differentiation of products, even for so homogeneous a commodity as rice. It requires a large-sized volume merely to list the various types of machine tools, a relatively nonhomogeneous type of commodity.

An obvious way to deal with the multiplicity of commodities and services is to freeze the prices of all commodities as of a given day—as was done under the General Maximum Price Regulation in the spring of 1942. The result is that the burden of proof for any rise of prices is put upon the seller; and when costs rise, the seller is forced to absorb the higher costs unless exceptions are made. In practice, however, many difficulties arise. One difficulty is that the legal price (i.e., the price freeze) is frequently unknown to sellers and buyers and a fortiori to the Price Administrator. The result is deficient enforcement. A second problem stems from the breaks in the price stabilization program—e.g., through wage increases, rise of transportation costs—which tend to jeopardize the freeze unless concessions are made to sellers.

A second approach to price-fixing is the formula price regulation. In these regulations which deal with nonhomogeneous commodities, the Administrator informs the seller how he is to calculate his prices. Here again evasion is a serious problem; and the formula price ceiling frequently provides (unlike the usual freeze) for automatic adjustments to certain rises in costs.

It might be assumed that the third important class of price regulations, the dollar-and-cents ceiling, would be particularly effective in protecting the buyer and in keeping profits down to a reasonable level. Actually, the dollar-and-cents price regulation has disappointed its supporters, though, on the whole, it is the most effective form of price control.

Obviously, the dollar-and-cents regulation is not easily applied when there are many varieties of a product; when prices vary greatly according to number of units sold, kinds of services offered (e.g., transportation and packaging) with the product, location of the seller and buyer, and the like. Again, the dollar-and-cents ceiling, as precise as it may be, often means a high price for the average consumer. The price must be set high enough to assure minimum profits to most suppliers. In the markets for essential products, the authorities cannot afford to eliminate a substantial part of the suppliers even if they are higher-cost producers. The result is that a dollar-and-cents ceiling allows large profits to the low-cost producers, whereas a formula ceiling may well pass on the savings of the low-cost producers in part to the buyer.

All types of price regulations are replete with difficulties. It is not easy to define a commodity precisely, with the result that sellers may evade the spirit of a price regulation by impairing the quality or denying services generally made available. Sellers who customarily absorb freight may favor buyers close by; sellers who ordinarily give credit may now deny credit; the buyer may have to indulge in cash and carry, whereas he was accustomed to credit and free delivery. To some extent, price regulations deal with problems of quality, performance, services, etc., but not by any means in a comprehensive and effective manner.

CONTRAST OF PRICE REGULATIONS

A contrast in effectiveness of price control is given by the controls of rent, on the one hand, and of clothing, on the other. In the control of rents, the price administrator deals with a commodity easily defined, the price of which is known to both buyer and seller. He can count on the co-operation of the buyer. Moreover, the OPA refused to grant individual adjustments as it frequently did in other areas. It is not surprising, then, that in 1945 rents were but 8.3 per cent above the 1936–39 level, whereas the general consumers' price index was up by 25.5 per cent. In 1949, the respective figures were 20.8 and 69.1 per cent. The rise was small, even if, as a Labor Committee claimed, the actual rise was somewhat greater than suggested by the Bureau of Labor Statistics (e.g., because of underweighting of new and high-priced rental units).

The plight of the landlord was not so serious as is frequently suggested. Against the small rise of rents, he profited from a reduction of repairs and maintenance (about 20 per cent over a four-year period), a reduction of vacancies, and fixed interest charges. Thus, whereas on June 30, 1943 rental income was 111.7 per cent (1939 = 100), *net operating income* was 126.8 per cent and *net income* rose substantially higher.

In general, the government defended a rent freeze on the grounds that in wartime the shortage of housing cannot be quickly corrected; and in the absence of a freeze, large inflation would result. The landlord has a genuine complaint in that his profits do not rise nearly as much as those of other types of business enterprise. Despite the continued recourse to rent control, however, the country has witnessed an unprecedented housing boom in the years 1946–50. Critics of rent control had warned the country that with reduced rents the construction of new housing would suffer. The boom of 1946–50 does not support their position. Perhaps in the absence of rent control, the multifamily house or apartment house might have increased much more than was actually the case.[5]

Price control of clothing was one of the least successful episodes, the explanation being largely the heterogeneity of the product, the multiplicity of sellers (price control is more effective the fewer the sellers), and the resulting difficulties of setting precise and enforceable price regulations. In the clothing field, the Administration had to depend on cost-plus (formula) regulations to a significant degree; and on the relatively effective dollar-and-cents regulations only to a small degree.

The results were disappointing in at least four respects:

1. By 1945, the price of apparel had risen by 46 per cent. Even food, the control of which was difficult as a result of pressure from farm groups, increased by but 39 per cent, rents by 8.3 per cent, all items by 28.4 per cent.

2. Price rises were especially large where the most prevalent, i.e., the cost-plus (formula) regulations were used. Thus, from September, 1942, to September, 1943, the increase for items under cost-plus regulations was 8.9 per cent (girls' inexpensive wool coats, 23.2 per cent); for items under the fairly popular general freeze and similar regulations, 5.1 per cent; and for items under dollar-and-cents regulations, which covered a small part of the field, 0.2 per cent (rayon hosiery, 4.3 per cent).

3. In the control of apparel, the government was hampered by the desertion of the low-end (low-priced) items, by the uptrading associated in part with the relatively increased demand for high-priced items in a prosperous economy and in part with the deterioration of products.

The President of W. T. Grant Company testified in 1944: "The present $1.98 cotton dress is the equivalent of the former 59-cent dress with approximately 10 cents of styling added. . . . The present $7.98 rayon dress is no better than the former $4.98."

According to the Meany-Thomas Report, Consumers Union, in a test of twelve national and private label brands of men's white broadcloth shirts, found thread count down 10 per cent, tensile strength down 10 per cent, and poor construction and inspection accounted for a further decline of 10 per cent in wearing quality.

4. As might be expected, profits rose greatly, both relative to 1936–39 and relative to other types of business enterprise. Moreover, the mark-ups, despite price control, increased greatly.

COTTON TEXTILE COMPANIES, SALES AND PROFITS

	1936–39	*1942*
Index of sales	100	234
Index of dollar profits before income tax:		
148 textile companies	100	963
2400 individual corporations	100	306
Index of dollar profits after taxes:		
148 textile companies	100	404
2400 industrial corporations	100	147
Profits of textile companies as per cent of sales	3.5	14.5
Profits of textile companies as per cent of net worth	4.3	37.4

Source: OPA, House Hearings on *Extension of Emergency Price Control Act,* 1944, p. 1562.

A comparison of corporate profits before federal taxes yields much larger rises for textiles and apparels than for all manufacturing. Yet, on the whole, the textile and apparel industries were less closely tied to war than other manufacturing industries. In the apparel industry, where, because of the differentiation of product, the low-end problem, deterioration, marking-up, the large number of sellers (and hence obstacles to enforcement), price control was especially difficult, the profits rose much more than in textiles.[6]

PERCENTAGE RISE OF CORPORATE PROFITS BEFORE TAXATION, 1936–39 TO 1942–45

All manufacturing	307
Textile mills	632
Apparel	818

Source: Calculated from *Survey of Current Business,* July, 1947.

THE RELEVANCE OF MILITARY PRICING

The military is interested primarily in supplies and date of delivery. They weigh prices much less heavily than the Price Agency. In a large part of the economic field, and particularly for military equipment—e.g., planes, tanks, munitions—the military are largely exempt from price control. Indeed, they try to keep prices as low as possible. In some respects they are in a strong position to keep prices down, e.g., they negotiate each contract on the basis of costs, time of delivery, past performance, costs of competitors, etc. They consider the proportion of overhead to be allocated to war goods, and economies of expanding output. Moreover, when, and especially in the experimental stage, prices are set too high, they can recover losses in part by renegotiation.[7]

Yet, when all of this is said, it still remains true that military pricing helps explain high prices and high profits in wartime.

In the years 1942–45, the federal government spent $297 billion on goods and services, of which $88 billion, or close to 30 per cent, went for personnel (inclusive of $64 billion, or 22 per cent for military payrolls). Of the remainder ($209 billion), a substantial part was spent for equipment not subject to price control. The $7 billion received back as a result of renegotiation ($1½ billion after allowance for losses of taxes on these $7 billion) were not large when compared with the more than $200 billion spent on goods, nor with the $100 billion of corporate profits before taxes and the $107 billion of income of unincorporated enterprise. The latter, however, was involved only to a small extent in military contracts.

Of 100 corporations with the largest amount of war business, the profits of those with highest returns in 1942 were as follows:

RISE OF PROFITS, 1942, IN RELATION TO THOSE OF 1936–39 *

Number of Corporations †	*Before Taxes*	*Number of Corporations* †	*After Taxes*
5	100 times or more	3	10 times or more
34	10 " " "	19	3 " " "
48	3 " " "	24	1–3 " " "

* 15 had deficits in 1936–39 and operating profits *before* taxes between 1 and 43 million dollars each in 1942; 12 with operating deficits in 1936–39 showed profits from 1 to 18 million dollars each *after* taxes.

† Cumulative.

Source: *Third Annual Report of the Truman Committee,* pp. 41–44.

As late as 1943, percentage return of net income *after* taxes to net worth was 37 per cent for aircraft and parts, 26 per cent for shipbuilding, 20 per cent for air transport and 18 per cent for automotive equipment.[8]

When corporations made vast profits, renegotiation and taxes reduced them; but frequently left them with substantial profits. Here are some extreme cases. The Truman Committee listed eight corporations manufacturing standard commercial articles. One such corporation in 1942 earned profits equal to 7,710 per cent of net worth before renegotiation; 3,580 per cent after renegotiation; and 1,030 per cent after renegotiation and taxes.[9]

KEEPING PRICES AND PROFITS DOWN

So far we have concentrated largely on the causes of higher prices and profits. But the main task of the control agencies was to keep prices down. In achieving this objective, they were bound to influence profits. In World War II, a sterile debate continued between the Congress and the OPA, the former contending that it was not the task of the OPA to fix profits. Indeed, it was not; but the test of equity was profits from 1936 to 1939, and price actions were bound to influence profits.

In shunning the cost-plus principle, as well as any close relation between costs or rises of costs and prices, the Price Agency sought to minimize the effects of rising costs. As a result, prices and profits were much smaller than they otherwise would have been.

We may discuss three of the techniques for isolating the price structure from the full effects of rises in costs.

1. The Price Agency never agreed to the principle that as output of less essential industries declined, the seller should be allowed to increase prices in proportion to the increase in overhead costs per unit. Should the OPA increase prices of gasoline to cover increased unit overhead costs of gas stations, associated with reduced sales, then that price action would retard the efflux of resources from less essential industries. Nor would the OPA agree to price concessions to textile firms that were troubled by shortages of materials and manpower in the latter part of the war, with attendant declines of output. Indeed, corporate profits before taxes of textile mills had declined from a peak of $863 million in 1942 to $774 million in 1945; but the latter sum was five times the average earnings of 1936–39. Lowering of the bars might have greatly increased the profits of textile firms. Surely, the termination of controls is one explanation of the rise of these profits to $1,435 million in 1946.

2. The theory of adjustments also reflected an unwillingness to tie costs too closely to prices. In general, the seller was required to absorb rises in costs (though as noted many formulas provided automatic passing on of higher costs). A textile manufacturer, confronted with a rise of wage rates and seeking higher prices, had to show that the effect would be to reduce profits below those in 1936–39; and, related to this, demonstrate that reductions in other costs would not offset the increase in the costs under consideration.

3. In a free economy, prices tend to be determined by the cost of the marginal (high-cost) producer. In wartime, the Price Administrator in various ways [(*a*) to (*d*) following] tries to circumvent the marginal principle.

(*a*) He will exclude the very high-cost producers from the market. Assume that the costs of units of 10 sellers each contributing about 10 per cent of the market supply, vary from $1 to $3, and that 20 per cent of the supplies are available at costs of $2 to $3. In a free market, the price would be $3. In a controlled market, the price might be set at $2, with the highest-cost producer being eliminated entirely and several other producers finding it unprofitable to maintain current output. If economies in use can be had, then output might very well decline somewhat. Otherwise, the low-cost producers will gradually usurp the market of the high-cost producers.

(*b*) It is possible in some degree to pay producers on the basis of their costs—i.e., differential pricing. When this is possible, large economies can be made.

The published price of standard iron ore at Lower Lake ports was $4.45 a ton in 1941. The industry was willing to agree on that as a maximum price for 1942. But as a matter of fact, only 27 per cent of the ore had brought $4.45 in 1941, 73 per cent of it had brought less than that, 60 per cent of it less than $4.25, 40 per cent of it less than $4.20, 20 per cent of it less than $4.10, 10 per cent of it less than $4, and some of it as little as $3.75. And at these prices, profits of the industry had ranged from 5 to 150 per cent on net worth, with one-tenth of the sales bringing 20 to 30 per cent and a tenth of them over 30 per cent.[10]

Much money could be saved if each producer in the iron and steel industry were paid according to *his costs*. In military contract negotiations, the tailoring of prices to costs is the principle involved. Actually, even under price control, the determination of prices on the basis of costs is not generally practical, and in many instances would be inflationary.

But when it becomes necessary to elicit additional high-cost materials in the midst of a war, then the differential principle may be applied. Thus, when the price of copper is 12 cents a pound and it is necessary to increase output by 10 per cent, the cost of additional units being 17 cents a pound, it would be a great mistake to allow the price of all units to rise to 17 cents. According to one high official, the application of the differential pricing system in nonferrous metals cost the government $80 million (subsidy to high-cost producers), but in the reduced over-all costs relative to a price system determined by marginal costs the savings were $1 billion yearly.[11]

Similar problems arose in the incentive program for farmers. When farmers were asked to increase output, the Price Agency insisted upon incentive payments for the *additional* output. The farmers, on the other hand, preferred the application of the marginal principle under which the price for the entire supply would be fixed at the high marginal costs. The resulting debate between the farm groups and the Price Agencies was one of the most bitter of the war.

(*c*) Where costs rose for part of the total supply, it was possible for the government or an agent appointed by the government to pool all units and sell at a price determined by the increase in costs allocated over all units. When ocean transportation became too dangerous and more costly land transportation of oil was substituted, the government provided for an averaging out of the increased costs. A variant of this method is to allocate high-cost items to sellers who can absorb higher costs (sellers of bristles to brush manufacturers), and low-cost items to those who absorb with difficulty (manufacturers of cordage).

(*d*) The government may pay outright subsidies to high-cost producers and thus enable them to sell at lower prices. This technique is related to differential pricing above. Examples are the purchase of high-priced metals by government abroad and sales at controlled (lower) prices at home; the sale of war-risk insurance at prices below costs as a means of precluding an over-all increase in import prices, and, when imports of high-cost items are substantial, an over-all rise in the prices of commodities.

More debatable is the use of subsidies as a means of keeping down the prices of important items in the consumer's budget. The famous food rollback program of 1943 is an instance. Here the government was primarily interested in stabilizing the price of food as a means of stabilizing wages and stopping the spiraling process.[12]

The table below illustrates the effects of subsidy and averaging programs.

	Prices (*Cents*)	*Total Outlay by Consumers* (*$ Million*)	*Savings to Consumers in Relation to Costs under Condition C* (*$ Million*)	*Loss to Government* (*$ Million*)
A. Subsidy	10	25	25	5
B. Averaging ..	12	30	20	—
C. No intervention ..	20	50	—	—

Source: *Price and Related Controls in the United States*, p. 228.

21. LESSONS OF WORLD WAR II

THE INTERRELATIONSHIPS OF INCOME POLICY, FISCAL POLICY, AND CONTROLS

Obviously the more incomes are allowed to rise, the more the burden put upon fiscal policy and controls to contain inflation. The substantial rise of wage payments in World War II, even if, as is contended, the major part of the rise was related to increased output and productivity, increased the pressure upon commodity markets. (Incomes rose much more than the supply of consumers' goods at stable prices.) Similarly, the insistence of the farm bloc on prices close to parity raised farm incomes and thus intensified inflationary pressures; and with higher farm prices, it became much more difficult to stabilize the price of food and raw materials. In fact, the struggle between OPA and the Agriculture Department and War Food Administration was one of the most intense of the war.

The problem is, then, to keep incomes from rising too much. In World War II, an increase of basic wage rates of but 20 to 25 per cent was consistent with a total rise of income payments of about 1½ times. From 1939 to 1945, national income rose by $110 billion, or more than 1½ times. With such large increases, to preclude a great inflation the only alternatives are:

1. A corresponding rise of consumption goods and services—an objective clearly out of line with the requirements of a war economy.

2. A vast increase of taxes and savings. An increase of taxes of $700 million with a rise of income of $17 billion in 1941 and of $2.7 billion of taxes, and $27 billion of income, in 1942 was clearly inadequate. In fact, with an expansion of income of these proportions, inflation and/or diversion of resources from war are bound to result. The resulting burden on fiscal policy (i.e., the required rise of taxes) and savings to prevent inflation is too great.

It would have been an achievement to remove two-thirds of a rise of income of $110 billion (e.g., from 1939 to 1945) through higher taxes and savings. To deal with the remainder would require control of prices and control of demand and supply. Even then the pressure of additional income not absorbed through increased supplies of consumption goods, fiscal policy, and additional savings would jeopardize price controls.

In the mobilization of the fifties as I contend elsewhere,[1] *rises* of taxes and savings on the World War II scale (i.e., a rise of 8 times) are not likely. Furthermore, we should demand a reduction of consumption. All these considerations point to a large inflationary gap only partly offset by the fact that output (and hence income) will not rise as much as in World War II. It is, therefore, imperative to discourage inflationary income policies—of labor, management, or farmers.

Unfortunately, it has become increasingly fashionable to tie wage rates to the cost of living. The result is, of course, that wage rates will rise with the cost of living and total wages, responding to increased employment, longer hours, upgrading, and overtime pay, will rise a fortiori. Insofar as wage rates rise with the cost of living, an increased burden is put upon fiscal policy and controls. To tie wage rates to the cost of living means that workers will claim more goods per hour of work and *all* workers' claims will rise greatly. If goods available to all workers are to decline, then the means would have to be severe taxes, large rises of savings, and sterilization of purchasing power through controls, which further add to savings.

Thus, assuming an average weekly wage of $50, we can predict the inflationary effect of a cost of living pay rise.

Assume a 10 per cent rise in the cost of living; weekly pay increase	$	5
Assume 50 weeks per year; annual pay increase		250
Assume 70 million workers; national income rise		17,500,000,000

It follows that the universal application of the cost of living guide, even with a 10 per cent rise in the cost of living, might raise wages by $17.5 billion. Another 10 per cent rise of income associated with high output in two years would add $25 billion to the income stream—about two-thirds going to workers. The important point is that the additional $17.5 billion requires a corresponding rise of taxes and savings to eliminate the inflationary pressures associated with an increase in the cost of living of but 10 per cent. That farm parity is tied to the prices farmers pay further adds to the inflationary effects of a rise in the cost of living.

Fortunately, the association of wage rates with the cost of living is not by any means universal, though most trade-union leaders seem to set this as a minimum goal in wartime. An automatic response of wage rates to increases in the cost of living would greatly strengthen the forces of inflation which are so often blocked by the lag in the rise of wages. I am surprised that my distinguished colleague, Professor Slichter, should urge the general application of this principle not only to wages but salaries and even to interest on the national debt. I cannot think of more effective ways of bringing about an inflation.

Many labor leaders seem to insist upon this association of cost of living and wages in wartime. Perhaps a compromise might be an increase of wages to offset the increase of the costs of an "iron ration"—that is, the costs of a rise of a *minimum* standard of living. Thus we might reduce these additional inflationary pressures by ½ to ⅔.

Inflation originating in the support of the parity principle is not likely to be so great as in World War II, the reason being that farm prices are now much higher, both relatively and absolutely, than in 1939. The parity ratio (the relative prices of purchases and sales by farmers) was 77 in 1939 and 97 in June, 1950.

INTEGRATION OF PRICE AND SUPPLY AND DEMAND CONTROLS

In stimulating output and excluding nonessential demand, the War Production Board (in World War II) or the Mobilization Director (1951) facilitates the work of the Stabilization Director. Control of prices and wages by the *Mobilization Director,* and hence better integration of these controls than was had in World War II, marks an advance over our administrative setup in 1941–45. Now one authority will be able to determine the extent to which reliance will be had on (say) allocations (i.e., directing supplies according to war objectives) against the price incentive.

It does not follow that merely because the functions are now entrusted to one over-all control that the optimum use will be made of the various controls. In World War II, for example, a point of contention revolved around the declining interest of producers in low-priced items. One of the pitfalls of price control is the "evasion" through increasing the relative output of high-priced items. It is possible to correct this tendency by raising the prices of low-end commodities; or by allocating materials to producers on the condition (say) that part of the leather provided is used to produce adult shoes costing $5 or less. One approach stresses the usual price and profit incentive but violates the stabilization objective; another capitalizes on "authority" bestowed on a war agency.

Within the mobilization office, there will continue to be splits between those who would demand the application of the price incentives and those who would seek authoritative measures. Differences *within* the agency would be substituted for differences *between* agencies.

Similarly, the conflict over standardization (simplification) and concentration (reducing the number of plants producing an item as a means of cutting unit costs) as adjuncts to price stabilization will spill over into the current mobilization. In World War II, the authorities were attentive to proposals to simplify and concentrate where important savings of resources might be made. The progress made, even with the objective in mind, was not great, however. Simplification and concentration, as programs to reduce costs and thus help maintain price ceilings, were not generally acceptable in the WPB.

How acceptable the simplification and concentration programs will be in the next few years will depend upon the severity of mobilization and (?) war, and hence upon the economies required. Should the crisis be more serious than in World War II, the Mobilization Director may be willing to proceed much further in concentrating output in a limited number of plants and imposing standardization programs. In a magazine article (*Atlantic Monthly,* January, 1950, *"How Much Is an Inch?"*), Senator Ralph E. Flanders struck the first blow against aggressive leadership by government under the stimulus of war toward further standardization.

THE SEQUENCE OF SUPPLY AND DEMAND CONTROLS

It required almost two and one-half years of controls by the WPB and predecessor agencies before a reasonably efficient system of controls of scarce materials was introduced. At a very early stage of mobilization of 1950–51, the government was prepared to launch a Controlled Materials Plan (CMP), the epitome of controls in World War II. Under this plan, the crucial materials are allocated among claimant agencies on the basis of the requirements of contractors and others who have claims on these agencies.

A plan for early use of the CMP explains also why in the emergency of 1950–51 the government did not shut down whole industries through L orders (e.g., automobiles), as in the early period of the emergency of World War II. Deny the civilian economy one-third of its copper and a paring of television output will follow. Other explanations of the failure to use L orders were: (1) an early use of some indirect controls, such as consumer credit control in 1950, conserved materials in short supply; and (2) the fear that a premature drastic curtailment of civilian output before the war contracts were let and industry was prepared to begin production would result in large amounts of unemployment.

Hence at the beginning of the Korean crisis, it was necessary only to exercise authority to force industry to accept defense contracts and to announce cuts in the use of materials in short supply. Many will, of course, criticize the government for allowing the housing and automobile boom to continue into 1951, even if there were gains in employment. Their criticism springs from the fear that this civilian boom has used up materials which might have been used with much greater effectiveness for furthering the war effort.

CONTROL OF PRICES, WAGES, AND MANPOWER

There is a general awareness today of the interdependence of prices and wages; in 1941–42, whatever the general comprehension of this interrelationship, the war authorities failed to integrate wage and price policy. It was, for example, a mistake to institute a price freeze without a wage freeze. That this mistake did not prove more costly is to be explained by the reduction of other costs (and hence financing higher wages out of economies associated with rising output), and the failure to achieve complete price stability. The contention at this point is not that the country should have had both a *wage* and a *price* freeze in April, 1942. One might argue persuasively that wage flexibility was a price to pay for the mobilization and the reallocation of manpower required for a shift from a peace to a war economy. I am contending, however, that a price freeze without a wage freeze seems unfair to sellers; and it results in labor absorbing the gains of reduced unit costs resulting from the expansion of output at the expense of consumers.

In the crisis of the fifties, the problems are somewhat different. Wages and employment are at a high level: the contribution of higher wages toward a rise in manpower is not likely to be large. It would be a mistake, however, to exclude relative wage movements as a means toward obtaining a reallocation of labor.

This problem leads us to a discussion of manpower control. In 1942–45 manpower control was rather primitive for a war economy. Fortunately, the War Labor Board never succeeded in stabilizing wages, though the upward movement was checked to a substantial degree. It is important that the current managers of the defense economy realize that any effective freeze of wages would be harmful unless accompanied by vigorous manpower control. The fact that the reservoir of unused labor is small in 1950–51 vis-à-vis 1940–42 emphasizes the point that the elimination of the price (i.e., higher wages) incentive as a means of redistributing labor makes manpower control an essential ingredient of an advanced mobilization program.

PRICE CONTROL AND SUPPLIES

We have noted elsewhere that, compared to the rise of prices in the war years, the increase of output was large indeed. Many would justify the degree of price flexibility in the war economy of 1941–42 on the grounds that the gains productionwise were more important than the losses inflationwise. Wage and price rises contributed toward the increase of 10 million on the labor market and the required realloca-tion of labor and other factors of production.

It is clear to most of us that price (and wage) inflation is required to a much smaller extent in the fifties than in the forties to elicit additional output. Against any losses associated with inflation, either on distributive grounds or in adverse effects on output, the gains productionwise will be small. That means the case for inflation and lax price control in the early fifties is much weaker than in the early forties.

We should note, however, an offset to this argument. In 1940–41, the war economy could mobilize large unemployed resources (9.5 million, or 17 per cent of the labor force in 1939), and excess capacity in plant and management. At the outburst of the Korean crisis, unemployment was but 3.4 million, or only 5 per cent of the labor force. A rise of prices is not a necessary cost for putting unemployed resources to work. Hence for a partial mobilization (i.e., putting the un-employed resources to work) a rise of prices was not required in 1940–41; but for putting additional factors to work, the increase of reward was a *sine qua non.*

HOW COMPREHENSIVE IS COVERAGE OF PRICE CONTROL TO BE?

For administrative reasons, it is easier to control all prices than to limit control to essential items. It is difficult to draw the line between essential and nonessential commodities and services. Anyone with experience in World War II knows what the problem is. Fur coats are a luxury, but what of the $100 muskrat; food is essential, but what of the luxury hoards of canned foods, or caviar, or pheasant, or porterhouse steaks. Is gasoline essential or nonessential? It depends—gaso-line for pleasure riding is not essential; for occupational use, it is essential. Restaurant food for the factory worker is essential; but at what point from the low-priced restaurant to the Stork Club does restaurant food become a luxury?

The case for comprehensive control rests partly on such considerations, but also on the theory that selective price control shunts excess purchasing power to the remaining free markets and, therefore, with rising prices in these markets, the pressure to extend controls increases. Perhaps the most important argument for comprehensive controls is that in their absence, the scarce factors of production tend to move into the noncontrolled or inefficiently controlled markets. These perverse movements explain in part the large increases in outlays for food in restaurants, alcoholic drinks, recreation, etc., in World War II.

In an all-out mobilization effort which we might well have in the fifties, the justification for selective controls may be much greater than in World War II. Indeed, administrative difficulties remain; but the essentiality line may be drawn very strictly to include the low-priced and the most necessary items—bread, cheap cuts of meat, milk, a few vegetables, utility clothing (e.g., low-priced coats, shoes, dresses, stockings, underwear).

The case for selective price controls would then rest on the following grounds: (*a*) With large sacrifices, the line could more easily be drawn between essentials and nonessentials. (*b*) In an all-out mobilization, the government in response to higher prices would prevent the movement of factors of production into the uncontrolled areas. (*c*) With heavy excise taxes (levied generally on high-priced units), the government would both discourage outlays on nonessentials and also intercept most of the additional profits made. Any net profits remaining would be largely absorbed by income and profits taxes.

COSTS, PRICES, AND PROFITS

In a price-control program, the major problem becomes one of preventing each rise of cost from being translated into an increase of prices, or even worse, from an increase for part of the total supply into a corresponding rise of prices for *all* units sold. *There is no doubt but that the scrapping of the marginal principle of cost determination in periods of stress makes an important contribution toward containing the inflation.*

In the limited area of controls in World War I, the authorities favored prices at a level which excluded the high-cost producers. In the more intensive war that followed, it was not feasible, as a rule, to eliminate the high-cost producers who might account for 5 to 25 per cent of total output. Yet it was not expedient to allow the high-cost producers, many of whom had to be enlisted in the course of the emergency, to raise prices for all producers.

The ways out were (*a*) to pool all supplies and distribute the increased costs of $1/x$ units over all units (averaging); (*b*) subsidizing the sellers of high-cost units (e.g., purchase of high-cost materials abroad by the government and sales at home at legal, i.e., lower prices); (*c*) paying according to differential costs (e.g., paying a premium of 5 cents to the copper producers who increase their output beyond a certain point, or setting prices on war contracts according to costs of each producer, or in relation to price ceilings encouraging the use of *individual* price adjustments on the basis of rises of costs).

All these ingenious approaches were used in World War II, but not nearly as much nor as consistently as they should have been. With large inflationary pressures resulting from vigorous attempts to raise supplies through increased imports from high-cost sources or through pressure on depleted natural resources, the need of scrapping the marginal principle in the fifties may well be greater than in the forties.

This brings me to the question of profits. Few will dispute the fact that profits in 1942–45 were out of line for a wartime economy and especially before taxes—the relevant variable in appraising the effectiveness of price control. One explanation of the high profits was the too frequent acceptance of the marginal principle; a second, the failure often to offset rises of costs against economies associated with increased output; a third explanation (related to the second) was the persistence with which sellers insisted upon a customary percentage markup, irrespective of the rise of output; a fourth, the frequent need of concentrating on supply considerations (e.g., military supplies) to the sacrifice of price stabilization; fifth, the necessary delay in imposing price control together with the later difficulties with rollbacks; sixth, technical obstacles to effective price control.

Relative to the problem of effectiveness, we comment briefly on the types of price regulations. The highest grade goes to dollar-and-cents regulations; but unless standardization proceeds much further than in World War II and control is limited to necessaries, dollars-and-cents ceilings are not likely to be very important. Their main advantage is enforceability; their great disadvantage is limited applicability and their difficulty of coping with varying costs.

The freeze is the easiest and the quickest regulation to impose. Its main advantage is that the burden of the proof for passing on high costs to the buyer is on the seller. Where the seller is likely to be confronted with increases of costs from many sources over which the Price Administrator may have little control, this feature of the freeze is very important.

In an economy with millions of differentiated products, the formula ceiling has proved to be most useful, although it is often vague, difficult to understand and enforce, and frequently the seller is automatically allowed to pass on increases in costs. Formula ceilings are popular because they provide the simplest approach to control of markets with much variation of products and costs. It is likely to be the most practical type of price regulation in the fifties, also.

PRICE CONTROL AND FISCAL POLICY

Our experience with price control in World War II suggests to the authorities of the emergency in the fifties that there should be greater dependence on fiscal policy as a means of keeping prices down. At best, price control is enforceable only within limits, and a genuine price freeze is out of the question. Even apparent stabilization obscures genuine rises in prices associated with deterioration, uptrading, and abandonment of supplementary services.

THE GENERALLY FAIR AND EQUITABLE CRITERION

One weapon available to the Price Administrator in 1941–45 is not going to be as potent in the fifties. The Administrator could generally deny price rises when profits were not in excess of those in 1936–39. In late 1950, the Economic Stabilization Director announced a similar test, but the relevant years were to be 1946–49. In 1936–39, however, *annual* corporate profits before taxes were $5 billion; in 1946–49, $29 billion. With some justice, the ESA might deny price increases even if the average of profits were *substantially less* than the 1946–49 level. In this manner, the Administration might neutralize inflationary factors more successfully. If the "generally fair and equitable" provision is related to 1946–49 profits, then the protection offered by this provision will probably be less than in World War II. In 1936–39, we started from a low price level and low profits, and hence the reference to this level in testing the propriety of price increases frequently would preclude a price rise. When the profits are high in the base period (1946–49), the obstacle of the base period is likely to be much less effective.

THE GAINS OF PRICE CONTROL

It is possible to compare the price rise in World War II with that of World War I and thus estimate the gains of price control. In World War II, this was a fashionable practice in the OPA. In view of the much larger percentage of resources used for war in World War II than in World War I, the rise in the cost of living in World War II of but 40 per cent of that of World War I was a great achievement.[2] But it should be noted that fiscal policies and other controls shared in this achievement.

Another important reservation is that what happens after the war is also of great importance. Immediately after World War I, prices soared. But in the twenties, wholesale prices settled at a level below the peak of World War I and cost of living somewhat above the war's peak. After World War II, even as late as mid-1950, the cost of living was about 35 per cent above the war peak and wholesale prices about 60 per cent above. In other words, the market forces were allowed relatively free play in World War I and therefore, except for the boom of 1919–20, the inflationary effects were exhausted by the end of 1920. In World War II, on the other hand, the gains of price control were spent in part in higher prices in 1946–50. Hence, in measuring the gains of World War II vis-à-vis World War I, we should allow for *later* effects when suppressed inflation gave way to open inflation.

Another approach to the problem of measuring gains is to compare prices of controlled as against noncontrolled commodities. Thus, for May, 1942, to May, 1943, the price of all foods at retail rose by 17.6 per cent, of uncontrolled foods by 74.7 per cent, of foods controlled under the general freeze by only 4.1 per cent. A caveat to this claim rests on the point that the rise in the prices of uncontrolled commodities springs in part from the release of purchasing power that otherwise would have been used in controlled markets.[3]

Part Seven

THE INCIDENCE OF INFLATION

22. THE UNEVEN INCIDENCE OF INFLATION

THE "FORTUNATE" FEW

ONE OF THE unfortunate aspects of inflation is that it falls with uneven incidence on different groups and activities. Many respond admirably well: the businessman, dependent upon profits, and the farmer obtain increases of income greater than the rise of prices. The explanation of the relative gains of profits is the lag of costs behind prices, as well as the increased business in periods of high activity; the explanation of farmers' gains, the quick response of raw material prices to anticipated shortages.

EFFECTS UPON WORKERS

Well-organized workers are also likely to obtain increases of wages equal to the rise of prices. Thus, from 1940, the first year of mobilization, hourly earnings of manufacturing rose more than the cost of living. But in the telephone industry, the rise in workers' hourly wages lagged behind that of the cost of living throughout the years 1939 to 1949. It is not, of course, the degree of organization alone that counts. Supply and demand conditions are relevant. Thus in the forties farm labor received an increase in wages much in excess of that received in the factories—partly because the wage level in 1939 was relatively very low, and partly because of the great scarcity of labor on the farms as farm labor moved into war production.

The rise in hourly earnings must, of course, be interpreted with care. In part, the increase was due to a larger proportion of work done at overtime rates, notably in the war period, and, in part, to upgrading, a phenomenon of scarce labor markets. (Upgrading results in a larger proportion of workers in the relatively high-paid occupations.)

Here is a breakdown of the rise of manufacturing payrolls in the period October, 1942, to May, 1943.

	Per Cent
1. Change in average weekly earnings	10.7
2. Contribution in hours of work per week	3.7
Contribution of increase in gross average hourly earnings due to all forces	7.0
(a) Due to increase in proportion of overtime pay	1.2
(b) Due to relative expansion of high-wage industries	1.9
(c) Due to other factors (Rise of output under incentive schemes, promotions, reclassifications, etc.)	3.9

Source: *Second Monthly Report of the War Labor Board,* June 1, 1943, p. 9.

That the rise of weekly wages is a compound of numerous factors in addition to rises in basic wage rates and an increase in hours is evident from the table below. From January, 1941, to July, 1945, weekly earnings in manufacturing rose from $26.64 to $45.54, or an increase of $18.90. The percentage rise of the total increase was as follows:

	Per Cent
1. Changes in basic wage rate	33
2. Liberal administration of merit increases, piece-rate adjustments, etc., and changes in provisions for premium pay, for overtime work and for work on extra shifts	12

3. Changes in distribution of workers as between regions, occupations, and shifts; and changes in provision for premium pay for overtime work and for work on extra shifts	11
4. Changes in distribution of workers as among industries	7
5. Extension of work week	26
6. Additional premium payment for overtime work	11
	100

Source: U.S. Dept. of Labor, *Problems and Policies of Dispute Settlement and Wage Stabilization During World War II,* 1951, p. 174.

From January, 1941, to September, 1947, the following changes occurred: [1]

	Per Cent
Gross earnings, weekly	+89.3
Gross earnings, hourly	+83.2
Estimated straight time hourly earnings	+82.7
Urban wage rates	+74.4

VARIATIONS AMONG WORKERS

Many do not fare as well as businessmen, farmers, and well-organized workers. The white-collar workers do not gain as much as the factory worker. In part, the explanation may be organization; in part, the greater gains of productivity of factory workers supported to a larger degree by machines; and, in part, the larger output of high school and especially college graduates who seek white-collar jobs. It is interesting that from 1940 to 1947–48 the median income of college graduates rose by 75 per cent and average earnings in industry for full-time employees by 99 per cent.[2] The difference may be associated with the increased pressure of numbers seeking employment palatable to college graduates and with their concentration on employment where pay in response to inflation does not rise as rapidly as in all employments—teaching, minor executive posts, law.

In all occupations, the figures are summarized below. Note that, in general, the rise of income has exceeded that in prices. But the gains vary greatly; the increase is associated, in part, with longer hours and upgrading; and the three groups containing a large proportion of white-collar workers did not gain as much as agriculture and manufacturing workers. Pay of workers in finance, real estate, etc., rose roughly as much as the cost of living; their real position was unchanged. Agricultural workers, on the other hand, obtained increased compensation equal to 3+ times as much as the rise in the cost of living. That the rise for *all* workers exceeded that in the cost of living reflects the movement into highly productive industries (e.g., durable goods) and perhaps some over-all gains in productivity. But we note, also, that in the war period the gain in real income was fictitious: workers received an increased number of dollars in 1939 purchasing power; but there were restrictions on their spending.

AVERAGE ANNUAL EARNINGS OF VARIOUS CATEGORIES OF EMPLOYMENT AND COST OF LIVING, 1939, 1944, AND 1949

	1939	*1944*	*1949*
All	$1269	$2120	$2869
Agriculture, forestry, etc.	403	983	1341
Manufacturing	1363	2507	3093
Finance, real estate, etc.	1761	2203	3084
Services	943	1517	2174
Government	1349	1961	2892
Prices, consumers' goods (1949 = 100)	58.8	76.7	100

Sources: *Survey of Current Business,* Annual Income Numbers, 1947 and 1950, and *Economic Report of President,* July, 1950.

EFFECTS ON ASSISTANCE, ANNUITIES, AND SAVINGS

All of this does not mean that each citizen was at least as well off in 1949 as in 1939. Far from it.

In 1949, there were about 11 million aged 65 or over. Most of these were not members of the labor market. They were dependent on old-age assistance, old-age annuities, weekly allowances from friends, and savings.

In all, there were 4.2 million receiving public assistance. This figure should be compared with the 38 to 39 million families and 8 million individuals not in families.[3]

In 1947, there were 2.3 million in receipt of old-age assistance. The average benefit paid was $37.42, as compared with $19.30 in 1939. The recipients of old-age assistance were able to obtain increases greater than that in the cost of living. The amounts were still not adequate and in the absence of inflation they would undoubtedly have achieved more. But their position has not deteriorated vis-à-vis 1939. (Similar remarks apply to the aid for dependent children.)

Recipients of old-age annuities did not fare as well as those on assistance. For example, whereas from January, 1941, to June, 1948, average monthly payments under old-age assistance rose by 86 per cent, retired workers under old-age and survivors' insurance received but 11 per cent more. At the latter date, those who participated in an insurance program received $25.13 on the average, as compared with $38.18 for old-age assistance. In 1950, there were 3 million annuitants under the old-age insurance program.[4]

Pensioners and annuitants are also an important element in our economic society. Thus, in 1950, there were almost 3 million receiving pensions from the U.S. Government, the total amounts paid out being $2.1 billion.[5]

Life insurance companies also pay annuities largely to the old. The average annuity paid was about $370 in 1941 and about $350 in 1949. A rise of annual payments from $671 million dollars to $1,173 million dollars was offset by an increase in number of annuitants from 1.8 million to 3.35 million. This suggests that the inflation may well have cut the real income received by each annuitant by almost 40 per cent from 1941 to 1949.[6]

It is scarcely necessary to add that insofar as the old or others depended on savings (cash, deposits, bonds) accumulated before 1941, they suffered reductions in real income of substantial proportions.

The following figures are relevant:

ESTIMATED LIQUID ASSET HOLDINGS OF INDIVIDUALS AND BUSINESSES
($ BILLION, END OF YEAR)

	1939	*1945*	*1948*
Total	69.0	226.8	238.8
Currency	5.8	25.5	24.7
Deposits	47.2	107.2	120.7
Savings and loan shares	4.0	7.2	10.8
U.S. Government securities	12.0	86.9	82.6
Business holdings, total	19.4	73.0	64.0
Personal holdings, total	49.6	154.5	174.8

Source: *Federal Reserve Bulletin,* July, 1949, p. 794.

These figures indicate the losses suffered by holders of liquid assets. The owners of $69 billion of liquid assets in 1939 had lost about $28 billion by 1949—as a result of a rise of prices of 69 per cent. The owners of $227 billion of liquid assets in 1945 had lost $47 billion by the end of 1949—as a result of a rise of prices of 27 per cent.

EFFECTS ON LOW-INCOME GROUPS GENERALLY

It is necessary to consider also the large proportion of the population with small incomes. As long ago as 1947, the government estimated that more than $3,000 were required in order to provide a decent standard of living for a family of four. Yet in 1948, there were 4 million families (10.6 per cent of all) with incomes of less than $1,000; 5.6 million with incomes of $1,000 to $2,000 (14.5 per cent); and 20.6 per cent with incomes of $2,000 to $3,000. In other words, close to one-half did not earn enough to obtain more than a minimum standard of living. Of the 6.3 million non-farm families with incomes of $2,000 or less, more than one-quarter were in the age group 65 or over. This quarter equaled one-half of all families in this older age group. These low-income groups are to be found especially in the unskilled and semiskilled groups (organized below national standards), among non-whites, the badly educated, and the disabled. In fact, there are more than 4.5 million disabled persons in the country, exclusive of children under 14, aged persons 65 years and over, and those in institutions. A large proportion of these are undoubtedly in the low-income groups. The large number of families with incomes of $3,000 or less and surely those with $2,000 or less, including largely those whose incomes are not likely to respond too well to rising prices—these stress the dangers of inflation. Their real income was too low even in 1950. The situation will become more serious with further rises of prices.

EFFECTS OF INFLATION ON LIFE INSURANCE GENERALLY

Insurance provides an important element of security for millions of Americans. The rise of prices in the forties and the accompanying fall in yield of investments have reduced the value of insurance. An examination of life insurance in force, of assets held by the insurance companies, of reserves held against liabilities shows that life insurance plays a smaller part in the economy and security of the country than it did 10 or 20 years ago. For example, the expansion of insurance in force from 1933 to 1949 was about 40 per cent of the increase of money income. The rise of benefit payments from 1940 to 1949 was less than half as much as that in the rise of prices: that is to say, the goods value of benefits had fallen by about one-fifth in a period when *real* income had risen by three-quarters. Indeed, a large part of the explanation of this decline in the state of insurance companies is the competition of government: veterans' insurance and social security. In 1950, the assets of the National Service Life insurance amounted to but $7.7 billion and the old-age and survivors' insurance fund in excess of $12 billion. These $20 billion equal about two-thirds of the deficiency in the rise of assets since the thirties for life insurance companies.[7] This is on the assumption that assets should have risen as much as income. Perhaps this is too much to expect. On the other hand, new insurance should rise much more than income relatively. This has not happened.

The problem is partly one of increased costs of insurance. The Committee on Public Debt Policy estimated that the net cost of insurance was from 10 to 30 per cent higher in 1947 than in 1930—the result of reduced earnings. But, of course, these losses are only part of those resulting from the inflation. Inflation has already washed away $46 billion (in goods value) from the $114 billion of insurance in force in 1939—minus, of course, allowances for any insurance lapsed or paid off in the interim. Additional losses of $13 billion have been incurred on insurance contracted since 1939. In other words, on the assumption of a stabilization of the 1950 price level, policyholders are insured for about $60 billion less in goods equivalent than at time of making their contract. In addition, the cost of a given amount of insurance has risen. Any further rise of prices or fall in the rate of interest will aggravate this situation.

Relevant figures on life insurance companies are as follows:

	Life Insurance in Force ($ *Billion*)	*Life Insurance Assets* ($ *Billion*)	*Policy Reserves* ($ *Billion*)	*Interest Earned* (*Per Cent*)	*Benefit Payments* ($ *Billion*)
1933	98	20.9	18.1	4.25	....
1939	114	29.2	25.8	3.54	2.664 (1940)
1949	220	59.6	51.5	3.04	3.468

Source: Institute of Life Insurance, *Life Insurance Fact Book, 1950,* pp. 11, 32, 46–48.

EFFECTS OF INFLATION ON STATE AND LOCAL GOVERNMENTS

In a war and inflationary period, services of various kinds tend to suffer. This is especially true of services dependent upon state and local government, philanthropic funds, endowments, and the like. Education, health, and other institutional services then deteriorate.

The reasons for the deterioration lie in the diversion of resources to government; in the high taxes and savings required by federal government; in the rise of prices; in any decline in the rate of interest; in the difficulties confronting state and local governments in increasing tax receipts *pari passu* with the rise of prices. The explanation of the last lies largely in the kind of revenues state and especially local governments depend upon. In the states, serious restrictions on the use of private automobiles, for example, may have serious effects on revenues; in local government, largely responsible for education, the general property tax, which is a most unresponsive tax to rising prices, provides about 90 per cent of the revenue.

Our experience with the last episode of war and inflation has not been reassuring for state and local governments. The response of income to growing responsibilities has been slow and inadequate. For example, even as late as 1946, the gross national product had risen by almost 100 per cent over prewar; but state and local receipts were up only 26 per cent and expenditures only 10 per cent. This meant a reduction of expenditures in goods equivalent of about 30 per cent. In fact, in the war period state and local governments had accumulated a deficiency of expenditures in relation to 1939 outlays corrected for prices of about $8 billion. If allowance is made for the rise in real output and the assumption is made that state and local governments should share in the general economic advance, then the additional deficiency may well have been 2 to 3 times the outlays of $9 billion in 1940.

That the inflation has serious effects on state and local finance is easily shown. This is reflected, for example, in the inflexibility of the general property tax. From 1932 to 1947, the yield of this tax rose by 30 per cent, but prices had gone up 75 per cent and income 400 per cent. It is not surprising then that school finance faced a serious crisis, with teachers being exploited and the service being deteriorated. Even in 1946, public school expenditures by 397 cities were but 8 per cent in excess of 1942. By 1949, the outlay per pupil in dollars of stable purchasing power had risen above the prewar, but according to the latest figures available, state and local outlays for public schools had fallen from 3.1 per cent of incomes in 1937–38 to 2.3 per cent in 1947–48. Indeed, this reflects a general decline in the relative resources being devoted to services provided by state and local government. By 1949, the purchasing power of goods and services by state and local government over prewar had risen only two-thirds as much as gross national product. And from 1933 to 1949, the rise of *all* purchases of goods and services was four times; of those by state and local government, only two times.[8]

CONCLUSION

If all prices and incomes would rise equally and simultaneously, the inflation would not be a problem. That the rise is uneven, is the essence of the inflationary problem. An increase of prices of 20 per cent may well increase profits by 100 per cent; but for the rentier, the pensioner, the poorly organized worker, the employee paid by employers whose incomes do not respond to rising prices, the net effect may well be a decline of real income of close to 17 per cent. A case study of the difficulties confronting institutions of higher learning in an inflationary economy, which is the theme of the next chapter, points to the difficulties confronting employers not able to raise incomes *pari passu* with rising prices. Here let me add that those who insist that a 10 per cent inflation per year need not be a great trial because all incomes should be adjusted accordingly are most unrealistic. The point is that the elasticity of income response varies greatly. As the mobilization proceeds and the civilian population has to sacrifice consumption standards, it becomes all the more important to fight an inflation which allows improved standards for those who thrive in inflationary periods and standards which are reduced all the more for others.

23. INSTITUTIONS OF HIGHER LEARNING

In Chapter 22, we discussed the incidence of inflation on various groups of the population. It is evident from the discussion in the last chapter that many lost from inflation. In *How Shall We Pay for Education?*, I discussed the problem of the lag of pay for teachers behind rising prices. Ultimately, the pay of school teachers caught up with the cost of living; but the slowness of the response and their failure to share in the gains of a rising standard of living were bound to result in dissatisfaction, demoralization, and a loss of talent. But with the help of organization and with the support of the tax power, this group of white-collar workers ultimately retrieved their absolute position. In part, however, the recouped losses were at the expense of standards—e.g., crowded classes.

My excuse for devoting a whole chapter to the effects of inflation on institutions of higher learning is not that the financial problems of these institutions are more important than (say) that of all white-collar workers, or public school teachers, or other weakly organized or positioned groups. Rather this is a problem which has greatly interested me, and I offer the discussion merely as a case study of the problems involved.

Our colleges and universities today face an unparalleled financial crisis. They have not by any means recovered from the inflation of the last ten years. Yet with a large deficit in 1950, they face another inflation and a large cut in enrollment;

and without the freedom to adjust prices which most sellers of products and services retain. Noneconomic considerations influence the prices of the product sold by colleges.

OUTLAYS

In the years since the depths of the depression, as prices and incomes have soared, institutions of higher learning have obtained increased funds also, but not in proportion to the rise of income.

In 1932, these institutions spent $421 million, or 1 per cent, of the national income. By 1947, outlays rose to $1,005 million and ½ of 1 per cent of the national income. In the last year or two, costs have increased further and enrollment and GI money have declined. For 1960, we anticipate outlays of $4.3 billion, or 1.5 per cent of the anticipated income. (These outlays, however, are based on rather optimistic projections of the President's Commission of Higher Education.) [1]

It is clear that the outlays have more than kept up with the rise of prices. On the assumption of no rise of prices from 1947 to 1960, higher education would make large gains in the next ten years. (Consider, however, later comments.) By 1947, the outlays were 40 per cent in excess of the 1932 amount, the latter adjusted for the rise of prices from 1932 to 1947. Since the enrollment in 1947 was roughly twice as great as in 1932, outlays per student in dollars of stable purchasing power had fallen by 30 per cent. This decline may reflect better use of capacity, but also a deterioration of the product.

STUDENT FEES

In order to contend with the rising price levels, institutions of higher learning were forced to raise tuition fees. This, of course, is unfortunate; for any increase tends to aggravate the problem of democratizing higher education. It is well known that students in institutions of higher learning are drawn predominantly from the higher-income groups. One study showed, for example, that for every good student entering college, another fails to get in, largely for financial reasons. Another reveals that potential students from parents in the $8,000-or-over income class had four times as good a chance to enter college as those in the average income class.[2]

The effect of raising tuition fees in a period of rising incomes was not a greater cost in terms of goods and certainly not in relation to average income. But for those with inflexible income, the costs rose; and the need of raising fees prevented the increase of incomes from greatly facilitating the entry of poorer students.

On the whole, the institutions showed restraint in their tuition policies. Even by 1949–50, according to a valuable survey (October 2, 1949) by the New York *Times* expert, Benjamin Fine, the increase in tuition from 1941–42 was 52.2 per cent in colleges, 45.5 per cent in professional schools, and 45 per cent in graduate colleges. In 1950–51, tuition rose 1 to 2 per cent further. This rise in tuition over 9 to 10 years was substantially less than that in prices. Students were getting their education cheaper than in prewar. Moreover, the higher institutions economized in other ways—e.g., by doubling up in rooms, introducing self-service in dining rooms, eliminating nonessential services. The result was that the estimated total cost per student had risen in these years from $572 to $877, or an increase of but 53 per cent (New York *Times,* November 27, 1950).

Even these increases would have met much more resistance without the aid offered by the GI Bill. Thus, in 1947, the federal government paid $301 million of the $565 million paid by students.[3] But by 1950–51 veteran enrollment was one-half of that in 1948–49 and freshman veterans but one-third the number in 1948–49.

TEACHERS' SALARIES

One of the distressing aspects of the inflation has been the failure of academic salaries to keep up with the rise in the cost of living. In terms of goods, the pay is less than prewar. Relative to the rise of per capita incomes of the working population, the rise of pay for college faculty has been disappointing indeed. For the country the rise of wages and salaries per employed member of the labor market from 1939 to 1949 was about 110 per cent; of college teachers, about 40 per cent. If allowance is also made for the large rise of employment in the general population, the relative deterioration for faculty members is even more serious. The impairment of the *real* position (dollars of stable purchasing power) for faculty members is about 20 per cent; that for the rest of the population, a rise of about 50 per cent. That is to say, the professional group has suffered a *relative* deterioration of close to one-half (150 versus 80).[4]

The significance of these figures lies in the loss of morale in college faculties; in a narrowing of the gap between the able and the mediocre as the lowest paid receive the major increases; and especially in the difficulties of recruitment of the men and women of ability required in the institutions of higher learning. On the narrowing of the range of pay differences and lessening of incentives, the following is of some interest. From 1923–24 to 1949–50 the median pay of professors, associate professors, assistant professors, and instructors in the Liberal Arts College at Northwestern University rose by 39, 64, 63, and 100 per cent, respectively. This is not typical. In the four city colleges (New York), the pay of professors rose by 7 per cent and instructors by 44 per cent.

EFFECTS ON THE FINANCIAL POSITION OF INSTITUTIONS OF HIGHER LEARNING

In the past, institutions of higher learning have depended largely upon government aid (state and municipal institutions), student fees, and endowment income and gifts (private institutions).

Inflation and war have had serious effects upon the financial position of these institutions. Costs have risen and it has been difficult to increase resources to offset the rise of prices, to improve standards, and to raise additional amounts required to cover the excess of costs over tuition per *additional* student enrolled. (In part the last is made up by economies resulting from increased use of capacity, that is, saving per student on overhead.)

The effects upon endowment income of the low-interest-rate policy have been especially serious. Thus a large sample of institutions earned 5.16 per cent on their endowment in 1926–32, 4.42 per cent in 1933–41, and 4.12 per cent in 1942–43. Another sample of 91 institutions suffered a reduction from 4.05 per cent in 1940–41 to 3.74 per cent in 1945–46. Even these figures understate the deterioration. They do not allow for the fact that in order to keep returns up, institutions of higher learning invest much more heavily in equity, that is, risky, securities. If allowance is made for added risks, the results are even less satisfactory. Moreover, allowance should be made for the rise of prices which results in a given income being worth less in goods and services. Thus, although Harvard's endowment rose by $68 million, or two-thirds, from 1928–29 to 1945–46, the University's income from investment (in goods value) was no larger than it was in 1928–29: the potential gains from a rise of endowment had been spilled in rising prices and falling yield. Furthermore, with the student body 50 per cent higher, the contribution of investment income per student was down by 33⅓ per cent.

The problem is, however, not merely one of yield. It is also one of obtaining gifts and endowment.

On the whole, institutions of higher learning have not been successful in maintaining their position in the quest for philanthropic funds. As I contended in *How Shall We Pay for Education?*, the explanation is partly the severe tax programs resulting largely from war and partly the losing fight waged by these institutions against competitors for these funds.

For example, the effective rates of federal individual income tax on incomes of $5,000, $25,000, and $100,000 were 0.2, 4.0, and 15.7 per cent in 1928 and 11.8, 34.1, and 62.3 per cent by 1945.[5]

The losing fight waged by institutions is suggested by the following:

1. In the first 30 years of the twentieth century, institutions of higher learning received $1.5 billion in endowment funds, an amount equal to about ⅛ of 1 per cent of the national income of the period.

2. Should they receive the same percentage of national income in the next 10 years as in the years 1900–30, they would obtain at least $2.5 billion, an amount in excess of endowments at the end of the war.

3. But on the basis of results in the years 1940–47, I would estimate the receipts in the forties at much less than $1 billion. In the fifties (aside from the effects of war), we would be overly optimistic to assume gifts of $1 billion. Receipts were inflated in the forties as a result of big endowment drives not likely to be repeated in the fifties.[6]

4. An average of $600 million in a decade is about what was received in each of the three decades, 1900–10, 1910–20, and 1920–30. Yet now prices are about 100 per cent higher than in 1900–30 (average) and the number of students about four times as high. Current gifts yield now about one-eighth as much in *goods equivalent per student* as in 1900–30, and even less when allowance is made for smaller yields.

THE FUTURE

It is clear that institutions of higher learning are facing a dark financial future. They have not as yet caught up with the past inflation and adverse effects of war generally. Now they are confronted with the prospects of another inflation. In his October 2, 1949, survey in the *Times,* Benjamin Fine noted that 20 per cent of higher institutions reporting were operating on a deficit. In his November 27, 1950, survey, a study of a sample twice as large revealed prospective deficits for close to one-half of all these institutions.

In a commentary on the Report of the President's Commission on Higher Education, I noted the difficulties of achieving the financial program issued by the Commission. This program would require annual outlays of $2.5 billion plus a generous federal scholarship program and a large capital expansion program to provide higher education for 4.6 million. To attain the goal the federal government would have to provide $2,061 million annually and state governments $1,433 million. Even in the absence of war, these governments could not afford outlays of these proportions. It follows, therefore, that the expansion of higher education proposed by the President's Commission will not be forthcoming unless private resources are found in vast amounts or tuition fees are raised greatly. Neither solution is practical. To substitute income on endowment for one-half of the additional sums asked of government would require $42 billion; and a large rise of tuition would reduce, not increase, enrollment.

Insofar as prices rise, the problem of finance will become even more difficult. Costs will increase more rapidly than income, both because of the rise of taxation, which finances state institutions, and the dependence upon earning of endowment funds, which do not keep up with the rise of prices; and, moreover, any rise of taxation to check inflation would further reduce gifts.

On top of the losses resulting from inflation, institutions of higher learning will also suffer from serious losses of students—in part because of the reduction in GI money but more largely because of the drains of manpower to the military. It is not easy, early in 1951, to estimate the extent of the losses. But even on the assumption that the military would increase its personnel to only 3 million and would drain almost exclusively those of college age, as they seem disposed to do, institutions of higher learning would lose about 400,000 students, or about 20 per cent of current enrollment. Losses for women's colleges would be negligible and for all-male colleges about 40 per cent. These are only rough estimates and relate only to 1951. For 1952, the loss should be at least one-third. The effects would be even more serious under universal military service, which might virtually wipe out two college classes. With a slowing-up of mobilization, the drop in enrollment may be less than here suggested.

A combination of (say) a loss of 25 per cent of students (to the military and industry) conservatively estimated and an inflation of 10 per cent per year would have serious effects. A 10 per cent rise per year is a possible development in the light of the military program, views on finance and controls in 1950–51, and past accomplishments. Of a budget of around 1 billion dollars for higher education, the result would then be a loss of about $120 million in tuition and (say) at least $150 million of additional costs per year within two years. The net effect on the assumption of a balanced budget in 1950 would be a deficit of $270 million. Strong institutions would undoubtedly be able to survive the storm by introducing policies of retrenchment and living on reserves. But there are not many which could survive a deficit equal to almost 30 per cent of receipts for many years; and a large proportion could not survive even 2 to 3 years of deficits of these proportions.

Indeed, the higher institutions will resist the rise of costs by economizing on services and not allowing pay of the academic staff to rise. But this also would have unfortunate effects. In a recent *Atlantic* article, Professor Slichter suggested tying tuition and pay to the cost of living. Unfortunately some noneconomic considerations militate against automatic rise of tuition and economic considerations suggest the unwisdom of introducing an automatic inflationary factor into the situation.

This survey underlines one important point. The financial plight of institutions of higher learning is one of many strong arguments for a courageous tax and anti-inflationary program.

Part Eight

WELFARE ASPECTS

24. WELFARE EXPENDITURES

THE PRESSURE TO CUT OUTLAYS FOR WELFARE

IN PERIODS of military mobilization or war, the pressure is on to prune all government outlays not directly connected with the military effort. The reasons are obvious. The more that can be saved through public economies, the less will have to be found through a rise of output, reduced consumption, or reduced private investment.

No one knows how large the military effort is going to be. But we can make three alternative assumptions, the second one perhaps being the most reasonable one.

The first is additional military outlays of $20 billion, to the amount likely to be spent in 1951; the second, $55 billion; the third, $125 billion—outlays equal to those at the peak of World War II, corrected for the rise of prices.

According to pessimistic estimates, these three efforts would require a reduction of private consumption of 8, 14, and 48 per cent from the 1950 level, and of consumption per hour of work by 12, 22, and 53 per cent. According to more optimistic estimates, the percentage reductions would be about one-half those given above. In other words, in contrast to World War II, when at the peak of the war a large rise of output made possible both $80 billion for war and $40 billion additional for consumption and the maintenance of consumption per hour of work, World War III requires a large cut in total consumption and in consumption per hour of work. Hence the great pressure to reduce outlays for the Welfare State.

SOME LESSONS FROM THE FORTIES

Before we discuss the pros and cons of "welfare policy," it would be well to emphasize certain aspects of our experience in the last ten to fifteen years. This was an inflationary period, with prices about 75 per cent above those of the depression low. It is most unlikely that we shall carry through a large mobilization effort requiring (conservatively) $200 billion in five years without an additional inflation of 25 per cent. (In the first nine months of war consumers' prices rose by 9 per cent.) On the basis of policies of 1950 and 1951 and considering the great demands to be superimposed on a strained economy, I anticipate an even larger inflation.

The coming inflation will aggravate the maladjustments originating largely in World War II and not yet fully corrected. Many groups are vulnerable to a further inflation. For example, there are 4.2 million receiving public assistance; the 2.7 million drawing benefits under the old-age insurance and survivors' program; the 4½ million disabled (aged fifteen to sixty-four and exclusive of those in institutions); the 4 million families with incomes of $1,000 or less; the 5.6 million families with incomes of $2,000 or less; the 7 to 9 million families with incomes of $3,000 or less. Note that figures are not additive, e.g., the annuitants are a significant part of the low-income groups. But those with low incomes and/or those dependent on aid or annuities are nevertheless numerous. Thus, families with incomes of $3,000 or less account for almost half the 38 to 39 million families in the nation. You will recall that the Bureau of Labor Statistics, on the basis of a study of 34 cities, estimated that a worker's family of four on prevailing standards required a minimum of $3,004 in New Orleans and a maximum of $3,458 in Washington, D.C., in June, 1947.[1]

In periods of inflation these groups are especially vulnerable. If they depend on pensions and annuities, the payments respond tardily, if at all, to higher prices. (Old-age assistance was a fortunate exception, in part explicable by the strong organizations representing the old.) Old-age insurance is an example of the disastrous effects of inflation. Thus, in January, 1941, the retired worker under old-age and survivors' insurance received $22.60; in June, 1948, he received $25.13. That is to say, in terms of goods and services, the worker received $15 of purchasing power as against $22.60 in 1941. Under the amendments of 1950, the old-age primary benefit (i.e., for the worker's share) will be raised from $26 to $45 or $46 monthly in 1951. The net result would then be a payment in dollars of stable purchasing power somewhat in excess of that received in 1941. But few would say the payment would be adequate. Budgets for twelve states estimated to show the minimum adequate budget for self-supporting women (and used for study of minimum-wage legislation) without dependents averaged close to $150 monthly.[2]

These low-income groups are heavily represented among the old, largely dependent on pensions and old-age assistance; among the poorly organized workers; among the non-whites; and among the poorly educated. They are especially vulnerable to rising prices and to the stresses on fair distribution which are felt in periods of pressure on available supplies. They will need protection in the next ten years.

I say this although the distribution of income improved over the last ten years, an improvement associated primarily with the reduction of unemployment and the accompanying rise of number of workers per family and the continued movement of workers into higher-paying occupations—e.g., from the farms into the city. Whereas in 1941, the fifth of household units with lowest incomes accounted for 3.5 per cent of incomes, in 1948 they accounted for 4.2 per cent. For the highest fifth, the respective figures were 49.6 and 46.9 per cent. A secondary factor was undoubtedly the changed pattern of government taxation and spending. An even more striking change in distribution is evident in Great Britain where from 1938 to 1948 per capita consumption in the working classes rose by 22 per cent and declined by 18 and 42 per cent for the middle class and the wealthy, respectively. Here again the explanation is primarily the change-over to a full-employment and a more productive economy, not government fiscal policy.[3]

HOW MUCH CAN WE AFFORD FOR WELFARE?

In the years since the collapse of the early thirties, this country has increased its outlays on social welfare, health, and security. Whereas all expenditures of government rose by 87 per cent from 1932 to 1941, outlays for welfare, hospitals, and corrections rose from $985 million to $4,389 million, or 346 per cent. This tendency to expand these outlays has continued into the present. Thus the total outlays for welfare alone in 1941 were $3 billion. For the latest year available the total was $4.3 billion.[4] Despite the increase, however, the amount available was but 90 per cent as much as in 1941 in stable dollars. In relation to national income, the amounts involved had declined from 5.2 per cent in 1941 to 2.5 per cent in 1949. It is clear, then, that the burden of welfare outlays has declined both absolutely and relatively. This, of course, might be expected, in a period of great prosperity; but it refutes the view that this is a welfare state. Surely spending 2½ per cent of income on welfare does not suggest the welfare state.

Modern government spends also for old-age insurance, for unemployment insurance, for hospitals, for housing, for education, for health, and for veterans. But these expenditures are generally accepted and are not now a subject of debate. The general view is, moreover, that the rise of outlay in recent years has not kept up with the growth of the economy. Thus, from the depression to the present, national output in dollars rose by four times; but state and local government expenditures have risen only two times. In other words, these governments largely responsible for education of our children, for a large part of welfare expenditures, for hospitals, etc., play a smaller part in the life of the community than they did ten or fifteen years ago. This reduction in the relative part played by these governments is partly the result of inflation which reduces the fiscal capacity of state, and especially local, governments. For example, the general property tax accounts for about 90 per cent of local government revenues. Yet this tax scarcely responds at all to rising prices and incomes. Hence the inability of local governments to meet their welfare and school bills adequately; and the greater pressure on state and especially federal governments. The rise of outlays by the last reflects in part the obstacles confronting local government in inflationary periods. Another inflationary period will raise further difficulties.

Many will point to the Federal Social Security program as another example of welfare outlays. Of course, the assistance program is included in the above estimates of total welfare outlays. But what of old-age and survivors' insurance and unemployment insurance? These should clearly not be included in welfare outlays. They are, in fact, transfer payments levied on employers and employees through payroll taxes. The employee receives part of his pay in old-age annuities and unemployment benefits.

This raises a general question concerning outlays for welfare. In a military economy, the main problem is to save scarce resources. This is much more important than the saving of dollars. Therefore, it is desirable to economize on outlays which involve using up scarce resources. From this viewpoint, we welcome any savings from the federal outlays (1951 budget) of $1,329 million for housing and community development, $436 million on rural electrification and communication, or

$2,220 million on natural resources ($817 for atomic energy), or the $1,640 million on transportation and communication ($530 million for highways), the $255 million for construction for veterans; or from state outlays (1949) on capital of $1,827 million, on natural resources of $290 million, or about $500 million of capital outlays by local government (1949). These expenditures of 8 to 9 billion dollars should be cut as much as possible in the midst of great scarcities. (The difficulties are discussed in Chapter 11.)

Transfer payments are another matter. Indeed the tax problem is serious in a period of great strain. But this is a financial, not a real, problem. It is important that the low-income groups more than maintain their relative position in periods of inflation and stress. This can be achieved, in part, by a tax policy which puts a heavy burden on those able to pay and, in part, by discouraging labor, agriculture, and capital from obtaining disproportionate gains. In order to preclude a maldistribution of income, it will be necessary to restrain trade-union leaders and the farm bloc and to control prices through proper negotiation of war contracts and ultimately through price control and heavy taxes on excess profits.

But these will not be enough. Profits and wages of well-organized workers will rise greatly. The more vulnerable groups—the unorganized and low-paid workers, the disabled, the old, the pensioners and annuitants generally, the others requiring assistance—all of these will need direct help through welfare outlays by government and private agencies. In general, private philanthropy does not contribute as much relatively as many years ago. The responsibility of government is therefore much greater; and government will have to do a much better job of tethering payments of low-income groups to price movements than has been done in the last ten years.

Hence, failing to keep prices down, the government will have to adjust welfare and social-security payments to rising prices, and to the increased number of those in distress in emergency periods. It will be the responsibility of the government to correct the injustices resulting from its financial policies, e.g., those accompanying inflation. Corrections will be required both because of the unfavorable effect on philanthropy resulting from higher taxes, and because of the rise of price and the increased number of dependent cases. The more effective the distributional measures—e.g., taxes, rationing, and price controls, the less these outlays will have to rise.

In two particulars the situation will deteriorate. First, an unfortunate failure to achieve a medical insurance program will make possible greater inequalities in accessibility to medical services. Medical facilities are already scarce. The average physician receives a net income of $12,000, about three times the depression low; and hospital charges are close to 100 per cent above prewar. Yet the proportion of sick and old will increase under the stress of the emergency; and especially if there is bombing. Second, the aging of the population continues.

We shall have to depend on the federal government largely, for the state and local governments are not going to be in a very expansive state. A minimum goal should be outlays rising with the increase of prices. Should we assume that the federal welfare budget is now $2.3 billion, then with a 25 per cent rise of prices, it should rise by at least $1 billion, to cover the increase of prices, the rise in numbers requiring help, and the reduced capacity of other governments. This sum would be but ⅓ of 1 per cent of our gross national product and would be more than offset by other cuts in spending for civilian purposes—e.g., roads. In addition, the government should make provisions for a much quicker adjustment to price movements for beneficiaries of insurance programs. The correct policy would be to reduce the standard of living of those above a minimum standard, as is required in a war economy, but to try to maintain the position, say, of the submerged quarter.[5]

SUMMARY AND CONCLUSIONS

In general we agree with the position that, in the midst of a great mobilization, it is necessary to economize on resources. This will be more important than in the last war because now the military will have to depend primarily on diversions from current output, not, as in the last war, on the rise of output.

But we distinguish these economies which conserve resources needed for war from those which involve transfers of income at the expense of high-income groups to those requiring help. The objective in the midst of mobilization and war should be to improve the relative position of the submerged quarter at the expense of the others, even though, in general, consumption must fall greatly. The major reductions of consumption will have to come from the three-quarters earning less than $5,000; but the lowest quarter should be saved as much as possible.

In order to achieve this objective of adequate standards for the low-income groups, the federal government may have to increase their outlays by $1 billion, or about 30 to 40 per cent. (I assume an added military program of $200 billion in five years and a 25 per cent inflation.) This rise in outlay will be more than offset by cutting expenditures (e.g., road building) which uses up resources.

By spending $1 billion additional the federal government will protect the position of those with incomes of $2,000 or less, inclusive of more than 4 million receiving aid and 4½ million disabled (not additive) and many others who will be squeezed by the inflation. The injustices resulting from the substantial inflation of the forties have not by any means been corrected. A further inflation could be disastrous.

With increased taxes and inflation, the contributions of

private philanthropy and state and local governments are bound to play a smaller part than in the past. The federal government will have to take up the slack. In addition, benefit payments in the social-security program should be somewhat better adjusted to rising prices than in the past.

CONCLUDING REMARKS

RISE OF OUTPUT AND PRICES

In a major mobilization the primary end is an increase of output. The managers of World War II economy can look back with satisfaction to a rise of gross national product (in stable prices) of about 50 to 70 per cent, accompanied by an increase of prices of but 25 per cent.

The record in the emergency of the fifties is not nearly so good. In fact, should one compare the achievements of the first eight months of the Korean War with those of World War II, one would find a record about one-tenth as satisfactory in 1950–51. Average annual price rise in the first eight months of the Korean War was 12 per cent (annual rate) and in World War II about 5 per cent—a ratio of 2½ to 1. Allow for the proportion of resources going to war (in excess of pre-Korea) in 1950–51 as compared with World War II (roughly one-quarter as high, relatively, in 1950–51), and the ratio of 1 to 10 is revealed. In these first eight months of the Korean War, output seems to have risen about 5 per cent, or approximately one-half of the percentage rise in prices. On this basis, the results in 1950–51 were one-fourth to one-sixth as satisfactory as in World War II. In relation to the developments in 1941 (a more appropriate comparison than with World War II), the ratio of gain of output to rise of prices was six times as high in 1941 as in 1950–51. (Again the 1950–51 record is based on that of the first eight months. A temporary flattening out of the price rise in the second quarter of 1951 seems evident. But too much reliance should not be put on this.)

This recent history is disconcerting—and especially since in previous emergencies the attack on inflation seems to have been better. Thus a comparison of price rises in relation to resources going to war yields the following. (The ratio in the Civil War is put at 100.)

Civil War	100 per cent
World War I	33 per cent
World War II	7 per cent

WHY THE DETERIORATION IN 1950–51?

Many reasons can be adduced for the failures of 1950–51, a poor record which is all the more to be lamented since inflation over a long-drawn-out emergency is more damaging than over a short period.

First, *there was the failure to introduce a tax program of the proportions required.* The significant feature of the inflation of 1950–51 was that it occurred despite a federal surplus. The corollary from this fact is that concentration on the federal budgetary situation does not solve all our problems. We have to concentrate also on private spending and saving. What is required is a fiscal policy (i.e., a surplus) which will offset the excess of investment over savings in the private economy. In 1950–51, the country did not profit from this kind of fiscal policy.

An examination of the over-all picture of the economy reveals at a glance the occasion for our deficiencies. In the first quarter of 1951, the excess of gross national product over that of the second quarter of 1950 was $44 billion. Here is how this sum was used:

	$ Billion
Rise of personal consumption	20
Rise of private investment	12
Rise of government purchase of goods and services	12

In other words, of the rise of output the government obtained but 27 per cent. Should we allow for the greater rise in the price of government goods and services than in civilian goods and services, the gain would be substantially less than one-quarter. No wonder that Mr. Edward Collins, of the New York *Times,* refers to the experience of the first year of the Korean War as *Inflation without Defense.* The weak tax policy in part explains the increase in consumption of roughly 5 per cent in stable dollars.

I have estimated that at 1951 incomes the government could raise $30 to 40 billion more in taxes than in 1949. This estimate is based on the achievements of World War II. For once, I am in agreement with the National Association of Manufacturers, which comes to similar conclusions—though their proposed tax structure is much different from mine. We shall be fortunate if Congress provides taxes equal to half the increase suggested here. A pay-as-you-go policy in 1951 is not enough, though in 195? a pay-as-you-go policy may not be feasible. At present, we can have much more than a pay-as-you-go policy.[1]

Taxes have indeed been inadequate. Nevertheless, we stress the point that starting from a high level of taxation, the government has performed better than in the early years of World War II. Thus, from the second quarter of 1950 to the first quarter of 1951, the rise of personal taxes was $7.2 billion (annual rate) or more than one-quarter of that of personal income. In part, the *relatively* favorable performance was the result of the improved built-in flexibility of our tax system. In 1940, the rise of personal taxes was but 3 per cent of that of personal income; in 1941, only 17 per cent. Lest the current managers of our economy be too much swayed by these figures, I hasten to add that in 1940–41 there was a great fear that heavy taxes would stop the rise of employment, a problem of less significance in 1950–51.

Second, *inadequate savings are part of the problem.* Despite a $27-billion rise of income, savings were unchanged at $10 billion (annual rate) in the first quarter of 1951. At real incomes roughly equivalent to World War II peak, the proportion of savings to income was less than one-fifth of the World War II peak. Moreover, the large response of savings to higher incomes proved to be a strong anti-inflationary influence in 1941 and 1942. In 1950–51, the growing awareness of the inflationary process and the threat of unavailability of goods stimulated scare buying. The proportion of personal savings to income declined from the low proportion of mid-1950.

On the basis of achievements in World War II, this country can save about $84 billion annually at anticipated incomes of 1951–54. Of this amount (again on World War II experience), $54 billion would be available for the Treasury security market. Approximately $13 billion would flow into private investments and about $17 billion would accumulate as cash and deposits (84 — 13 — 17 = 54). Since private investments should continue at about 10 per cent of GNP so long as the war is restricted, the amounts available for Treasury securities would be around $40 billion. Even this amount will not be required, it is hoped, for a long time. In 1951 and 1952 it will be necessary to encourage the flow of funds into the Treasury market in order to redeem maturing issues and borrow additional sums.

Obviously, strong measures would be required to provide $84 billion of savings. The problem is not only that of increasing savings; but also that of channeling them into the market for Treasury issues. Relevant is the fact that inflationary pressures would be much smaller had the government taken stronger measures to curb nonessential investment. Gross private investment of $48.5 billion in 1950, and $60 billion (annual rate) in the two quarters ending March 31, 1951, are way beyond what is necessary to sustain a healthy economy for the long pull, both for civilian and military needs. Indeed, the country requires much more than the less than 4 per cent going into investment in 1943–45; but much less than the 20 per cent of the first year of the Korean War.

Savings available to the Treasury will rise as private investment is curbed; as the country is assured of genuine stabilization policies; and as consumer goods become unavailable. More heroic measures may be required. Professor Slichter's support of the escalator clause (i.e., redemption values increase with the rise of prices) in government bond contracts is one approach. I have suggested some objections to this proposal. One of the defects is that the differential will be available to all irrespective of whether it is required; another is that there would be a desertion of other investments in order to obtain an "escalator" bond. Professor Slichter deals with the danger of deserting other markets by suggesting that limitations would be put upon amounts of "escalator" bonds to be purchased (e.g., related to income), and also the privilege of cashing in would be available only after (say) five years.

Another approach is the compulsory loan. The case for this technique is less strong than in World War II, because in a long-drawn-out struggle, the government should not be encumbered with obligations maturing within, say, 5 to 10 years. Yet it seems to me that Professor Hart, relying on similar arguments in his interesting book, dismisses the forced loan too readily. The compulsory loan impairs incentives, because it is a form of tax; and yet even if the repayment date may have to be pushed forward, it still has advantages for the taxpayer over ordinary taxes.[2]

Finally, the suggestion has been made that higher rates of interest on government securities would increase savings and divert them to the government security markets. (In 1950–51, the problem was one of increasing savings; in the future, it is likely to be one also of channeling savings into the government securities markets.) Unfortunately, it is not clear that a *practical* rise of the rate of interest, with the public anticipating an inflation of 10 per cent a year, would elicit the required rise and diversion of savings. Professor Slichter's proposal for a government security guaranteed against a rise in the price of commodities is in fact a *disguised* rise in the rate of interest. For example, had such securities been issued in 1940 and redeemed in 1950, the rate of interest would have been in fact 9 per cent, and not the actual 2 to 3 per cent.

Third, *we stress the problem of supplies and manpower.* These are bound to be a serious problem for the new effort is built on an economy close to fully employed and one seriously short of vital materials. In a recent article in *Foreign Affairs,* Dr. Bissell pointed out that the requirements for industrial materials in the Western world, even before the Korean War, were 1½ times those of prewar. Yet the Western world is confronted with serious shortages in iron, aluminum, nonferrous metals, and many other indispensable items; the underdeveloped areas which provide a large part of the materials have not fully recovered from the war, and are handicapped by continued warfare and political dissensions. In addition, the competition of iron-curtain countries is germane.

In no field is the threatened shortage so serious as in manpower. The unavailability of 10 million unemployed and an additional reservoir of 10 million, as in World War II, means greater inflationary pressures as the effort gains momentum. Even the 5 million additional needed for war work and the military in 1951 promises to disrupt the economy. These shortages interfere with output and facilitate price and income inflation. Since it is theoretically possible to increase our manpower for the military and war output by the equivalent of more than 30 million, the shortages promised even for late 1951 are disconcerting. To make 30 million additional available would require much more heroic measures than were forthcoming in World War II; and nothing short of an atomic war would justify the extreme measures required. Among these would be a drastic reduction of employment in the distributive trade and in all nonessential production. So far, the actions taken are scarcely adequate to deal even with the manpower problems of 1951–52.

Fourth, *a large effort requires a substantial cut of investment and consumption.* Inflationary pressures in 1950–51 stem in part from the failure to prune investment and consumption in anticipation of the large reductions required by 1952–53. Incidentally, I doubt the wisdom of the Wilson Policy, which promises, once the war effort has been tooled up, a rich civilian life by 1953. No one can say what the requirements of the war effort will be in 1953 and later years. It would be better to prepare the public for sacrifices than to lull them into co-operation with the promise of an even more abundant life later.

The contrast between World War II and the current emergency is striking. In World War II, an $84-billion effort (at the peak) was consistent with a $44-billion gain of consumption. The worker received an unchanged basket of goods for every hour worked. In the current effort, even a $60-billion effort means sacrifices by the public. How much sacrifice depends upon the rise of output and the limitations put upon private investment. In the longer run, of course, *high* investment brings larger flows of consumers' goods. The more output rises and the less investment, the less the sacrifices of consumption in the immediate years ahead. But the higher the output, the greater the inflationary pressures; and, therefore, the greater the need for strong fiscal and saving measures to siphon off the excess of income over the supply of consumption goods available. In 1950–51, the inflation resulted in part from a rise of income not adequately offset by an expansion of consumption goods produced and/or a rise of taxes and savings.

As the effort grows, the need for vigorous tax and savings policies grows. Thus, a $600-billion program over a period of six years might be financed by taxes ($400), non-inflationary savings ($100), inflationary purchases of government securities ($100). The tax burden would be heavy indeed even on World

War II standards. The government would then require more than $100 billion of taxes per year. Consumption would decline greatly, and especially per hour of work. A rise of $60 billion of taxes on top of the tax load of June, 1950, reflected in large part in reduced consumption, would be hard to swallow. Yet the suggested rise of monetary expansion of $100 billion, on top of the monetary expansion and inflation of the forties, would be a serious threat to our stabilization program.

It is well to note that, although the burden of the debt is exaggerated, it is unfortunate to have a second emergency follow so soon upon the emergency of the forties. After the Civil War, two-thirds of the national debt was paid off and income rose by 4 times. Even after World War I, one-third of the debt was redeemed. But prior to the Korean War the reduction of World War II indebtedness was but a few per cent. This debt now overhangs the market, a fact which emphasizes once more the need of a strong tax policy.

In this book, I have assumed conservatively that a $120-billion (annual) military program would be an all-out program. On World War II standards, $120 billion is not a high estimate. Actually, with a GNP averaging $340 billion in 1951–54, an all-out effort might more reasonably be put at $250 billion. This figure is obtained by assuming that the 1932 standard of living is the minimum. The amount figured at 1951–54 prices would be $600 per capita for 150 million people, or $90 billion. Therefore, the war effort would absorb $250 billion, or almost 75 per cent of the national income. Of course, in order to obtain the required $250 billion, the government would have to take drastic measures to move factors of production. And the government would fail in part because of their unwillingness to act and because factors available to the civilian economy cannot all be transferred to essential uses. World War II revealed, however, the possibility of a war taking 50 per cent of the nation's output. An all-out war might well use up 60 per cent, say, $200 billion.[3]

In summary, a pruning of investment and consumption is a condition for a stable economy. This curtailment in turn requires heavy taxes and large savings.

Fifth, *the country suffers from inflationary income policies.* Insofar as incomes rise, the inflationary pressures grow. An ideal plan would be a stabilization of all incomes at June, 1950, levels. But this is obviously impossible, for incentives are required in order to achieve a redistribution of labor and increased output.

Inflation of labor income is an especially serious problem. The shortage of manpower and the increased strength of labor contribute to this difficulty. It is interesting that during the Civil War wage rates rose one-third as much as the cost of living; in World War I, 1.4 times as much; in World War II, 1.8 times as much. Labor income will rise in response to longer hours, up-grading, increased overtime pay, and a rise in employment. As a result, labor income will increase without changes in basic wage rates. It would be well if rises in wage rates could be limited to the increased cost of an "iron" ration —e.g., when the cost of living rises by 10 per cent, the average worker obtaining $60 per week would receive an "iron" bonus of 5 per cent; and the $1,500-a-year worker, one of 10 per cent. Actually, labor demands as a minimum a tying of wages to a cost of living index number. They thus would maintain the purchasing power of an hour of work. In 1951, labor demanded even more than this, and under political pressures, the Labor Board makes concessions. As the supply of consumption goods available declines, the allowance of rises in wage rates equal to or exceeding the increase in the cost of living brings to labor more goods per hour of work and a fortiori for all hours of work, and hence means deprivations for workers not well organized or others whose incomes do not rise with prices.

Similar issues arise in the determination of farm incomes. But like labor, farmers need an incentive to increase output, and since their hourly pay is less than one-half that of city workers, they have special claims on the national income. Nevertheless, the Defense Production Act is too favorable to farmers.

One approach to the wage problem would be a stronger attack on excessive profits. Many of the arguments used against profit control seem weak. Business does not need vast profits for investment purposes: they are investing too much. The excess profits tax does not militate against the interests of the small businessman; it does not result in great wastages of economic resources; and it does not interfere with output. Note the large gains of small business, the small outlays for advertising, the large rises of output in 1941–45, the years of excess profits tax, as against the results before and after. So long as corporate profits are running at an annual rate of $50 billion, the demands upon labor for a restrained income policy will fall on deaf ears: the reply of labor is, if we deny ourselves, profits rise. Ultimately, increased taxes and controls will solve the problem of excessive profits; but the record in 1950–51 is not good.

Sixth, *control policies have been weak*. In view of the large excesses of demand, related to inflationary income and inadequate fiscal and savings policies, the gaps in the control program are particularly unfortunate. Had income policy been more restrained, had taxes and savings been larger, then the burden on controls would have been much less. In fact, controls might have been applied only to deficient markets. In the light of the defects of other facets of stabilization policy, controls become more important though, unfortunately, less effective also.

Viewing the mistakes of 1950–51, one wonders whether those in charge ever read the copious records of World War II. They have missed very few traps. An elementary rule is that price fixing will not be effective if those who write the regulations are recruited from the industries and firms to be regulated. The price executive should not be both base runner and umpire. Here are some other fundamental rules that have been violated:

1. Do not allow the highest-cost units to determine prices. The correct principle is to cover the additional costs of *only* high-cost units which are required to serve the defense or war economy. Here the difficulty lies with the Defense Production Act as well as with the OPS.

2. Force absorption of rising costs out of profits where principles of equity are not violated. In the first year of the Korean War, the absorption principle made little progress—a technique used with great effectiveness in World War II.

3. Treat the problem of quality, provision of low-end (cheap) items, economies of output as essential parts of a price control program. Progress was not notable in World War II in these areas and seems even less so in 1950–51. As scarcities spread, the $4.95 dress, the $5 pair of shoes, and the $1 pair of stockings will become unavailable. These issues underline the general problem which troubled the policy-makers in World War II: the failure to obtain better integration of those responsible for supply and control of demand, and those responsible for price regulations.

4. Do not introduce a general freeze until a large part of the excess purchasing power is siphoned off. The Administration can make out a case for the January, 1951, freeze on the grounds that the freeze was necessary to stop scare buying. But unless supplementary measures are taken, the relief will be temporary indeed. And the weak tax policy of 1951 may in part be traced to the imposition of the freeze.

5. Where large excesses of purchasing power prevail, price regulation of essentials without control of demand may be disastrous. It is highly doubtful, for example, that the control of meat prices will succeed, given the excess of purchasing

power, the unavailability of consumers' durables, and the absence of rationing.

In summary, the first year of the war economy has been disappointing in the degree of inflation relative to the rise of output. Too much attention has been given to monetary policy and particularly to the needs of higher interest rates, with neglect of more important issues. Undoubtedly, the monetary expansion contributed to the rise of prices. But it is not at all clear that a feasible rate of interest would have stimulated savings and reduced investments adequately without *seriously* unstabilizing the government bond market. Effective monetary policy is more likely to lie in the direction of sheltering the government security market from adverse effects of large rises in the interest rate and dealing with excessive demands for credit through rationing of credit. With adequate control of investment, with sensible income policies and the required controls, the supply of money, responding to curtailed demands for money, will cease to be an inflationary factor.

A rigid price level is out of the question. The real issue is, shall we have a rise of 2 to 3 per cent a year or one of 10 per cent? Our system will be in jeopardy from a 50 per cent inflation over the next 5 years on top of a 75 per cent inflation in the forties. For proper use of incentives, an average rise of 2 to 3 per cent should be adequate.[4] The experience in 1942–45 is of relevance here. What makes the problem serious is that powerful groups support inflation; and in the absence of a major war and with concentration of inflation over a short period, the opposing forces do not mobilize.

In the first year, output has satisfactorily expanded by 9 per cent; but consumption and non-essential investment are too high and war output too low. The country has shown its usual aversion to non-inflationary finance and controls—aggravated by uncertainty concerning the duration of the crises.

A BIBLIOGRAPHICAL NOTE

This note is necessarily brief. The reader will find much bibliographical material in the footnotes to this volume, and in my other books listed in the prefatory note.

I. GENERAL BOOKS ON WAR ECONOMICS

Elliott, W. Y., *Mobilization Planning and the National Security (1950–1960)*, Senate Doc. No. 209, 1950.

An excellent survey of the broad problems by one of the most distinguished and knowledgeable operational officers of World War II.

Lincoln, G. E., Stone, W. S., and Harvey, T. H. (Eds.), *Economics of National Security,* Prentice-Hall, 1950.

A comprehensive and useful volume by faculty members of West Point.

Mendershausen, H., *The Economics of War,* Prentice-Hall, 1940.

One of the better elementary treatments.

Nathan, R. R., *Mobilizing for Abundance,* Whittlesey House, 1944.

A useful volume by one of the economic strategists of World War II.

Nef, Wright, Leland, *et al., Economic Problems of War and Its Aftermath* (C. W. Wright, Ed.), University of Chicago Press, 1942.

Useful survey of wars before 1939 and application to more modern wars.

Novick, Anshen, and Truppner, *Wartime Production Controls,* Columbia University Press, 1949.

Indispensable analysis of techniques.

Pigou, A. C., *The Political Economy of War,* London, Macmillan and Co., 1939 (Rev. Ed.).

A classic theoretical presentation.

Spiegel, H. W., *The Economics of Total War,* Appleton-Century, 1942.

An early and helpful analysis of the mobilization for total war.

Stein and Backman (Eds.), *War Economics,* Farrar and Rinehart, 1942.

A comprehensive treatment of the major problems.

Steiner, G. A. (Ed.), *Economic Problems of War,* John Wiley and Co., 1942.

Twenty-eight experts discuss many facets of war economics.

Walker, E. R., *War-Time Economics,* Melbourne University Press, 1939.

This is an excellent brief statement of the problems, although a little out of date now.

II. BOOKS DEALING WITH PARTICULAR EPISODES

Baruch, B. M., *American Industry in the War,* Prentice-Hall, 1941.

This is a report of the War Industries Board, which was responsible for many mobilization problems of World War I.

Clark, J. M., *The Costs of the World War to the American People,* Yale University Press, 1931.

The best American discussion of the economics of World War I.

Hancock, W. K., and Gowing, M. M., *British War Economy,* H. M. Stationery Office, 1949.

The first of a series of studies to be published under

government sponsorship. The first volume promises well for the series.

Mitchell, W. C., *The History of the Greenbacks,* University of Chicago Press, 1903.

Still a classic on the Civil War economy, although written almost a half century ago.

Oxford University, Institute of Statistics, *Studies in War Economics,* 1947.

This volume includes many superb essays, both theoretical and statistical, on the major problems of the British war economy.

I shall not list the hundreds of wartime volumes planned or issued by the historical records offices of various agencies: WPB, OPA, Department of Agriculture, etc. Any student of war economics will find them very helpful, although at times they reflect the attack on problems as the operational officer put them in the record rather than the genuine problems, or the genuine manner of meeting them.

III. SPECIAL ASPECTS OF WAR ECONOMICS

I shall not list even examples of the excellent studies on many aspects of war economics: agriculture, labor and wage rates, economic warfare, price control, etc. But I list a few of the more important volumes on finance and stabilization.

Crowther, G., *Ways and Means of War,* Oxford, The Clarendon Press, 1940.

Well presented and elementary.

Durbin, E. F. M., *How to Pay for the War,* Routledge, 1939.

A thoughtful discussion of war finance.

Hart, Allen, *et al., Paying for Defense,* The Blakiston Co., 1941.

One of the most forceful pleas for a noninflationary fiscal program.

Keynes, J. M., *How to Pay for War,* Macmillan, 1940.

Still a classic. The first forceful presentation of the need of a forced loan.

Worsley, T. B., *Wartime Economic Stabilization and the Efficiency of Government Procurement,* U.S. Government Printing Office, 1949.

The government published this private investigation of the problems of stabilization. This book covers much ground.

IV. OFFICIAL DOCUMENTS

Aside from the vast number of documents issued by war agencies, the publications issued during war and after by government departments, agencies, and legislative bodies are all illuminating. For example, the OPA, the WPB, and the Labor Department issued thousands of documents; also of importance are the Annual Reports of the Treasury, the Annual Budget Statement, the Reports of the CCC, the Hearings before House and Senate Congressional Committees, the House and Senate Reports (e.g., the Truman Committee Reports), the monthly publications (e.g., *Federal Reserve Bulletin, Survey of Current Business, The Social Security Bulletin, The Treasury Bulletin, The Monthly Labor Review*). In Great Britain, the *Annual Budget Statement* and the *Annual Survey of National Income and Expenditures* are especially helpful.

NOTES

CHAPTER 1

1. *The Economics of National Defense: Fifth Annual Report to the President by the Council of Economic Advisers,* December, 1950, p. 11.

2. U.S. Dept. of Agr., Washington, D.C., Speech at Outlook Conference, October 30, 1950, pp. 13–15 (mimeographed). "These are not forecasts but broad approximations of the course of the indicated possible aggregates under specific assumptions."

3. McNair, Learned, Lintner, and Bursk in *Harvard Business Review,* January, 1951.

4. New York *Times,* November 28, 1950.

5. See S. Kuznets, *National Product in Wartime,* National Bureau of Economic Research, 1945, especially p. 51; and "Symposium on National Product, War and Pre-War," by M. Gilbert, S. Kuznets, and others, in *Review of Economics and Statistics,* August, 1944, pp. 109–135.

6. *Fortune,* December, 1950, p. 75; cf. *General Credit Control, Debt Management, and Economic Mobilization,* Report of the Joint Congressional Committee on Economics, 1951, pp. 27–33, for discussion of price rises of military items since April, 1950.

7. For further discussion see the excellent statement by C. Daugherty, "Wage Controls," *Dun's Review,* January, 1951; also U.S. Dept. of Labor, Bureau of Labor Statistics, *Problems and Policies of Dispute Settlement and Wage Stabilization during World War II,* Bull. No. 1009, 1951; and my *Inflation and the American Economy,* 1945, Chapters 19–22.

8. M. S. Eccles, "The Defense of the Dollar," *Fortune,* November, 1950, p. 81.

9. S. Kuznets, *National Product in Wartime,* pp. 96, 102.

10. Calculated from Bur. of Labor Statistics, Bull. No. 699, p. 44; *Report of the Secretary of the Treasury,* 1949, p. 445; *Federal Reserve Bulletin,* July, 1950, *Mid-Year Economic Report of the President,* July, 1950, and *Treasury Bulletin.*

11. See *Fortune,* December, 1950.

12. *Review of Economics and Statistics,* February, 1950.

13. Cf. review of Douglas and Goldenweiser in *Review of Economics and Statistics,* February, 1950; and L. Chandler in *Proceedings of American Economic Society,* 1951.

CHAPTER 2

1. See Learned, McNair, Lintner, and Bursk, "Thinking Ahead," *Harvard Business Review,* January, 1951; *The Economic Report of the President,* Janu-

ary, 1951, pp. 70–81; and D. B. Woodward, *Outlook for 1951*, Paper delivered at annual meeting of the American Statistical Association, December 28, 1950.

The President's Council estimated a rise of GNP to $310 billion for 1951 (1950 prices), or 7 per cent in excess of the end of 1950 rate and more than 10 per cent in excess of the 1950 annual output. Approximately $20 billion were to come from additional employment and hours, and $10 billion from a rise of productivity. For five years, the gains would be 25 per cent. Mr. Woodward found that the average of estimates for 1951 was $295 billion (a rise of $20 billion over the estimated $275 billion for 1950).

CHAPTER 3

1. I do not include here the effects of conversion of part-time to full-time workers—an issue discussed in the closing section.

2. BLS, *Factors Determining Part-Time Job Transfers and Unemployment*, Serial R 1620 (from *Monthly Labor Review*, February, 1944).

3. Figures from *Survey of Current Business*, Income Numbers, July, 1947, and July, 1950.

4. U.S. Census, *School Enrollment of Workers in the United States*, October, 1949, p. 6.

5. Robert C. Goodwin, *Agricultural and Defense Manpower*, Address given in Chicago, Illinois, December 11, 1950, p. 3 (mimeographed).

6. Figures from U.S. Census, *Forecasts of the Population, 1945–1975*, p. 49.

7. BLS, *Tables of Working Life*, August, 1950, p. 37.

8. U.S. Census, *The Monthly Report on the Labor Force*, October, 1950, p. 10.

9. Calculations based on *The Monthly Report on the Labor Force*, October, 1950, p. 10, and *School Enrollment of Workers in the United States*, May 3, 1950, p. 7. Cf. also T. Hitch in *Review of Economics and Statistics*, February, 1951. Hitch's estimate of involuntary short-time employment is substantially less, but he does not consider the effects of an emergency.

10. A survey in *Life*, apparently based on official estimates, puts the rise in the armed forces at 11.7 million; the rise of defense workers, 10.5 million. The number of civilian nonfarm workers would fall from 51.9 to 38 million, or 13 million (*Life*, January 1, 1951, p. 14).

11. For further discussions of some of the issues raised in this paragraph, see the excellent paper by W. Haber, "Appraisal of Current Manpower Problems," *Proceedings of American Economic Association*, 1951.

CHAPTER 4

1. *A Water Policy for the American People*, President's Water Resources Policy Commission Report, 1950, pp. 92–93; *The President's Budget Message for 1952*, pp. M7, M37.

2. Committee on Interior and Insular Affairs, Senate Hearings on *National Resources Policy*, 1949, pp. 6–7.

3. Twentieth Century Fund, *America's Needs and Resources*, 1947, Chapter 23.

4. Committee on Public Lands, Senate Hearings on *Investigation of National Resources*, 1947, pp. 175–184 (Table, p. 183); Twentieth Century Fund,

America's Needs and Resources, pp. 184–190 and 574–579; J. A. Krug, *National Resources and Foreign Aid,* 1947, pp. 11–14.

5. Legislation summarized in Senate Report No. 140, *ECA and Strategic Materials,* Report of the Joint Committee on Foreign Economic Cooperation, March 22, 1949, pp. 8–10; and *An Analysis of the ECA Program,* Senate Doc. No. 142 (81:2), 1950, p. 11.

6. *Ibid.*, p. 11; and *Budget of the U.S. Government for the Fiscal Year Ending June 30, 1951,* pp. M27–M28, M34, 1117 and [same] *1942,* p. M14; *Report to the President on Foreign Economic Policies under ECA,* 1950, pp. 59–60.

7. *ECA and Strategic Materials,* Senate Report No. 140, p. 33; *An Analysis of the ECA Program,* Senate Doc. No. 142, pp. 11–14; S. E. Harris, *Foreign Aid and Our Economy,* 1950, pp. 17–19.

8. C. L. Nau in *Saving American Capitalism* (S. E. Harris, Ed.), p. 167.

9. Figures from U.S. Dept. of State, *Energy Resources of the World,* 1949, pp. 7–8, 27, 30.

10. *A Water Policy for the American People,* I, p. 239 (see 1, above).

11. Senate Hearings on *National Resources Policy,* 1949, p. 245.

12. See especially House Report No. 1845, *Final Report on Foreign Aid,* 1948, pp. 869–879.

CHAPTER 5

1. CCC, *Report of Financial Conditions and Operations as of September 30, 1950.*

2. Cf. U.S. Dept. of Agr., *Farm Production Practices, Costs and Returns,* Statistical Bulletin No. 83, 1949, p. 70.

3. Figures from *ibid.*, pp. 44, 49, 73 and *Agricultural Outlook Charts—1950,* p. 23.

4. Report of Fiscal Branch, CCC, *Review of CCC Price Support and Section 32 Operations as of September 30, 1950.*

5. Secretary Brannan, before the House Committee on Agriculture, April 7, 1949.

6. Cf. U.S. Dept. of Agr., Bur. of Agr. Econ., *Agricultural Wage Stabilization in World War II,* by A. J. Holmaas (Agr. Monograph No. 1).

7. L. J. Ducoff, *Outlook for Farm Wages* (mimeographed), November, 1950.

CHAPTER 6

1. U.S. Dept. of Commerce, *International Transactions of the United States during the War, 1940–1945,* 1948, p. 15; and Committee on Finance, *Foreign Assets and Liabilities of the United States and Its Balance of International Transactions* (A Report to the Senate Committee by the National Advisory Council on International Monetary and Financial Problems, December 15, 1947), 1948, p. 17.

2. See my *Price and Related Controls,* Chapter 15.

3. FEA, *First Report to Congress,* p. 24.

4. U.S. Dept. of Commerce, *International Transactions of the United States during the War, 1940–1945,* 1948, p. 15.

5. My *Inflation in the American Economy,* p. 143.

6. My *The European Recovery Program,* 1948, especially Chapter 14 and my *Foreign Economic Policies for the United States,* 1948, especially Parts I, II,

and IV; and *Report to the President on Foreign Economic Policies*, especially p. 106.

7. For discussions of the relevance and presence of dollar shortage, see S. E. Harris, *The European Recovery Program*, 1948, Chapter 4 and references there; also see C. R. Kindleberger, *Dollar Shortage*, 1950; and H. S. Ellis, *The Economics of Freedom*, 1950.

8. See E. Bloch, "European Rearmament and United States Foreign Aid," *Review of Economics and Statistics*, November, 1950, pp. 342–346.

9. Estimates based on *The European Recovery Program*, pp. 86–89; *Second Report of the OEEC*, pp. 34–35; *The Mid-Year Economic Report of the President*, July, 1950, p. 115.

10. Cf. *Foreign Aid and Our Economy*, 1950, for further discussion of these problems; also see *Report to the President on Foreign Economic Policies*, pp. 66–72.

11. In addition to the references quoted in this chapter, the following will be helpful: Economic Commission for Europe, *A Survey of the Economic Situation and Prospects of Europe*, Geneva, 1948, and *Economic Survey of Europe in 1948*, Geneva, 1949; the ECA, European Recovery Program, *Report of the ECA-Commerce Mission*, October, 1949; the Department of State, *Point Four*, 1950; also the *Quarterly Reports of the ECA*, the House and Senate Foreign Relations and Appropriation Committees, Hearings on *ERP and ECA*, 1948–50; also, U.N., *National and International Measures for Full Employment*, 1949; C. R. Kindleberger, *Dollar Shortage*, 1950; and H. S. Ellis, *The Economics of Freedom*, 1950.

CHAPTER 9

1. *President's Budget Message*, Jan. 6, 1943, pp. XV–XVI.

CHAPTER 11

1. See the excellent statement by E. B. Staats, Assistant Director of the Bureau of the Budget, *Budgetary Implications of the Defense Program*, Nov. 1, 1950 (mimeographed).

2. Figures from *Survey of Current Business*, Annual Income Numbers.

CHAPTER 12

1. *Annual Report of the Secretary of the Treasury on the State of the Finances for the Fiscal Year Ended June 30, 1948*, p. 52; Secretary Snyder's *Statement before the House Ways and Means Committee*, February 5, 1951.

2. Cf. my *Inflation and the American Economy*, pp. 226–228, and the *Economics of America at War*, pp. 183–184, and S. H. Slichter, "Business and Armament," *Atlantic Monthly*, November, 1950, p. 41.

3. OPA, *Civilian Spending and Saving*, 1941 and 1942 (March, 1943). Charts accompanying Secretary Snyder's *Statement before the House Ways and Means Committee*, February 5, 1951.

4. G. Colm, *Who Pays the Taxes?* TNEC Monograph.

5. Figures for United Kingdom from *National Income and Expenditure of the United Kingdom, 1946 to 1949*, Cmd. 7933, pp. 6, 34, 43, and *Survey of Current Business*, July, 1950. Figures for the two countries are not strictly comparable.

6. All figures based on *Survey of Current Business,* July, 1950, and my estimates. Dr. Paradiso, of the Department of Commerce in an address "Current Factors in Consumer Purchasing" (New York City, November 3, 1950, typewritten), estimated a rise of 5 per cent in the third quarter in GNP over second quarter and 7½ per cent by November, 1950, and a 5 per cent rise of output in 1951. My estimate for personal income is a 6 per cent rise in the second half of 1950 and 5 per cent in 1951.

7. Secretary Snyder's estimate was $37 billion for 1950, *Statement before The House Ways and Means Committee,* November 15, 1950.

8. On Social Security, see Ways and Means Committee, *Actuarial Cost Estimates for Old-Age and Survivors' Insurance System as Modified by the Social Security Act Amendments of 1950,* July 27, 1950; *Summary of Principal Changes in the Old-Age and Survivors' Insurance System under H.R. 6000, According to Conference Agreement,* July 25, 1950; *Recommendations for Social Security Legislation: The Report of the Advisory Council on Social Security to the Senate Committee on Finance,* Senate Doc. No. 208, 1949, especially pp. 143–144; *Social Security Bulletin,* September, 1950.

9. To a large extent, I have allowed for this interdependence, for the income, corporation, and excess profits tax yield in World War II, upon which I base my estimates, reflected the adverse effect of each of these taxes on the yield of the other. Insofar as I propose a rise of the corporate tax over 1945 levels, the interdependence is not allowed for. In his testimony before the Ways and Means Committee in November, 1950, Secretary Snyder emphasized the point that the $40 billion yield of the excess profits tax in World War II provided the Treasury $16 billion returns. That is to say, $24 billion could have been captured under the corporate tax and other financial measures.

CHAPTER 13

1. I assume a 5 per cent rise of output in the first (1951) and second (1952) years, and no rise of output in the third and fourth; and an average rise of 5 per cent in prices each year. Actually the increases in output and prices are likely to be higher in the first two years and may well be less in the last two years (1953–54) than here indicated.

2. Corporate income, GNP, corporate taxes from *SCB,* Annual Income Number; yield of excess profits tax from Bureau of Internal Revenue, *Statistics of Income for 1946;* Federal tax receipts from *Annual Report of the Secretary of the Treasury on the State of Finances,* 1948.

3. In 1940, for example, income originating in business services amounted to $656 million; in 1945, $1,241 million; in 1949, $1,926 million. In relation to income, the respective percentages were 81, 62, and 89. (This is a more inclusive item than advertising.) *Survey of Current Business,* National Income Numbers, 1945, 1949. Also see W. H. Mullen, "Measurement of National Advertising," *Harvard Business Review,* September, 1949, p. 644.

4. Cf. my *Inflation and the American Economy,* Chapters 19–21.

5. Cf. Mr. Edward Collins, in New York *Times,* November 19, 1950.

6. See, for example, K. J. Curran, *Excess Profits Tax* (American Council of Public Affairs), 1944; R. Magill, *The Impact of Federal Taxes,* 1943, Chapter V; H. N. Groves, *Production, Jobs and Taxes,* 1944, Chapter IV; and also see Machinery and Allied Production Institute, *Bulletin No. 2292* (October 30,

1950) for some suggestions for relief under the 1950 legislation. (I would not by any means support all of the suggestions.)

7. See *Secretary Snyder's Statement before the Ways and Means Committee,* November 15, 1950, Exhibit I, pp. 1–2.

8. See my *Inflation in the American Economy,* pp. 281–284; Truman Committee *Renegotiation of War Contracts,* Senate Report No. 10, March, 1943; *Joint Statement of War, Navy and Treasury Departments and the Maritime Commission; Sixth Supplemental National Defense Appropriation Act of 1942,* March 31, 1943; House Report No. 733 on *Renegotiation of War Contracts* (October, 1943); and my *Price and Related Controls,* Chapters 19–20.

9. D. S. Smith, "Role of Invested Capital in Excess Profits Taxation," in Tax Institute Symposium on Excess Profits Taxation, December 9, 1950.

10. See *Excess Profits Tax Act of 1950,* House Report No. 3142, December 2, 1950; *Excess Profits Tax Act of 1950,* Senate Report No. 2679, December 18, 1950; *Excess Profits Tax Act of 1950,* House Report No. 3231, December 22, 1950; *Excess Profits Tax Act of 1950,* Public Law 909, 81st Congress [HR 9827].

CHAPTER 14

1. There are some statistical discrepancies in these figures which are not of great importance.

2. *Federal Reserve Bulletin,* October, 1944.

CHAPTER 15

1. *Survey of Current Business,* April, 1944, and February, 1945; cf. *Budget, 1946,* p. 7 and *First Report by the Director of War Mobilization and Reconversion,* p. 19.

2. *Survey of Current Business.*

3. *Survey of Current Business, Federal Reserve Bulletin, Treasury Bulletin.*

CHAPTER 16

1. Cf. my *National Debt and the New Economics* for further discussion of some of the issues.

CHAPTER 20

1. Cf. p. 109.

2. See my *Price and Related Controls of the United States,* pp. 13–15.

3. S. Kuznets, *National Product in Wartime,* New York, 1945, p. 65.

4. *Steel's War Record,* 1944, p. 75; and F. C. Mills, *Prices in a War Economy,* p. 23.

5. See, especially, House Hearings on *Extension of Emergency Price Control Act (1944),* pp. 2156–2169; and Senate Hearings on *Emergency Price Control Act,* p. 119; OPA, *Questions and Answers on Federal Rent Control,* January, 1944; *Cost of Living,* by G. Meany and R. J. Thomas, later Members of the Presidential Committee on the Cost of Living, 1944, pp. 40–48; Bureau of Labor Statistics, *The Cost of Living,* February 25, 1944, pp. 32–42.

6. For materials in this section, see especially Senate and House Hearings on *Extension of Emergency Price Control Act,* 1944; G. Meany and R. J. Thomas,

op. cit.; and my *Prices and Related Controls in the United States,* Chapter 13.

7. See *Prices and Related Controls in the United States,* Chapters 19 and 20, and *Inflation and the American Economy,* pp. 281–284.

8. House Hearings on *Extension of Emergency Price Control Act,* p. 666.

9. Truman Committee, *Renegotiation of War Contracts, passim.*

10. OPA, *A Manual of Price Control* (S. E. Harris, Ed.), p. 161.

11. J. H. Sumner, "Differential Pricing of Non-Ferrous Metals," *Proceedings of the American Economic Association,* March, 1943, pp. 279 ff.

12. For further discussion, see my *Price and Related Controls in the United States,* Chapters 11, 18, and my Monograph for the OPA Historical Office, *Stabilization Subsidies 1942–1946,* and *A Manual of Price Control* (S. E. Harris, Ed.).

CHAPTER 21

1. See Chapters 12, 15.

2. See OPA Price Control Report 12, *The Accomplishment of Price Control,* January 15, 1943.

3. For other reservations, see *Price and Related Controls in the United States,* pp. 17–19.

CHAPTER 22

1. National Security Resources Board, *Wartime Economic Stabilization and the Efficiency of Government Procurement,* by T. W. Worsley, 1949, p. 376.

2. F. L. Babcock, *The U.S. College Graduate,* 1941, pp. 30–31; *Preliminary Report on the U.S. College Graduate* (1949), p. 12; and issues of *Survey of Current Business;* also my *Market for College Graduates.*

3. Bureau of the Budget, *The Federal Budget in Brief, Fiscal Year, 1951,* p. 16.

4. Figures from *Recommendations for Social Security Legislation: The Reports of the Advisory Council on Social Security,* Senate Doc. No. 208, 1949, p. 97; Conference Board, *The Social Security Almanac,* 1949, p. 38; and *Social Security Bulletin,* October, 1950.

5. *The President's Budget Message,* 1950, p. M30.

6. *Life Insurance Fact Book,* 1950, pp. 24–25.

7. *Social Security Bulletin,* August, 1950; *The President's Budget Message,* 1950.

8. Material based on the Council of State Governments, *The Forty-Eight State School Systems,* 1949; my *How Shall We Pay for Education?; Survey of Current Business,* Annual Income Numbers; various Census publications on finance—e.g., *Summary of State Government Finances in 1949;* The Tax Foundation, *Facts and Figures on Government Finance, 1948–49.*

CHAPTER 23

1. See my estimates in "The Future of Higher Education in the United States," *The Harvard Educational Review,* Fall 1948, p. 204. The 1960 estimate is based on the recommendations of the President's Commission on Higher Education. I have adjusted the income estimate upward from the figure given in the 1948 article.

2. See my *How Shall We Pay for Education?,* Harper, 1948, Introduction to Chapter 12.

3. For further details on this problem, see the President's Commission, Vols. V–VI; my *How Shall We Pay for Education?,* especially Part V, and my *The Future of Higher Education in the United States,* pp. 202–203.

4. See my *How Shall We Pay for Education?,* Chapters 4, 11, and my "Professorial Salaries and Tuition, 1947–48: Background and Proposals," *Bulletin of the American Association of University Professors,* Vol. 34, No. 1, Spring 1948.

5. *How Shall We Pay for Education?,* especially Chapters 8 and 9.

6. J. P. Jones, *Philanthropy Today,* 1949 Supplement to Chapter 12, p. 69.

CHAPTER 24

1. Figures from the Report of the Joint Committee on Economics, *Low Income Families and Economic Stability,* 1949, pp. 3, 19–20; *The Federal Budget in Brief, Fiscal Year 1951,* p. 16; Bureau of Labor Statistics, *Workers' Budgets in the United States, City Families and Single Persons,* Bull. No. 927, 1948, p. 22.

2. Eightieth Congress, 2d Sess., *Recommendations for Social Security Legislation,* Senate Doc. No. 208, 1949, p. 97. Committee on Ways and Means, *Actuarial Cost Estimates for the Old-Age and Survivors' Insurance System as Modified by the Social Security Act Amendments of 1950,* p. 8; and Bureau of Labor Statistics, *Workers' Budgets in the United States,* Bull. No. 927, 1948, pp. 52–53.

3. H. P. Miller, "Factors Related to Recent Changes in Income Distribution in the United States" (to be published in the *Review of Economics and Statistics,* August, 1951); and F. Weaver, "Taxation and Redistribution in the United Kingdom," *ibid.,* August, 1950, p. 212.

4. This is a low estimate, since figures are available only for 397 cities with population in excess of 25,000. Federal figures are for 1950–51 (estimate), state for 1949, city for 1948, in *dollars of stable purchasing power* (and allowing for an underestimation of $150 million).

5. Statistics in this section from: *The Federal Budget in Brief, Fiscal Year 1951;* Bureau of the Census, *Financing Federal, State, and Local Governments,* 1941, especially p. 54; *Compendium of City Government Finances in 1948; Summary of State Government Finances in 1949;* The Tax Foundation, *Facts and Figures on Government Finance,* 1948–49.

CONCLUDING REMARKS

1. Cf. NAM, *Paying-as-We-Go,* Economic Policy Division Series No. 38, February, 1951, p. 16; and S. H. Slichter, "Should We Pay as We Go?" New York *Times,* Sunday Magazine Section, February 4, 1951.

2. A. G. Hart, *Defense without Inflation,* pp. 122–123.

3. For an able presentation of the economy of full mobilization, see E. S. Shaw and L. Tarshis, "A Program for Economic Mobilization," *American Economic Review,* March, 1951, pp. 30–50.

4. Cf. A. G. Hart, *op. cit.,* pp. 9–10. Professor Hart here presents some unusual arguments for inflation. He sees an advantage in inflation, for example, in that the inflation will drive those not on the labor market and expropriated by inflation into the labor market. But what about those too old to work and those already on the labor market who suffer from inflation?

INDEX

[*cont.*